The Deregulated Society

D1601532

Of Related Interest

Public Policy and Politics in America, Second Edition
James E. Anderson, David W. Brady, Charles S. Bullock,
Joseph Stewart, Jr.

Public Policy in the Eighties
Charles S. Bullock, James E. Anderson, David W. Brady

An Introduction to the Study of Public Policy, Third Edition
˙arles O. Jones

> **and the Bureaucracy:**
> ˙˙ing in the Fourth Branch
> ˙nt, Second Edition
> ˙ər

> **˙ivil Rights Policy**

The Deregulated Society

Larry N. Gerston
San Jose State University, San Jose

Cynthia Fraleigh

Robert Schwab

Brooks/Cole Publishing Company
Pacific Grove, California

Brooks/Cole Publishing Company
A Division of Wadsworth, Inc.

Printed in the United States of America

10 9 8 7 6 5 4 3 2 1

Library of Congress Cataloging-in-Publication Data

Gerston, Larry N.
  The deregulated society.

  Bibliography: p.
  Includes index.
  1. Deregulation—United States. I. Fraleigh,
Cynthia, [date]. II. Schwab, Robert, [date].
HD3616.U47G47 1987   338.973   87-5116
ISBN 0-534-08208-4

Sponsoring Editor: Cynthia C. Stormer
Marketing Representative: Tina Allen
Editorial Assistant: Linda Loba
Production Editor: S. M. Bailey
Manuscript Editor: S. M. Bailey
Permissions Editor: Carline Haga
Interior Design: Roy R. Neuhaus
Cover Design and Illustration: Roy R. Neuhaus
Art Coordinator: Lisa Torri
Interior Illustration: Judith Macdonald
Photo Researcher: Marquita Flemming
Typesetting: Kachina Typesetting, Inc., Tempe, Arizona
Printing and Binding: R. R. Donnelley, Crawfordsville, Indiana

PHOTO CREDITS   Chapter Opening Photos
1, Gerard Fritz, Monkmeyer Press Photo Service. 2, Illustrator's Photos. 3, Christopher Morrow, Stock, Boston. 4,
Paul Conklin, Monkmeyer Press Photo Service. 5, George R. Fry, *Los Angeles Times*. 6, Bill Anderson,
Monkmeyer Press Photo Service. 7, U.S. Department of Transportation, National Highway Traffic Safety Ad-
ministration. 8, Michael Hayman, Stock, Boston. 9, Ellis Herwig, Stock, Boston. 10, Daniel Brody, Stock,
Boston.

This book is dedicated to

Elisa,
friend, wife, critic

and

Loy Laney,
grandfather and teacher

Almost everybody loves shortcuts, unless they bring more confusion than clarity. Such an appreciation extends to the English language, where the prefix *de-* has become a handy antonym. Placed before another word, de- suggests the undoing of the concept to which it is connected. To *detach* is to uncouple; to *demote* is to send down; to *devalue* is to make something worthless. To *deregulate,* however, means more than the reversal of government obligations—it means the adoption of new values.

In the United States today, there is a movement committed to the deregulation of society. Sometimes couched in the phrases "regulatory relief" or "privatization," deregulation refers to the wholesale rearrangement of the connections that bind the public, the private sector, and government institutions.

To deregulate means for the government to exercise less control over public goals and private pursuits. Less governmental oversight portends more opportunities for private gain, competition, and individualism. In fact, the slogan "less is best" may have become the modern demand to reverse the oppression associated with the growth of government at home.

The call for deregulation has antecedents throughout American history. The political framework of the United States originally placed constraints on government to guarantee individual liberty. So important were these concerns that the Bill of Rights, the first ten amendments to the Constitution, focused on the *limitations* of government. This refrain has been repeated again and again in association with the concept of independence. Yet, even the most sacred values can change.

Society has become far more complex over the past 200 years than the framers ever could have foreseen. Concomitant with this, government has increased its involvement in our lives. Bit by bit, issue by issue, policy area by policy area, governmental regulatory institutions—commonly known as agencies, boards, or commissions—have been created to smooth out the conflicts between private aspirations and the public good. Although such wrinkles may have been the unexpected glitches of industrialization, governmental responses through regulation have been purposeful and intentional.

At first, the regulatory movement seemed the zenith of governmental responsibility. Who could argue against creation of the Food and Drug Administration to combat food poisoning or drug defects? Who would oppose the Federal Reserve Board as a means of guaranteeing economic tranquility in place of traumatic "boom-and-bust" cycles? Yet for many, the original goals of the FDA or the FED have never matched the ambiguities connected with the Environmental Protection Agency or the Occupational Safety and Health Administration.

Once-cautious reviews have now become strident reactions. The proliferation of regulatory agencies provided the basis for reassessment and subsequent demands for a "back-to-the-basics" government. By the 1970s, the calls for deregulation were no longer considered to be the cries of revisionist kooks; today such demands come from the center of American political thought.

But for many observers, the movement to deregulate has created more problems than solutions. They argue that although removal of governmental controls may mean economic freedom for some, it may augur economic instability for others. They worry that fewer public controls may bring about more private abuses. They fear that although caveat emptor ("let the buyer beware") may work for used car purchases, it does not sit well with communities ravaged by the effects of toxic waste.

At what point does deregulation become more devastating than desirable, more burdensome than beneficial? Does deregulation remove wasteful government, promote disparity, or both? These questions and more are explored in *The Deregulated Society*.

In the following pages, we discuss the relevance of deregulation to everyday life. Once restricted to esoteric economic journals, deregulation has moved onto the front pages of daily newspapers. Accordingly, we shed some light on the topic by focusing on the theory of deregulation, the origins of regulation and deregulation, and selected examples of deregulation efforts. Our goal is to provide the student with the necessary tools to understand the phenomenon of deregulation as it applies to contemporary political life.

Chapter 1 introduces the concept of deregulation. Far from a fad, deregulation follows 100 years of increased governmental activity. The introductory chapter not only traces regulatory developments but also examines relevant political actors.

In chapter 2, regulation is examined as a political corollary to the economic growth and development of the United States. Given the conflict between individual liberty and governmental oversight, the chapter examines the factors most responsible for the growth of regulatory activity.

The elements, key institutions, and changing conditions responsible for the deregulatory climate are examined in chapter 3. In addition to the activities of the Reagan administration, the chapter traces the presidential initiatives of Richard Nixon, Gerald Ford, and Jimmy Carter.

Chapter 4 turns to the major theories of regulation and deregulation. Such constructs are valuable for both their logic and their application. As with any fundamental shift, many deregulatory efforts are explained, in fact, by more than one theory. Yet an understanding of these frameworks allows us to go beyond the analyses in this book to examples elsewhere in the political arena.

Chapters 5 through 8 contain examinations of issue areas we have selected for more detailed study. Two examples of economic regulation—the airlines and financial-services industries—are discussed in chapters 5 and 6. In chapters 7 and 8, we address the controversies associated with social regulation, examining the auto industry's approach to the air-bag standard and the case of occupational safety and health.

Regulation and deregulation are the most common responses of government to troublesome economic and social conditions. But they are not the only answers to public policy difficulties. Chapter 9 focuses on other possible ways of coping with inequities and uncertainties in the American polity.

In chapter 10, we assess the deregulation efforts in an increasingly regulated environment. Given the composition of the U.S. political system, we suggest that deregulation is likely to be every bit as inconsistent and controversial as has regulation itself.

The success of this effort is due in large part to the assistance and advice of several people throughout the project's development. At Brooks/Cole, our thanks go to Executive Editor Craig Barth and Political Science Editor Cindy Stormer for their initial support, encouragement, and patience as we struggled to deliver a comprehensive and up-to-date manuscript. Finally, S. M. Bailey used his editing skills to give our ideas a clarity they would not have otherwise enjoyed.

A group of excellent reviewers gave us considerable guidance in honing a rough manuscript into finished product. These people include Edgar Litt, the University of Connecticut; Barry Mitnick, the University of Pittsburgh; Eric Moskowitz, the College of Wooster in Wooster, Ohio; Larry Regens, the University of Georgia; Walter Rosenbaum, the University of Florida; and William West, Texas A&M University. At San Jose State University, Peter Haas was particularly helpful with his suggestions for chapter 4.

Finally, we are indebted to Linda Chromik and Wendy Greer for their careful preparation of the manuscript. Confronted with draft after draft, they typed with meticulous attention and good spirit. And when the authors' editorial eyes tired beyond repair, Linda and Wendy picked up the slack.

Larry N. Gerston
Cynthia Fraleigh
Robert Schwab

CONTENTS

ACRONYMS

ALPA   Air Line Pilots Association
CAB   Civil Aeronautics Board
CEA   Council of Economic Advisors
CEQ   Council on Environmental Quality
COWPS   Council on Wage and Price Stability
CPSC   Consumer Product Safety Commission
DOT   Department of Transportation
EEOC   Equal Employment Opportunity Commission
EPA   Environmental Protection Agency
FAA   Federal Aviation Administration
FCC   Federal Communications Commission
FDA   Food and Drug Administration
FDIC   Federal Deposit Insurance Corporation
FED (or FRB)   Federal Reserve Board
FERC   Federal Energy Regulatory Commission
FHLBB   Federal Home Loan Bank Board
FMVSS   Federal Motor Vehicle Safety Standard
FPC   Federal Power Commission
FSLIC   Federal Savings and Loan Insurance Corporation
FTC   Federal Trade Commission

ICC   Interstate Commerce Commission
IIHS   Insurance Institute for Highway Safety
IIS   Inflation Impact Statement
MTB   Materials Transportation Bureau
MESA   Mining Enforcement and Safety Administration
NHSB   National Highway Safety Board
NHTSA   National Highway Traffic Safety Administration
NIH   National Institute of Health
NIOSH   National Institute of Occupational Safety and Health
NRC   Nuclear Regulatory Commission
NTSB   National Transportation Safety Board
OIRA   Office of Information and Regulatory Affairs
OMB   Office of Management and Budget
OSHA   Occupational Safety and Health Administration
OSM   Office of Surface Mining
PATCO   Professional Air Traffic Controllers Association
RARG   Regulatory Analysis Review Group
SEC   Securities and Exchange Commission
TVA   Tennessee Valley Authority
USDA   United States Department of Agriculture

PART ONE

Understanding Deregulation

CHAPTER 1

Understanding Deregulation:
American Politics Reexamined

Deregulation is a theme of the 1980s, referring to the de-emphasis of governmental oversight of activities in the private sector. At a time when public functions have become increasingly intertwined with private functions, the deregulation movement has come to represent an effort at minimizing governmental impact on society, for the cost of regulation has been great in both dollars and manpower. Thus, proposals for deregulation have the potential for great change.

Regulation is an effort through governmental authority to control certain aspects of the private sector for a public purpose. Such work is commonly managed by a government regulatory agency, a decision-making body designed to alter economic life or social conditions in order to satisfy specific political needs or values. Society contains numerous private interests as well as competing interpretations of the public good. Therefore, the efforts to regulate or, in recent years, deregulate various aspects of life are often controversial.

Regulatory Agencies: An Overview

The bodies we know as regulatory agencies have been given a variety of names. In some cases they are indeed called *agencies,* but they are also known as *boards, commissions,* or *administrations.* Regardless, the differences in surname are basically cosmetic. The importance of a regulatory unit lies not so much in its name, but in the powers conferred upon it. *Agency* is used as a general term to separate these entities from the traditional three branches of government. Today, some forty-plus agencies fit under the regulatory umbrella at the national level of government.

One important distinction separates *independent* agencies from others. Independent agencies are created by Congress to assume complete responsibility for a given policy area or issue. As quasi-judicial units, they have the power to investigate, deliberate, and execute policy decisions. Each unit is governed by a small number of commissioners (usually between five and ten) who are appointed by the president and confirmed by the United States Senate. The terms of these members are fixed, overlap with one another, and usually last longer than the four-year tenure of the president. Inasmuch as these policy makers cannot be fired, they enjoy relatively independent status.

A second cluster of agencies regulates policy, but with strings controlled by the president or one of his cabinet officers. The Environmental Protection Agency (EPA), for example, has an administrator who serves at the pleasure of the president. In a variation of this theme, the National Highway Safety Traffic Administration (NHSTA) has a chief administrator who serves under the secretary of transportation. In both of these instances, the administrators are assigned responsibility for carrying out congressional mandates. If they do not perform adequately, they may be removed by the president, although Congress may demand an explanation as to why such action has been taken.

The Evolution of Values

As with any serious political trend, the concept of deregulation has had a lengthy gestation period. In fact, the reconsideration of regulatory power has been, as much as anything else, a reaction to the expansion of government. With passage of the Interstate Commerce Act of 1887, the national government determined that private interests could be subject to governmental regulation if their activities posed a threat to the *public interest*. Determining how best to protect the public and under what conditions have been debated ever since this first key piece of regulatory legislation. At each subsequent juncture of regulation, the debate has been rekindled as the values of individualism have collided with the public good in one or another of the governmental arenas of power.

At both the national and state levels, the development of regulatory policies and agencies originally followed from a common concern—that unrestrained private enterprise could not, or would not, deal with the economic and social problems created by conflict between the pursuits of private profits and public goals. Depending upon the issue at stake, proponents of regulation argued that corporate management had sacrificed worker safety, public health, or product safety for production goals and favorable balance sheets.

The corporate sector appeared to remain indifferent to public concern over its activities. Clinging to the treasured ethic that the least government was the best government, corporate leaders seemed "reluctant to devote scarce decision-making resources to clarify problems which [were] only peripheral to them."[1] The public's perception of such attitudes ultimately led to the development of such regulatory agencies as the Interstate Commerce Commission (ICC) in 1887 and the Food and Drug Administration (FDA) in 1931. In these and other instances, Congress determined that the "invisible hand" of the marketplace did not function as an independent balance, despite the teachings of Adam Smith, and that regulatory agencies were thus required to assure corporate reliability and responsiveness.

Until the middle of the twentieth century, government regulation had been confined mainly to economic interests. But the growth of a modern nation seemed to invite broadened regulatory dimensions. By the 1960s, regulation had expanded from narrow economic concerns to include quality-of-life issues that affected society at large. Today, a plethora of federal agencies regulates such diverse interests as air quality, banking practices, the flow of commerce, miners' working environments, nuclear-waste disposal, and automobile safety; thousands of other industries, products, and conditions are also regulated. Almost every element of the population thus has been affected in some way by regulatory activities.

Although a variety of regulatory agencies and commissions has been created at all levels of government, the efforts of national policy makers have had the most substantial impacts on society. Legislative enactments, executive orders, and judicial decisions at the federal level have resulted in the redirection of commitments, opportunities, and obligations.

Some regulations have been welcomed over the years as necessary and good; others have been embroiled in controversy from the earliest stages of discussion through the implementation of policy. Yet out of the regulatory movement, one general consequence has persisted: The more that government has extended its influence, the more that previously unaffected sectors of society have been brought under the umbrella of public control. As new forms of regulation have been added to the old, critics have increasingly challenged the possible overuse of government clout. It is one thing for a public agency to regulate such narrow concerns

---

Living with Regulation

Consider how a typical college student is impacted by federal regulatory activity:

Roger Rules awakened early Monday to attend his classes at Regulation University. It was so cold in his apartment that even his electric blanket (endorsed by the *Consumer Product Safety Commission*) failed to keep him warm. So, Roger turned up the thermostat on his natural gas heater (no longer regulated by the *Federal Energy Regulatory Commission*).

On this morning, Roger was hampered by allergies. He took a decongestant (approved by the *Food and Drug Administration*) as he watched the network news on television (authorized by the *Federal Communications Commission*). While driving his automobile to the university (under the auspices of the *National Highway Traffic Safety Administration*), Roger decided to have breakfast at a local fast-food restaurant (where the food was approved by the *U.S. Department of Agriculture*). But realizing he had no money, Roger stopped first at his bank's instant teller machine (governed by the *Federal Deposit Insurance Corporation*) to withdraw some cash for the day.

Finally, Roger arrived at his newly renovated economics classroom (as ordered by the *Occupational Safety and Health Administration*). The day's topic? Life in a "free market" economy.

---

as commodities futures or media monopolies; it is quite another for a public agency to require national standards for drug efficacy or to establish industrywide air-pollution criteria.

There is little doubt that much of the regulatory activity of the twentieth century has been in response to unfairness and inequity. But at the same time, the increased interaction between public agencies and the private sector has generated calls for the reassessment of government's proper role in the domestic arena. The deregulation movement's simplest demand is for government to retreat from the marketplace and from people's lives so that individual freedoms are enhanced. The retraction of government involvement, the argument goes, promotes greater efficiency and a direct, unencumbered relationship between producers and consumers.

Yet, government policies are rarely neutral. The same governmental retrenchment that some believe would reestablish individual freedom is seen by others as an abandonment of society's protection from the excesses of such freedom. Thus, any reconsideration of current regulatory practices raises the question, What do we want from government? Which is more desirable—government as the guardian of individual liberties or as the protector of the public interest? Must the accomplishment of one objective be at the expense of the other? Regulation has developed over the years as a mechanism to ensure the attainment of both goals. But now some critics assert that what began as "fine tuning" has resulted in sour notes for American society. Once a technical issue of concern only to economists, regulation now simmers as a general issue on the front burner of America's political stove.

The history of American politics is replete with critical clashes over the appropriate direction of government. The bloodiest of these struggles took place in the name of states' rights and resulted in the Civil War. Similarly, dramatic temblors shook the country during the Great Depression and again with major international conflicts. The current debate over domestic government activity also portends a turning point of great importance, for in its purest form, deregulation calls for nothing less than the wholesale rearrangement of America's political structure. This book addresses the issue and examines the consequences associated with such changes in regulatory agencies and policy.

The Origins of Regulation

From its beginning, American society moved forward with bold assumptions and expectations. All indications were that "the first new nation" would be guided by its unique conditions.[2] Rich land assured agricultural independence, and an abundance of raw materials would help nourish the industrial age. For the restless and adventurous, the breadth of an entire continent permitted westward expansion. Waves of immigrants inundated the young country whose Constitution promoted equality and liberty over class and servitude, and upon arrival, the new Americans became immersed in a culture that was deeply attached to the Protestant work ethic. Success through hard work became an important corollary to the American value of personal accomplishment.

The combination of manpower, resources, and opportunity allowed the young nation to prosper at a pace then unrivaled by any other. The creed of individualism militated against collective responsibilities and obligations, preventing both the emplacement of an aristocracy and the unwarranted intrusion of government. So constrained, in fact, was the position of national government after the War of Independence that the Founders waited more than a decade before they acquiesced to the necessity of a common national currency! Indeed, in its early days, the national government was known more for what it was *not* permitted to do than for what it was.

Minimal government activity went hand in hand with the development of a free-wheeling capitalist economy that witnessed the widespread distribution of private power rather than its excessive concentration. Given these conditions, John Kenneth Galbraith writes, "there could be no misuse of private power because no one had power to misuse. An innocuous role was assigned to government because there was little that was useful that a government could do."[3] Unrestrained competition and minimal government involvement seemed to be the requisite conditions for keeping American society on the move.

Insulated from the world's problems by two mighty oceans, the young nation excelled. If England was the birthplace of the Industrial Revolution, then America was the site of its perfection, and by the late 1800s, the United States had evolved from an agricultural society to an industrial giant. Except for a few dispossessed farmers, unskilled laborers, and floundering immigrants, most Americans thrived as the economy came of age.

But industrialization brought a series of changes in both society and government. Urbanization reorganized large populations within close quarters and tight living conditions. The growth of massive assembly plants typically placed hundreds, sometimes thousands, of formerly independent craftsmen under a single roof. The emergence of multimillion-dollar corporations consolidated economic power into the hands of a few. And the economy, once fairly stable if unexciting, was increasingly subject to severe recessions following boom periods.

An unpredictable economy brought trouble to both society at large and its political institutions. Although many observers longed for stability, they were reluctant to accept the use of government as a means of achieving it. Whatever its possible benefits, surrendering the free-market mechanisms of control to government seemed to many to be too high a price to pay for economic stability. Yet the pressure for some kind of change mounted.

Perhaps the earliest disappointments were suffered by those most responsible for the massive industrialization of America. The captains of industry were displeased with their companies' erratic performances, and as corporations began to issue public stock, similar complaints were heard from corporate stockholders and management alike. Meanwhile, those at the bottom of the economic scale were even more disconsolate about their fate, which seemed to be beyond the control of individuals.

Competition among corporations often brought disaster for the losers and their employees. As an individual company, for example, reorganized its production means in search of desired profit levels, its employees often faced either a reduction in wages or outright dismissal. Political and social repercussions were inevitable. Whereas conventional wisdom viewed unrestrained competition as an adequate "self-generating regulatory force,"[4] the market conditions of the late nineteenth century were not responding efficiently or appropriately. Nevertheless, any discussion of government as a stabilizing economic force was usually viewed by the private sector as an affront to individualism.

Clientele Cabinet Departments: Regulatory Forerunners

The development of federal regulatory agencies with specific powers over particular industries accelerated during the 1930s. But their structures were in large part determined by the development of clientele cabinet departments within the executive branch. In 1903, Congress had created the Department of Commerce and Labor, which was split into separate departments ten years later. The tasks of these cabinet offices were narrow in scope: to provide assistance, not hindrance, to their respective constituencies where necessary. The Department of Commerce quickly became an agency known for its statistics, charts, and maps. Its responsibilities were so limited because "government and business regarded each other as adversaries, not as potential partners."[5] Similar functions were assigned to the Department of Labor, which represented a workforce whose members were "more laissez faire than business."[6] These two cabinet departments had functions like that of the Department of Agriculture, a cabinet-level agency created in 1862 to promote the welfare of farmers while keeping government interference at bay.[7]

These newest cabinet departments did not have significant regulatory authority, yet there was something unique about their genesis. They were not organized along the lines of early cabinet posts, which were constitutionally established. The first departments were responsible for such national concerns as justice, postal delivery, and defense. The new cabinet positions, however, responded to specific groups. At first, these groups worked within government to keep it from their spheres of interest. Later, they actively sought governmental action to solve private problems through public policies. The "second generation" cabinet departments signified a new administrative relationship between government and sizable portions of the private sector.

Early Agency Development at the State Level

The first federal agencies were modeled after those of some individual states. During the second half of the nineteenth century, these states had vigorously assumed a number of regulatory functions. Because they were not viewed as intrusions of the national government, these state powers were routinely validated by the U.S. Supreme Court.[8] States were particularly active in setting professional standards by creating licensing boards to maintain the qualifications of attorneys, physicians, plumbers, beauticians, and dozens of other occupations.

The early state efforts had not been without their critics. Some viewed the licensing boards as public institutions in name only. This opinion has been held by modern students of government, such as James Wilson, who has written that such state agencies represented "the possession of public power by persons who use it for private purposes. They . . . benefited those in the profession in the sincere but unsubstantiated conviction that doing so would benefit the public generally."[9] These themes were echoed by the critics of federal agencies a century later. Nevertheless, the appeal of industry self-regulation through these agencies was so great at the state level that they became the prototypes for subsequent federal agency development.

Whether inspired by state forerunners or clientele cabinet posts at the federal level, the growth of regulatory agencies was simultaneous with the expansion of national government and was just as sporadic.

The Great Depression and the
Growth of National Regulatory Agencies

The first regulatory agencies had limited objectives and were defensive of their clientele industries. The original purpose of the new governmental bodies, writes David B. Truman, was to assure access for the privileged.[10] Thus, when the ICC determined rates and conditions of transportation, it set minimum prices and exceedingly generous criteria to meet the industry's requirements. Likewise, although the Federal Trade Commission (FTC) was mandated to oversee conditions of food preparation and production, it assumed similar responsibility as a service agency for the industry. Such developments were not necessarily "anti-public"; rather, they followed from a desire to protect the public good only through the cooperation of the industries involved.

On those occasions when Congress misconstrued its regulatory function, the U.S. Supreme Court was able and willing to recast Congress'
intent in a more appropriate—i.e., narrow—format. As Michael Reagan
and John Sanzone note, throughout the late nineteenth and early twentieth
century, "the Court narrowly defined commerce and stated that the
commerce clause [of the U.S. Constitution] stopped where the Tenth
Amendment began."[11] Wherever possible, the Court seemed to say, the
nation's domestic issues were to be managed by the states. To the extent
that Congress elected to dispute that treasured relationship, its work had
to be both narrow and to the benefit of those economic interests affected
by any such regulatory policy.

With the onset of the Great Depression, virtually all aspects of national
government and power were reassessed. The potential virtues of regulation drew a considerable part of that attention. As the nation unravelled
financially, many feared that the failure of some parts of the economy
would bring down the whole structure and even society itself. Regulation
of commerce for the producers' sake no longer seemed adequate to
protect the nation as a whole. The use of regulation, therefore, changed
from protecting private interests to protecting the public interest. With
this, regulatory activity assumed a new significance for the nation.

Regulatory actions during the 1930s opened the opportunity for the use
of government in new and unforeseen ways. Given the complexity of the
modern economy, relying on the states for various regulatory functions
no longer seemed appropriate; moreover, narrow regulation of specific
industries did not guarantee that society would benefit. Thus, Congress
began to create regulatory agencies that provided national relief related to
overall market conditions rather than to particular products. Described by
Theodore J. Lowi as the "whole-market approach," the new regulatory
philosophy was first applied to the communications industry and then
quickly extended to air traffic and motor-carrier traffic.[12] Ultimately, this
philosophy was applied to atomic energy and satellite communications.
The protection of society was now given a wider context than was
previously thought to be acceptable in American politics.

Several legislative acts illustrate the shift of regulatory activity from
narrow objectives to national purposes. Passage of the Robinson–Patman
Act in 1938 gave expanded power to the FTC. Similarly broad
responsibilities were granted to the Securities and Exchange Commission
(SEC) between 1933 and 1935. Whereas the agency was originally
designed to protect investors on Wall Street, "significant additions were
made to the legislative authority and regulatory jurisdiction of the SEC by
1935,"[13] thus increasing its clout.

In addition to increased regulatory activity, the crisis of the Great
Depression brought major institutional changes. One such shift occurred
with the U.S. Supreme Court. For more than a century, the Court had
emphasized very limited federal authority in the domestic sphere. During

his first term, President Franklin D. Roosevelt repeatedly criticized the Court for this attitude, which he characterized as out of touch with the needs of the time. So incensed did he become that in 1937 he proposed to add six more justices so that the nine already on the Court might be relieved of some of their burdens. Critics were outraged, calling the proposal "court packing," but within weeks of the proposal, the Court acquiesced to executive pressure and began to uphold the constitutionality of expanded federal power in virtually all areas, including regulation. The effects of that benchmark period remain to this day.

The Court's new outlook suggested the possibility of broad powers for the national government, particularly for the executive branch. Fearing an overzealous president, the architects in Congress devised regulatory agencies as major policy-making bodies that could affect national policy in an environment beyond the reach of the chief executive. In the words of one observer, "the assignment of regulatory duties to commissions was held to be one way of checking the discretionary powers of the president."[14] Thus, in the process of redistributing power at the national level, regulatory agencies emerged as policy-making authorities acceptable to all three branches of government. The agencies seemed to be the one way for the national government's influence to grow without disturbing the equilibrium among the traditional branches of authority.

The Regulatory Explosion of the 1960s and '70s

The most recent flurry of regulatory activity occurred during the late 1960s and early '70s. At first, the national government seemed intent on strengthening those agencies already in place. One early indication of the new activity took place with the FDA. First created in 1931 to suggest standards for food additives and drugs, the administration was given enforcement ability in 1962 through a premarket certification process. With its newfound power, the FDA assumed a "gatekeeper" role (that is, kept out those undesirable elements that might tamper with the goals of the agency and its clientele) for the public rather than for the drug companies.

In 1966, Congress created another agency, the NHTSA, to increase motor-vehicle safety both in equipment and operation. The powers of and controversies involving this agency are discussed at length in chapter 7. Of importance here, however, is that the NHTSA's powers paralleled those of the new FDA. Manufacturers of automobiles and automobile-related products had to comply with agency-established standards before marketing their goods.

By the mid-1970s, a series of new regulatory agencies had been established specifically to protect the public good. The EPA was created in 1970 to set standards for toxic waste as well as air- and water-pollution control. Also that year, Congress established the Occupational Safety and

Health Administration (OSHA) to develop and enforce safety and health standards in the workplace. Finally, in 1972, Congress established the Consumer Product Safety Commission (CPSC), whose purpose was to protect consumers from hazardous and poisonous products.

Three critical political trends had set the tone for the creation of these and many other regulatory agencies and commissions throughout the 1960s and 1970s. First, support for the agencies had an unusually bipartisan quality. Although Democrats John Kennedy and Lyndon Johnson held the presidency during the beginning of the new regulatory period, Republican Richard Nixon held office toward its end; furthermore, in Congress, most of the new agencies were approved by lopsided votes that transcended political party division. Second, government assumed a positive role in creating proper conditions for the public good rather than continuing its role as a "rubber stamp" for producers—that is, the agencies were designed to set standards for the public that, in turn, would be met by the private sector. Although such agency responsibilities led to "courtships" by the regulated elements, the regulated still had to comply with conditions set forth by the regulating agenc', not vice versa. Third, the new agencies had distinctly social rather than economic purposes, that is, protecting the public rather than promoting profit. By the mid-1970s, regulation was recognized as a vital component of governmental activity.

Regulation Reconsidered

Given the American values of equality and individualism, regulation was controversial from the start, and the antiregulatory movement began almost simultaneously with the concept's introduction. In the late nineteenth and early twentieth centuries, some critics outside government feared that the relationship between agencies and regulated industries would permit special treatment of private interests. Others worried that government regulatory policies would discourage, if not destroy, competition. That deregulation had gained momentum by the 1970s shows that these views were never far from the surface of American political thought. To the extent that deregulation has taken place, these themes have gained credence.

The Growth of Resistance

By the 1930s, antiregulatory sentiment emerged within as well as outside of government. Legislative leaders were ambivalent about regulation as a policy-making tool. On the one hand, they welcomed regulation as a means of carrying out national goals while denying further authority to an increasingly powerful presidency. On the other hand, "the scope of

discretion exercised by commissions often aroused [c]ongressional suspicion."[15] But national efforts to stimulate the economy seemed more
important than did congressional jealousies in the 1930s. As the nation's
financial condition improved, however, some critics questioned whether
the proliferation of regulatory power had been at the expense of traditional legislative authority.

Post–World War II assessments further focused on regulation as a
potential abuse of the policy-making process. In reviewing what he
describes as "interest-group liberalism," Theodore J. Lowi has criticized
the evolution of regulation from the narrow, categorical management of
specific industries to the broad, prescriptive advocacy of the public good:
"As regulation moved from the denotation to the connotation of what is
subject to public policy, discretion inevitably increased."[16] Clear rules
and order had given way to inconsistent bargaining between regulatory
agencies and their clientele industries. Those opposed to such a relationship, ranging from academics such as Lowi to public-interest advocates
such as Ralph Nader, worried that public environments characterized by
negotiation and abstraction were likely to produce irresponsible agency
behavior.

By the late 1970s, antiregulation had become a rallying cry for those
opposed to "big government." Opponents of regulation criticized agency
activity for a variety of excesses, including the following:

- The Civil Aeronautics Board's regulation of air fares was cited by
  some as an example of the production of artificially high prices,
  while other critics argued that the CAB was a captive of the major air
  carriers.
- Establishment of minimum freight rates by the ICC was blamed for
  discouraging competition by entrepreneurs who would have entered
  the market at reduced rates.
- The FDA was lambasted because of its premarket requirements for
  drug safety, which made drugs unnecessarily costly and discouraged
  further research, according to the agency's critics.
- OSHA and EPA were alleged to have set standards that were deemed
  unrealistic and cost inefficient.[17]

Other critics cited unnecessary duplication and overlap throughout the
regulatory network.

In 1977, the deregulation movement scored its first victory. Under the
provisions of the Natural Gas Policy Act, the Federal Power Commission
(FPC) was stripped of its authority to establish rates for the wholesale
prices of natural gas in interstate commerce. The government-imposed
price levels, criticized by industry spokespersons and their allies as
unnecessarily low, were phased out by Congress over an eight-year
period. The FPC, however, has continued to administer other agency
activities.

One year later, Congress actually voted to phase out one federal agency, the CAB, over a seven-year period. As of 1983, the board lost all authority over structures of and rates for domestic airline routes, thus freeing the industry from all economic regulation. Further deregulation of transportation occurred in 1980 with the Staggers Rail Act (railroad freight) and the Motor Carrier Reform Act (interstate bus-fare structure). By the mid-1980s, much of the regulation of the nation's transportation industry had been eliminated. For deregulation's proponents, these were but the first of many direct hits to come.

Deregulation in the 1980s

In the past decade, deregulation has emerged as a critical issue on the public agenda. During the 1980 presidential campaign, both incumbent Jimmy Carter and challenger Ronald Reagan repeatedly focused on the problems of overregulation. Whereas Carter spoke of his administration's successes, Reagan charged that the incumbent's actions had barely scratched the surface of regulatory reform. Reagan's subsequent victory set the tone for an active period of deregulation during his two terms of office. Although some of his objectives were met, others, however, were scuttled by Congress and the courts. The battles among the various branches of government reveal two facts: first, that it can be just as difficult to enact deregulatory change as to initiate regulation itself, and second, that all major federal institutions have a stake in the deregulation issue.

The Executive Branch

The presidency is important in the deregulatory question for two reasons. The president not only appoints a number of agency heads and commissioners (usually subject to legislative confirmation) but also controls several agencies directly. In setting his own political agenda, President Reagan has embraced a particular philosophy of deregulation, and that viewpoint has been echoed by his appointees. Thus, by the decade's midpoint, a Reagan-appointed majority on the Federal Communications Commission (FCC) had loosened requirements for the renewal of broadcast licenses, while the commission's chairman argued publicly against the equal time doctrine for political candidates.[18] Within the administration's direct sphere of influence, the EPA had elected to decentralize some of its responsibility by relinquishing the regulation of toxic chemical gases to the states.[19] Perhaps CPSC chairman Terrence Scanlon best summarized the Reagan administration philosophy when he stated, "We are stressing voluntary development of standards. We want to work with companies to solve problems, not against them."[20]

The Judicial Branch

After decades of upholding the right of the federal government to regulate various facets of economic life, the Supreme Court has signalled a change in direction. The Department of Justice sued to break up American Telephone and Telegraph (AT&T) in 1974 on the grounds that the giant utility controlled virtually the entire telephone market and discriminated against non–AT&T equipment. In 1983, the Court sided with the government and the breakup was ordered. Since then, the Court has considered other regulation questions, and in 1985, the justices unanimously voted that the SEC could not regulate investment letters of the fast-growing independent brokerage industry.[21]

The Legislative Branch

In recent years, Congress has behaved inconsistently toward regulation. Legislators have felt caught in the middle between those seeking to protect the public from abuse *(protective regulation)* and those seeking special consideration for favored industries or economic interests *(competitive regulation)*.[22] At the crucial moment, quite often the most vocal expression of interest had had the greatest impact on congressional action. In 1984, for example, Congress discovered that the ICC was allowing trucking companies to expand their operations in violation of federal safety standards. In response, Congress passed protective legislation that required the ICC to deny new routes to carriers who failed to pass safety inspections. Conversely, Congress enacted the Federal Trade Commission Improvements Act of 1980 to restrain the FTC from actions that Congress felt did not comply with the commission's mandate. The bill included a section that required the commission to inform Congress of any trade-regulation rule ninety days in advance of any action. The legislative intent was to help specific economic interests.

The examples cited attest to the "checks and balance" difficulties associated with deregulation. The call for a deregulated society may be the hot political topic of the 1980s, but dismantling the federal regulatory structure may be as difficult as it was to build.

A Look Ahead

The chapters that follow attempt to explain the mysteries of deregulation. As with any important topic, the concept must be examined in theory as well as in application. For the remainder of Part I, chapter 2 examines the waves of regulatory activity from past to present; chapter 3 compares the approaches to deregulation as undertaken by the Nixon, Ford, Carter, and Reagan administrations; and chapter 4 discusses the leading theories behind regulatory and deregulatory activities.

Part II of *The Deregulated Society* presents a series of case studies. Two economic areas—airlines and financial institutions—are discussed in chapters 5 and 6. Issues that have a sizable impact on society at large—auto safety and worker safety—are analyzed in chapters 7 and 8.

In Part III, we use chapter 9 to suggest possible alternatives to deregulation. Finally, in chapter 10, we consider the consequences of deregulation for society, its economy, and its political system.

Notes

1. John T. Scholz, "Reliability, Responsiveness, and Regulatory Policy," *Public Administration Review*, 44, no. 2 (March/April 1984): 146.
2. In *The First New Nation* (Garden City, N.Y.: Doubleday, 1963), Seymour Martin Lipset writes that the weakness of aristocratic traditions and the presence of the work ethic cushioned the young government from the difficulties associated with early political development. These elements separated the United States from other nascent societies. See pp. 61–68.
3. John Kenneth Galbraith, *American Capitalism* (Boston: Houghton Mifflin, 1952), p. 12. For a somewhat less kind interpretation of this period, see Max Weber, who described the American economy of the nineteenth century as a ruthless struggle that left the individual powerless: "The capitalist economy . . . is an immense cosmos into which the individual is born, and which presents itself to him, at least as an individual, as an unalterable order of things in which he must live. . . . The manufacturer who in the long run acts counter to these norms, will just as inevitably be eliminated from the economic scene as the worker who cannot or will not adapt himself to them will be thrown into the streets without a job." *The Protestant Ethic and the Spirit of Capitalism* (New York: Scribner's, 1958), pp. 54–55.
4. Galbraith, *Capitalism,* pp. 112–113.
5. Harold Seidman, *Politics, Position, and Power: The Dynamics of Federal Organization,* 2d ed. (New York: Oxford University Press, 1976), as reprinted in *Bureaucratic Power in National Politics,* 3d ed., Francis E. Rourke, ed. (Boston: Little, Brown, 1978), p. 340.
6. Theodore J. Lowi, *The End of Liberalism* (New York: Norton, 1969), p. 118.
7. See Grant McConnell, *Private Power and American Democracy* (New York: Knopf, 1967), who writes that the department's early farm constituency insisted "upon voluntary action and cooperation" (p. 76).
8. David B. Walker acknowledges that the federal courts sanctioned a strong role for Congress in matters of commerce throughout the nineteenth century. But "the states continued to exercise a near-exclusive authority . . . in the areas of family and criminal law, elections, control over local government and commercial law." See *Toward a Functioning Federalism* (Boston: Little, Brown, 1981), p. 60.
9. James Q. Wilson, "The Rise of the Bureaucratic State," *The Public Interest,* no. 41 (Fall 1975): 90.
10. David B. Truman, *The Governmental Process* (New York: Knopf, 1951), pp. 418–419.
11. *The New Federalism,* 2d ed. (New York: University Press, 1981), p. 21.
12. Lowi, *Liberalism,* p. 142.
13. Marver H. Bernstein, *Regulating Business by Independent Commission* (Princeton, N.J.: Princeton University Press, 1955), p. 79.
14. *Ibid.,* p. 58.
15. *Ibid.,* p. 56.

16. Lowi, *Liberalism,* pp. 143–144.
17. For a summary of the antiregulatory movement, see James E. Anderson, David W. Brady, Charles S. Bullock III, and Joseph Stewart, *Public Policy and Politics in America,* 2d ed. (Monterey, Calif.: Brooks/Cole Publishing Company, 1984), pp. 290–296.
18. *Christian Science Monitor,* May 20, 1985.
19. *Wall Street Journal,* June 4, 1985.
20. *U.S. News and World Report,* April 15, 1985.
21. *Wall Street Journal,* June 11, 1985.
22. For a thorough discussion of the differences in regulatory approach, see Roger H. Davidson and Walter J. Oleszek, *Congress and Its Members,* 2d ed. (Washington, D.C.: Congressional Quarterly Press, 1985), pp. 414–417.

CHAPTER 2

The History of
Regulation in America

In 1776, the year in which the United States declared their independence from England, Adam Smith wrote *The Wealth of Nations*.[1] Smith's economic arguments seemed to weave perfectly with the political objectives of revolutionaries in search of freedom, describing how producers and consumers, acting without the intervention of government, could achieve the best outcome for society as a whole. Smith's treatise set the tone for a doctrine of separation of the functions of government from the rights of producers.

The American Revolution and the themes of mainstream economics intertwined as elements of the emerging nation's most cherished value— freedom. Ever since that tumultuous period, most Americans have viewed a market economy free of government control as an essential ingredient of democracy. Instead of government managing resources and goods, Americans have relied on competition as the ideal means to deliver the best products to consumers. Competition fits in well with the political and social values of self-reliance, hard work, and the pursuit of private property.

Indeed, much of this thought has been drawn together by Milton Friedman, a twentieth-century economist. In *Capitalism and Freedom,* his modern classic, Friedman writes: "The kind of economic organization that provides economic freedom directly, namely, competitive capitalism, also promotes political freedom because it separates economic power from political power and in this way enables the one to offset the other."[2] Not only does a free market act as the best guarantor of a free society, but also the very tension between private interests and government serves to limit both.

Despite the primacy of economic freedom, government has never left business entirely alone; but neither has business always wanted to be left alone. If, as David Truman writes, "governmental decisions are the resultant of effective access by various interests,"[3] then public policies may benefit selected private interests not because of competition but, rather, because of special relationships.

Scholars differ over the cause-and-effect relationship between private interests and government. In pointing to organized elements as the forces of initiation, E. E. Schattschneider argues that "the flight to government is perpetual. . . . It is the losers in intrabusiness conflict who seek redress from public authority."[4] Opposing the Schattschneider theory, Theodore Lowi asserts that government pursues private interests: "The role of government is one of ensuring access particularly to the most effectively organized."[5] Regardless of order, the relationship between the private and public sectors seems to be purposive in nature. The foregoing suggests that competition includes the struggle for government favor, a political outcome decidedly different from the proclaimed struggle for separation and self-reliance.

The erratic behaviors of the forces for and against regulation become particularly difficult to understand when assessed in the dual contexts of economic and social activity. Some commentators find the distinctions between the two forms of regulation—social and economic—blurred, if not entirely arbitrary.[6] Although it may be difficult at any one time to distinguish clearly between economic and social regulatory policies, the fact remains that the two exist, overlap notwithstanding. Moreover, the motivations for and results of both forms of regulation are usually quite different. These differences are critical and are often confused in the quest to understand an increasingly deregulated society.

Often inconsistent and haphazard, the development of regulatory policy has taken place despite demands for governmental nonintervention. Because of conflicts within and between the economic and social spheres, regulatory policies have often worked against one another. Thus, while the National Institute of Health (NIH) has branded tobacco a social ill, the U.S. Department of Agriculture (USDA) has continued to provide economic support to tobacco growers. While lower fares from a dismantled CAB have provided economic benefits, deregulation has also led to increasingly crowded skies and an increase in the loss of lives and finances from air disasters. In the following sections, we attempt to make sense of these contradictions and trace the evolution of regulation in both the economic and social policy areas.

Interest Groups as Catalysts of Regulation

Much of the growth of government regulation corresponds to the development of organized interests in American society. Industrialization led to vast changes both in the workplace and social structure. One does not have to be a student of interest-group theory to appreciate the changing role of these groups in the political process as well. Interest groups have developed to compensate for the loss of influence by individuals. Their size and presence have given interest groups access to government on a more powerful level than that enjoyed by most individuals. Moreover, as their individual members lose control of their own enterprises through increasingly complicated economic and social networks, organized interests find it possible to enlist the assistance of governments to meet their objectives.

Observers of interest groups point to them as responsible for guaranteeing equilibrium, or balance, in the democratic process. As David Truman has remarked, "Disturbances growing out of the market cannot all be settled directly [or privately] by trade associations or monopolistic economic groups. These groups must supplement direct action by making claims through or upon some mediating institutionalized group whose primary characteristic is its wider powers."[7] That independent authority is government.

As the nature of interest groups has changed, so have the types of regulatory demands and policies. During the late nineteenth century and through the early part of the twentieth century, regulatory policies responded to the narrow economic concerns of farmers, businessmen, and, initially, workers. In each instance, the agency and its authority was created to promote the economic well-being of the affected groups.[8] As the Great Depression developed, organized labor gained the attention of the federal government, with Congress passing the National Labor Relations Act in 1935 in an attempt to right perceived imbalances.[9] And more recently, during the late 1960s and early 1970s, civil rights organizations and environmental groups were most instrumental in gaining governmental attention, once again changing the constellation of interests that are most influential upon government.[10]

Clearly, various interest groups and their goals have become intertwined with the objectives of government over the years. Although the issues and interests were basically of an economic nature early on, they have gradually become social in orientation. Despite this shift, one fact about the behavior of interest groups remains indisputable—their numbers have grown rapidly over the years. Kay Schlozman and John Tierney have indicated, for example, that 25 percent of the organizations represented in Washington have been founded since 1970. Moreover, the predominance of new organizations has altered the political balance, at least in terms of numbers. According to Schlozman and Tierney, "57 percent of the citizens' groups and 51 percent of the social welfare and poor people's organizations but only 23 percent of the trade and other business associations and 6 percent of the corporations were founded since 1970."[11] The changing patterns of representation, likewise, have affected the regulatory agenda in terms of pressures, if not in policies.

The First Wave: Economic Regulation

With an early bent toward agrarianism and decentralized government, the first American policy makers had little concern for regulation. The late 1700s and early 1800s brought little economic development. Although urban centers of commerce developed, the pace was slow, the persistence of rural values and the ethic of self-reliance ensuring that society would organize around small economic and social units.

Regulation of businesses did not become an important issue until the late nineteenth century. Because the nation lacked a cohesive system of transportation to allow inexpensive and speedy shipments of goods, local trade had come to dominate interstate commerce. And state governments "regulated" business only through the granting of charters to corporations.

The development of a national railroad system had a significant impact on both travel and interstate business activity. The behavior of the railroad companies suddenly tested the free-market philosophy. Lacking competition, the railroads could set freight rates as they pleased— and they did, to the dismay of farmers. Responding to railroad power, farmers organized the National Grange of the Patrons of Husbandry in 1867. They lobbied state governments to regulate freight rates, and several states complied, including Illinois and Kansas.[12] But not all farm states responded to the call for railroad regulation in the same way. Some remained aligned with the railroads, unsympathetic to the needs of farmers. In many eastern states, competition from other means of transportation kept railroad rates low and regulation unnecessary.

Two events led to the replacement of the state system of rail regulation with a federal agency. In 1886, in *Wabash, St. Louis and Pacific Railway* v. *Illinois,* the U.S. Supreme Court ruled that if a railroad faced different regulations in several states, freedom of commerce could be seriously harmed.[13] This decision opened the way for federal oversight. Feeling armed with law, farmers immediately intensified their lobbying efforts in Congress. But as long-term beneficiaries of favorable government policies, the railroads continued to ignore the increasingly loud public outcry for responsible rate setting, and enhanced by massive land and monetary grants, railroad power soon had no parallel. Although mergers expanded corporate power, public opinion against the industry hardened, helped along by the conspicuous displays of wealth of rail tycoons.[14]

In 1887, President Grover Cleveland signed the Interstate Commerce Act, federal legislation designed to reduce private railroad power through government action. The ICC, the first independent federal regulatory commission, was empowered to set reasonable railroad rates, protect consumers from price discrimination, force the posting of rates, and prohibit a variety of anticompetitive practices.[15]

The establishment of the ICC was truly a landmark in economic regulation. With its commissioners appointed by the president and confirmed by the Senate, the ICC became a model for the structure of future agencies. Isolated from immediate pressures, commission members were given quasi-judicial power to determine a variety of policies. At last, politicians and consumers thought they had created a way to tame a huge industry that had removed itself from the public interest. In effecting this policy, government leaders abandoned the market as the best mechanism for defining key economic and political values. Moreover, they had set a standard by which subsequent economic crises might be resolved by governmental regulatory responses.

Justification for Economic Regulation

Economic regulation varies with the particular industry, nature of the public concern, and regulatory body. Although no two regulatory arrangements are identical, certain factors are common in economic regulation. Initially, public authorities ascertain the existence of an unacceptable relationship between producers and consumers. In response, an agency or independent commission is established to direct the activities of the industry, such as railroads or banking. The regulatory body sets minimum or maximum levels for services previously determined by the marketplace, including price, level of output, entry into and exit from the industry, rate of return, and market to serve. In return for regulation, firms are usually allowed to receive a *fair rate of return,* although the commission and industry sometimes differ on the definition of "fair."

Since the creation of the ICC, several rationales have been offered to support regulation. Primary among these justifications has been the claim of market failure, a condition that sometimes accompanies the existence of a natural monopoly. When an industry has very high fixed costs in establishing service, such as electricity, it may not make sense for several companies to offer parallel service. The costs of wiring a city two or three times over would far exceed the benefits of competition, and a free market would be unlikely to offer a competitive outcome. But such a monopoly would have tremendous power over its market. It could easily set a price well above the competitive price for its product, and consumers would have little choice but to pay.

A second justification for regulation follows from the perceived need for a central authority to allocate a common resource. Without some means of assigning radio frequencies, for example, the market would create chaos. Several stations might choose to broadcast on the same frequency, and none of their signals would be heard. Regulation helps to ensure that a limited common resource is used efficiently and is not depleted by one producer to the detriment of society.

Some social thinkers have postulated a third justification for economic regulation: Certain industries provide basic services that should be available to everyone. Without regulation, the costs of providing power, telephone service, and perhaps airline service to remote areas would be prohibitive. Regulators allow their industries to charge higher rates to low-cost consumers (e.g., urban electricity users) in order to pay for the higher costs of service to marginal customers (e.g., rural electricity users). This practice is called *cross subsidization.* If the government imposes a universal service requirement, it must also control entry into the industry, or new unregulated firms will simply provide service to consumers where the cost is low, forcing the regulated firm to serve the remaining unprofitable market. Small communities, rural residents, and low-income consumers are often the beneficiaries of cross subsidization.

The fourth justification for intervention was especially popular in the early years of economic regulation. As we have seen, as the size of industries increased toward the end of the nineteenth century, competitive practices were often cutthroat. Price wars designed to force competitors out of business were standard economic practices. Although prices might be low during the war, the victorious firm would emerge with tremendous power, and a quick rise in prices would follow. The instability in such markets worried both consumers and government officials. Control over pricing policies to prevent price discrimination, price wars, or other unstable conditions thus became a common rationale for regulation. These reasons are seldom advanced today; businesses seem to have learned to better control their competitive instincts.

Encouraging the growth of industries during vulnerable stages of development became a fifth justification for economic regulation. Such protection often occurred when industries were new and the successes of their products were uncertain. If policy makers determined that an industry was critical to economic development or to national security, rules might be imposed to lessen the risk to investors. The risky enterprises of aviation and nuclear power were both regulated in this way to ensure their development.

Finally, past regulation has often proved to be the sixth justification for continued or new economic regulation. Once an industry has been placed under federal control, its investors are assumed to have certain property rights. Regulation may continue and expand to keep currently regulated firms from suffering losses, thus protecting as much as regulating the industry. The trucking industry became regulated in this manner, primarily because it threatened the already regulated railroads. As discussed in the previous chapter, an agency can, over time, begin to identify closely with the industry it regulates. The agency, in fact, may go to great lengths to ensure the health of its charge.[16]

These six justifications have constituted the principal bulwark of economic regulation. When more than one has been advanced at the same time, the need for regulatory activity has seemed to be more critical. Early telephone service is a case in point. The expenses of fixed costs (justification one), acknowledgement of the basic rights associated with the service (justification three), early monopolistic tendencies (justification four), and encouragement to grow (justification five), brought together numerous forces in and out of government to work toward regulation. Such justifications do not necessarily sit well with a historic anathema toward regulation. Nevertheless, they are just as much a part of our economic history as Adam Smith's call for strict separation between producers and consumers.

The Growth of Economic Regulation

As the twentieth century began, it appeared that the ICC might handle all aspects of economic regulation. Its very title, "Interstate Commerce," suggested an expansive range of responsibilities, and this seemed to be confirmed when Congress assigned the regulation of telegraphs and telephones to the young commission in 1910.[17] But the regulatory zeal connected with the Progressive Era began to point economic regulation in new directions.

In 1913, the banking industry became the next significant economic interest to fall under federal control.[18] Because many public officials believed that the largely unregulated private banking system was a primary cause of serious economic fluctuations, Congress established the Federal Reserve Board (FED) to assure an even flow of money, low rates of inflation, and stable economic growth. The independent regulatory commission (this time with seven members and staggered fourteen-year terms), was again chosen as the instrument of economic reliability.[19]

The call for further economic regulation waned during the 1920s. An expanding economy restored public faith in the ability of the free market to act as a guarantor of growth and wealth. The only significant economic regulatory agency established during this period was the Federal Radio Commission in 1927, later to be known as the Federal Communications Commission (FCC).[20] For a time, it appeared that federal policy makers were content to organize the economy as a modest mix of free enterprise and select regulation.

But the bubble of faith in market mechanisms burst in 1929. Economic collapse and the subsequent depression destroyed public confidence in the ability of the business community to act responsibly without federal guidance. From 1932 to 1934, the financial-services industry saw four new major agencies formed to help prevent future economic catastrophes. The Federal Home Loan Bank Board was established to regulate savings-and-loan associations and to help increase the availability of mortgage credit. The Federal Deposit Insurance Corporation (FDIC) was formed to guarantee bank deposits to help restore confidence in the nation's banks and to further regulate the banking industry. The Federal Savings and Loan Insurance Corporation (FSLIC) was established to similarly regulate savings-and-loan associations and savings banks.[21] And the newly created Securities and Exchange Commission (SEC) began to regulate U.S. stock exchanges, which had to be licensed by the commission, with the rates their members charging the public thus becoming controlled.[22]

The 1930s also brought increased regulation to the transportation industries. With the Motor Carrier Act of 1935, the ICC was allowed to control major segments of the trucking industry including entry, types of commodities transported, and rates.[23] And in 1938, Congress placed the young civilian aviation industry under regulatory control as well, creating the Civil Aeronautics Authority, replacing it with the Civil Aeronautics Board two years later. Airline routes, prices, and entry and exit thus fell under the regulatory umbrella.[24]

Many other regulatory commissions were created as Franklin Roosevelt's New Deal attempted to cope with the Great Depression. Within a decade, the federal government regulated steamships, airlines, trucks, and trains; telephones, telegraphs, radios, and televisions; pipelines, dams, and electricity; banks, savings-and-loan associations, savings banks, and stock exchanges.[25] Faith in the marketplace and free enterprise had been replaced by a new belief in a changed relationship between the federal government and the private sector.

The compelling needs associated with World War II led to a cessation of additional regulatory activity, and even after hostilities ended, policy makers allowed the economy to find its own equilibrium without further governmental intervention. Although there were sporadic efforts at economic regulation during the 1960s and '70s, the changes were minimal compared to those of the first third of the twentieth century.

The Second Wave: Social Regulation

Until the 1960s, most regulation was directed toward control of the economic sector. From the mid-1960s to the present, however, regulatory initiatives have been primarily designed to provide increased protection for the environment, the consumer, and the worker. Largely societal in orientation, the agenda of the past two decades has been so significantly different from earlier governmental involvements that it has often been called the *new regulation*.

The differences between economic and social regulation are substantially more than a change of labels. Economic regulation has given government control over major economic decisions, including price, rate of return, and entry and exit. Although tailored for specific industries, economic agencies usually have broad mandates. Simply put, economic regulation places government in the driver's seat with respect to the economic direction and performance of the regulated industry.

Social regulation assumes different goals and objectives from its economic counterpart. Policies associated with social regulation focus on specific attributes of products, such as safety levels, without directly controlling major economic decisions. Unlike the industry-by-industry orientation of economic regulation, social regulation attends to a problem that may impact several industries—pollution, for example. Despite the depth of focus, social regulatory agencies have narrow mandates; they have little room for discretion. They are less concerned with an industry or segment of production than with the general welfare of society.[26]

The importance of the rise of social regulation cannot be overstated. Prior to 1964, only one regulatory agency, the FDA, had been established with the primary goal of protecting the well-being—as opposed to the economic interests—of consumers, workers, or the public. Between 1964 and 1977, eleven regulatory agencies were created to meet these goals: the Equal Employment Opportunity Commission (EEOC) (1964), the National Transportation Safety Board (NTSB) (1966), the Council on Environmental Quality (1969), the EPA and OSHA (1970), the CPSC (1972), the Mining Enforcement and Safety Administration (1973), the Nuclear Regulatory Commission (NRC) (1974), the Materials Transportation Bureau (1975), and the Office of Strip Mining Regulation and Enforcement (1977).[27]

The new social regulations have made critical contributions to overall federal regulatory growth. In 1970, expenditures by social and economic regulatory agencies amounted to $500 million and $300 million respectively. By 1980, the budgets for social regulatory agencies had increased by more than ten times to $5.1 billion, while economic regulatory agency budgets had more than tripled to about $1 billion.[28] The increase in the numbers of federal regulatory employees also can be attributed in large part to the new social regulation. In 1970, personnel in social and economic regulatory agencies were split 9,700 (35%) social to 18,000 (65%) economic. But by 1980, the split was 66,400 (73%) for social agencies and 24,100 (27%) for economic agencies.[29] By whichever standard one chooses—agency budgets or personnel, pages in *The Federal Register* (proposed rules) or *The Code of Federal Regulations* (actual rules), or the number of agencies or statutes—the growth in federal regulatory activity has been so dramatic that the Center for the Study of American Business has declared that it "has perhaps no counterpart in governmental expansion in the peacetime history of this nation."[30] Figure 2-1 shows the upward swing in agency growth that began in the 1960s.

Although most of the social regulation originated in the late 1960s and early 1970s, some regulatory statutes were passed during the Progressive Era and the New Deal. The Progressive Era, a period of increased economic regulation, took its name from efforts by laborers, consumers, and farmers to change the relationship between government and business. But far beyond the relationship between government and business, Progressive philosophy embraced new social and political values that rejected laissez-faire and justified public control of social and economic institutions according to the principles of liberal democracy. Regulation, then, held new social implications in addition to its assumed economic meanings. Important regulatory acts passed during the Progressive Era included the Food and Drug Act of 1906 and the Federal Trade Commission Act of 1914, which established the FTC as an independent administrative agency.

During the first six years of the New Deal, 1933 to 1938, regulatory

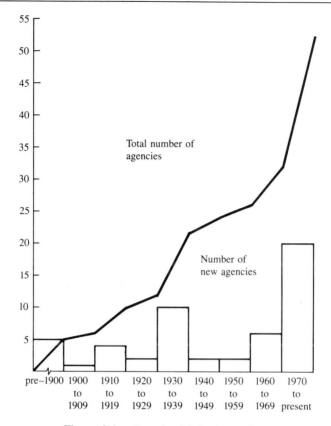

Figure 2-1. Growth of federal agencies
Source: Murray Weidenbaum, "The Benefits of Regulatory Reform," in
Regulation and Deregulation, Jules Backman, ed. (Indianapolis: Bobbs-
Merrill Educational Publishing Company, 1981), p. 54.

activity was primarily directed at restoring the U.S. economy. The Great
Depression, however, challenged the nation's social values as much as its
economic framework. Yet, of the many reform measures passed by
Congress, only three held social importance: the 1935 Wagner Housing
Act, the 1938 Fair Labor Standards Act, and the 1938 Food, Drug, and
Cosmetic Act; each of these was substantially weakened in the face of
business opposition.[31] Increasing government interest in social issues,
however, was apparent.

The most recent period of social regulatory activism can be distinguished from the Progressive Era and New Deal by three characteristics. First, the sheer volume of recent regulatory actions and statutes has
dwarfed earlier reforms. David Vogel notes that in the area of consumer
safety and health the federal government enacted five laws during the
Progressive Era and eleven during the New Deal, but sixty-two between
1965 and 1979. In the worker-safety field, only five statutes were enacted

during both the Progressive Era and the New Deal, while twenty-one laws were passed between 1960 and 1978. Similar trends are seen in the regulation of energy and the environment: Two statutes became law in the Progressive Era, five during the New Deal, but thirty-two since the late 1960s.[32]

The change in origin of these regulatory initiatives provides the second distinguishing characteristic. During the first two periods, most of the social legislation had been sponsored by strong, activist presidents: Theodore Roosevelt and Woodrow Wilson during the Progressive Era and Franklin Roosevelt during the New Deal. By contrast, the most recent period of regulatory action has been dominated by the Congress. In the words of one authority, "Unlike the situation in previous eras, the source of most of the recent regulatory initiatives was Congress itself, . . . and the legion of congressional staff members on the lookout for issues through which their principals—particular congressmen and senators—could attain visibility and national prominence."[33] Each issue subject to regulation seemed to have its own sponsors. While Sen. Edmund Muskie (D.–Maine) watched over the environmental movement, Sen. Warren Magnuson (D.–Wash.) and Rep. John Moss (D.–Calif.) concerned themselves with consumer issues. Meanwhile, Sen. Edward Kennedy (D.–Mass.) became the congressional watchdog for health care.[34]

The third characteristic of the latest regulatory initiatives has been their specificity. The federal government has become involved in almost all facets of the production process. For example, OSHA often sets not only performance standards, but also specific engineering controls that must be adopted; likewise, the CPSC requires not only that products be safe but also that they possess certain specific features, such as a "deadman" switch on a lawnmower.[35] Criteria such as these underscore the approach of social regulation. Performance standards do not tell companies what to do, but rather the results they must achieve. As a result, "(r)egulatory officials began routinely to shape and influence virtually every important decision made by virtually every firm."[36] Regulators in various commissions throughout the bureaucracy have collectively become formidable policy makers.

Justification for Social Regulation

The social regulation movement did not begin in a vacuum. Rather, various attempts to redress the nation's economic ills over a long period of time left many critics dissatisfied with the results. Despite post–World War II promises of "the good life," prosperity developed more slowly for some than for others. By the 1960s, a constellation of interests began to demand change in all arenas of power, including regulation. Elements within society who were dissatisfied with race relations joined first with those who opposed the war in Vietnam, and later with those who were concerned with the environment; altogether, they sought to reorganize the nation's political, economic, and social systems. In his chronology of crisis and regulatory reform, Robert Rabin connects long-term dissent with demands for new governmental responses in areas previously untouched:

> [T]hese sustained groundswells of protest and dissent [created] an atmosphere in which previously unnoticed consequences of industrialism were subjected to the same close scrutiny as the promises and performance of political and business leaders in other spheres of activity. And given the temper of the time, once the largely ignored social landscape of industrial development was subjected to close scrutiny, a new wave of regulatory activity was virtually a foregone conclusion.[37]

The demands for social regulatory activities, then, developed in reaction to politically unsatisfactory economic policies.

Two principle justifications for social regulation have emerged in response to market failure, or where the market economy fails to work satisfactorily. The first argument stresses the economic theme of *externality,* a situation said to exist when the actions of a producer or consumer impose costs on society not accounted for in the costs of production or consumption. If a widget factory dumps waste into a river, for example, everyone is hurt by the loss of clean water. The cleanup costs of the river should be borne by the producers and consumers of widgets, but they are not; the cost is said to be *external* to production. If widget-production problems seem remote, the consequences of pollution in general are no longer seen as distant. Rabin points out that until the regulatory demands of the 1970s, "the only weapons available to victims of pollution were an ineffectual common law remedy, the tort of private nuisance, and a collection of weak federal and state antipollution statutes."[38] Hence, advocates of "the public interest" pressured Congress and the executive branch for meaningful regulatory response.

The problem of air pollution presents a classic illustration of externality. Many industrial producers consider air a free commodity, yet their production processes often leave the surrounding community with unhealthy air. The offending industries have little motivation to take corrective action, especially when such efforts are likely to be costly. Moreover, companies that voluntarily attempt to mitigate negative production effects often find themselves at a competitive disadvantage. Consider pollution as a result of automobile emissions: The prudent industry response may be no response at all. John Riccardo, former president of Chrysler Corporation, explains: "Any manufacturer who installs and charges for such equipment while his competition doesn't soon finds he is losing sales and customers. In cases like this, a government standard requiring everyone to have such equipment is the only way to protect both the public and the manufacturer."[39] With externalities, there is no place in the free-market environment for a producer to assume the bill, much less admit responsibility. The government therefore must intercede to rectify those conditions that are not obtained in marketplace relationships; that adjustment comes through regulatory activity.

The second justification for social regulation involves *imperfect information*. A key assumption underlying the theory of an efficient market economy is that producers, consumers, and workers all have sufficient information about the benefits and costs of their possible actions and are thus able to make rational decisions.[40] But the failure of this assumption is two-fold.

First, correct and complete information may not be available to those who seek it. For example, business is unlikely to provide information that would reduce sales or result in increased wages to employees in compensation for unsafe work conditions. This problem can sometimes be mitigated by governmental intervention, such as federal labeling and disclosure requirements. Examples include the labeling of ingredients in food and drugs, warning labels on possibly dangerous products, and energy-efficiency labeling of electrical appliances.

Second, the public may not be able to accurately assess the available information. Consumers and workers may not understand it if they have it and, even if they do, may not apply it correctly. Many studies have shown that most people do not naturally understand statistics.[41] And even if the public could adequately comprehend the effects of its decisions, such decisions often involve significant costs. For the most part, people have little time and few resources to determine the safety of the various products they purchase. Most people would rather not worry each day about the toxicity of the food they eat or the concentration of carcinogenic agents in their workplaces. Because of this lack of general public involvement, the federal government has set minimum standards in various areas. For example, the FDA requires that all drugs undergo extensive tests to ensure that they are not only effective but also safe. Similarly, the CPSC requires that children's sleepware be treated with a flame retardant, and the FAA sets standards to ensure that airline pilots are qualified and that planes are mechanically sound.

Social regulation was not proposed merely as a convenient alternative to economic regulation; rather, it represented a fundamental shift in priorities from narrow oversight of selected industries to broad control over basic objectives, and from concern with efficient production to promotion of the public good.

The Push for Social Regulation

As various segments of society organized to protest the status quo, advocates of social regulation gained allies in their quest for new governmental intervention in the economic and social systems. Inasmuch as social regulation constitutes more fundamental change than does its economic counterpart, it is understandable that its advocates have had an uphill battle. Nevertheless, two factors contributed to the delayed arrival of social regulation.

First, the public grew increasingly aware of the dangers involved with the products of modern life. Although Americans have seen their life-spans lengthen through the twentieth century, they have become increasingly cognizant of the life-threatening conditions connected with post–industrial society. True enough, there were some unsafe products on the market early in the century, including adulterated meats and unsafe drugs. But by the 1960s, modern technology had created many more new products, many of which were of dubious benefit. Some of those that have allegedly caused unacceptable levels of harm to the public include: diethyl stilbestrol or DES (toxic poisoning), Tris (flammable clothing), leaded gasoline (brain damage), vinyl chloride (brain damage), the pesticide DDT (toxicity), tobacco products (lung and other cancers), fluorocarbon propellants (environmental damage and breathing difficulties), tampons (Toxic Shock Syndrome), phosphates (water pollution), poisonous household cleaners, Firestone radial tires (premature punctures at high speeds), and even aircraft such as the SST, or supersonic transport (environmental damage at high speeds), and the DC-10 (inferior design).[42]

The new concern for safety has been facilitated by scientific advances that allow the use of increasingly sophisticated techniques to measure product hazards. For example, food products such as saccharin and cyclamates were long thought to be safe but are now suspected to be carcinogenic, as are such substances in the workplace as asbestos and benzene. As David Vogel notes, we are now "dealing with a level of public consciousness about environmental, consumer, and occupational hazards that appears to be of a different order of magnitude from public outrage over such issues during both the Progressive Era and the New Deal."[43] In short, life-style issues have been added to the public agenda as questions worthy of government concern.

The second factor in the ascendancy of social concerns during this time period has been the emergence of public-interest groups as major political forces. Examples of such important public-interest consumer and environmental organizations include the Friends of the Earth, the Consumers Union, the Environmental Defense Fund, Common Cause, and Public Citizen. The growth of these groups has often been dramatic. Between 1970 and 1971, for example, the five largest environmental associations increased their membership by 400,000, or 33 percent.[44]

The ability of public-interest groups to influence policy makers was enhanced by three factors. First, these organizations were able to effectively pressure policy makers through their use of media, grass-roots organizing, and sophisticated lobbying techniques. Second, these groups were helped by the Supreme Court's broadening of the rules governing standing to sue. This has allowed many consumer and environmental groups to file suit on behalf of the public. Third, business, for the most part, has failed to match the aggressive lobbying of these groups.

Former FTC commissioner Michael Pertschuk concluded in 1982 that corporations and business interests ignored the political impact of social and environmental movements. They placed their faith in trade and other umbrella organizations, even though these bodies had long ago lost their commitment: "While young public-interest volunteers worked well into the night, spurred by conviction and a sense of political momentum (if not manifest destiny), the business lobbyist, on the defensive, . . . earned his pay and reserved his commitment for the fifth hole at the congressional country club."[45] Moreover, if all defensive efforts failed, the leaders of regulated industries felt consolation in knowing that any costs connected with regulation would be passed on to consumers with little harm to their industries.

The Third Wave: Resistance

The effects of social regulation have changed the landscape of American politics. Whereas many businesses initially perceived the latest wave of regulation as neutral, if not benign, their relationships with the new regulatory agencies became increasingly hostile as the public units asserted their power over the private sector. And agency power seemed to be sweeping in scope. The fledgling regulatory bodies dealt not with just one industry but across industries. They significantly expanded governmental intervention into quarters of the private sector unaccustomed to such supervision.

Unlike the feelings of "protection" associated with early economic regulation, business leaders now began to equate social regulation with unnecessary interference. Many executives sensed a loss of control, believing that the new agencies were telling them who to hire, who not to fire, and how to produce, all of them decisions previously made solely by the private sector. Now on the defensive, corporate leaders were accused of promoting dangerous products, discriminating against minorities, endangering workers, and despoiling the environment.

Anger in the private sector mounted not only over the loss of control but also over the added expenses. Cleaning up the environment usually meant adding the extra costs to their products; improved working conditions translated into higher operating outlays. Moreover, the volumes of paperwork involved with compliance consumed endless amounts of time, money, and patience, all of which interrupted the natural flow of commerce. Business leaders, never more than lukewarm in their endorse-

ment of social regulation, now became the first to retreat. Their senti-
ments were soon echoed by members of Congress and even the regulatory
agencies themselves.

Business Fights Back

Business representatives chose to fight social regulation along several
avenues. Because regulation was no longer industry-specific, business
leaders saw the need to answer broad-based rules with equally broad-
based organizations. For hundreds of companies to respond individually
to each rule would be confusing and counterproductive. Thus, in order to
channel their energies in a more rewarding fashion, some of the largest
corporations formed an umbrella organization, the Business Roundtable,
in 1972. The Roundtable sought to increase the political visibility of
business by bringing corporate chief executive officers together with
leaders in Washington and by lobbying Congress and federal agencies for
rules that would be more compatible with the needs of business.[46]

But individual companies and industries did not rely solely upon the
Roundtable's efforts. Corporate presence in Washington skyrocketed
during the 1970s. Public-affairs offices of private organizations increased
fivefold, while many staffs tripled in size.[47] At both individual and group
levels, business fought back by disseminating information about the
harms from regulation. In addition, in questions of environmental protection, tobacco control, and auto safety, business turned to the courts for
the purpose of slowing or reversing regulatory trends.

Paying the Price: The Problem of Cost

During the late 1970s, the American economy slumped substantially.
Inflation and interest rates hit new highs, and unemployment failed to
provide its usual braking effect. Business and others blamed regulation as
one significant cause of the economic morass.[48] Many critics traced the
economic ills of the time to regulation. For example, Barry Bosworth,
former chair of the Council on Wage and Price Stability, cited regulation
as the source of a ¾ to 1½ percent increase in the cost of living each
year.[49] As inflation and its cures led to unemployment, regulation was
once again targeted as a major culprit.

The long-run impacts of regulation became a troublesome issue to
critics and policy makers alike. Businesses were often forced to invest
large amounts of time and money in complying with specific federal
directives. In the process, business leaders claimed, they had less money
available for research and development.[50] Although the effect might not
be immediately noticeable, businesses feared they would lose their competitive advantage. Eventually, lower levels of research and productivity
would combine to limit growth of the U.S. economy for years to come.

When regulation did not "go away," business interests organized a serious counteroffensive. Specific groups and industries complained of special burdens. Small businesses contended that they could not comply with the same rules and amount of paperwork that were imposed on giant corporations, while large corporations claimed that they were being penalized for their success. Other critics of regulation charged that the burdens for a cleaner environment and safer products and workplaces fell primarily on the poor, who might prefer higher wages and lower prices to regulated "amenities."

The business claims were not completely without merit. Regulation undoubtedly imposes significant costs on society, but its proponents have always contended that the substantial benefits easily outweigh these costs. A number of studies that focused on the harm done by regulation drew considerable attention, the most famous of them by Murray Weidenbaum, a prominent conservative economist who once headed the Council of Economic Advisors. Weidenbaum estimated that regulation cost the private sector $120 billion in 1980.[51] An earlier study by the Business Roundtable calculated the costs to forty-eight corporations of regulations by the EPA, EEOC, OSHA, FTC, and the Departments of Energy and Labor. The report found the direct cost of regulation to be $2.6 billion. Indirect costs were not calculated, and the study did not intend to be comprehensive. Still, it had identified the significant expenses associated with new federal rules.[52]

"Unreasonableness" and "cost" became the rallying cries for business elements opposed to social regulation. Coupled with the traditional American predisposition to a free-market economy as the economic guarantor of democracy, regulation opponents now had a powerful arsenal of weapons with which to attack the pitfalls of excessive government.

Regulation in Transition?

While it is true that regulation has imposed substantial financial burdens, the industry-sponsored studies of costs and other problems have seldom told the whole story. Most economic regulation provides direct monetary benefits to those regulated, but business studies seldom mention this. In effect, the corporate opposition to governmental intervention is often selective. Helpful governmental policies, while perhaps not the hallmark of free enterprise, are seldom opposed.

One observer of regulatory policies provides an example of the inconsistency of industry criticism of governmental involvement. Walter Gellhorn examined a 1980 steel-industry report that focused on "excessive regulation" as the principal cause of the industry's woes. The report argued that governmental rules and interference with free-market activities forced the steel industry to divert funds that otherwise would have been used for the purchase of modern equipment and expanded production. The needed solutions, the industry argued, "are friendly tax laws, lessened environmental and other regulation, and *increased regulation* of foreign competition" (italics added).[53] The conclusion indicates that even within the boardrooms of the corporate sector, regulation has its place. To some critics and defenders alike, it then becomes a question of determining "good" from "bad" regulation, a distinction that is inherently subjective and often self-serving.

Consumer advocate Joan Claybrook summarizes the conflicting feelings that business often has about government regulation: "Uncle Sam is fine when he plays Uncle Sugar. . . . It is compellingly clear that many corporations welcome government when it is the subsidizer of last resort, guarantor of last resort, insurer of last resort, and cartel-defender of last resort. But when Uncle Sugar becomes Uncle Sam, people protector of last resort, the corporate tiger bares his teeth and snarls."[54]

As we have seen, the distinction between economic and social regulation is important. Business often derives direct benefits from economic regulation, and some elements within a given industry may well lose from deregulation. The motives for economic deregulation are often different from those for social deregulation. The technological conditions that initially spawn much economic regulation often evolve into new conditions in which regulation is no longer required. Long-distance telephone service was at one time a natural monopoly, and it made good sense to regulate the service; but the advent of satellite transmissions encouraged competition, to the profit of both consumers and new firms. Changes in the financial-services industries, which we will discuss in chapter 8, made the old system of economic regulation both outdated and unworkable. Finally, both conservatives and liberals alike have come to question the use of economic regulation where there is no compelling justification for its use. Society checks the power of major corporations in many ways not available a century ago, and economic regulation is no longer the only answer to problems created by business.

Social regulation is another matter. Although the costs of regulation are easily identified and often fall heavily on business, the benefits are not easily measured and accrue to the population in general; this does not make these benefits any less real or important. The Center for Policy Alternatives at the Massachusetts Institute of Technology (MIT) prepared a study for the U.S. Senate and found that social regulation at the federal level directly saved billions of dollars each year. The study examined regulations issued by EPA, OSHA, CPSC, FDA, NHTSA, and the Food Safety and Quality Service, and found that the lives saved, injuries prevented, and productivity increases from regulation saved billions of dollars each year for society.[55]

Comparing the costs and benefits of social regulation is much harder than it is for economic regulation. The FDA is a good example of the difficulty in evaluating the costs and benefits of social deregulation. A number of the administration's critics have argued that its drug-efficacy laws are so stringent that many beneficial pharmaceuticals are needlessly kept from the U.S. market. The FDA has responded to these charges by noting that rigorous testing requirements are necessary to prevent such health disasters as the Thalidomide incident in which thousands of infants were born with gross deformities, the consequences of an improperly tested drug. It is hard to say who is correct; proving that present regulations are not too stringent might be to risk another such disaster.

The changes wrought by regulation over the last century have been massive. By the mid-1970s, however, observers both in and out of government began to reconsider once-acceptable policies. First economic and then social regulation became topics for serious debate. The regulated society had lost favor, and the taming of big government had become a political issue of virtue to both Republicans and Democrats.

Notes

1. Adam Smith, *The Wealth of Nations,* Modern Library Edition (New York: Random House, 1937).
2. Milton Friedman, *Capitalism and Freedom* (Chicago: University of Chicago Press, 1962), p. 9.
3. David B. Truman, *The Governmental Process* (New York: Knopf, 1951), p. 507.
4. E. E. Schattschneider, *The Semisovereign People* (New York: Holt, Rinehart & Winston, 1960), p. 40.
5. Theodore J. Lowi, *The End of Liberalism* (New York: Norton, 1969), p. 71.
6. See Alan Stone, *Regulation and Its Alternatives,* (Washington, D.C.: Congressional Quarterly Press, 1982), p. 41.
7. Truman, *Governmental Process,* pp. 104–105.
8. Marver H. Bernstein, *Regulating Business by Independent Commission* (Westport, Conn.: Greenwood Press, 1955), pp. 117–119.
9. Frances Fox Piven and Richard A. Cloward, *Regulating the Poor* (New York: Vintage Books, 1971), p. 90.
10. For an excellent chronology of the rise and fall of interest-group clout and governmental responses, see Robert L. Rabin, "Federal Regulation in Historical Perspective," *Stanford Law Review,* 38-1189 (May 1986): 1189–1326.
11. Kay Lehman Schlozman and John T. Tierney, *Organized Interests and American Democracy* (New York: Harper & Row, 1986), p. 75.
12. Louis M. Kohlmeier, Jr., *The Regulators* (New York: Harper & Row, 1969), pp. 11–12.
13. Congressional Quarterly (CQ), *Regulation: Process and Politics* (Washington, D.C.: Congressional Quarterly, Inc., 1982), pp. 11–12.
14. Kohlmeier, *Regulators,* p. 12.
15. CQ, *Regulation,* p. 12.
16. This section draws heavily from the excellent review of the justifications for regulation found in *Study on Federal Regulation,* vol. 6, "Framework for Regulation," U.S. Congress. Senate Committee on Governmental Affairs, December 1978.
17. Kohlmeier, *Regulators,* p. 14.
18. Stone, *Regulation,* p. 31.
19. CQ, *Regulation,* p. 14.

20. Bernstein, *Regulating Business*, pp. 22–23.
21. CQ, *Regulation*, p. 15.
22. Kohlmeier, *Regulators*, pp. 117–118.
23. CQ, *Regulation*, p. 15.
24. *Ibid.*
25. Kohlmeier, *Regulators*, pp. 105–106.
26. For other explanations of the differences between economic and social regulation, see William Lilley III and James C. Miller III, "The New 'Social Revolution,'" *Public Interest*, no. 47 (Spring 1977): 52–53; Jules Backman, "The Problem of Regulation," in *Regulation and Deregulation*, Jules Backman, ed. (Indianapolis: Bobbs–Merrill, 1981), p. 9; and *Study on Federal Regulation*, p. 32.
27. David Vogel, "The 'New' Social Regulation in Historical and Comparative Perspective," in *Regulation in Perspective*, Thomas K. McCraw, ed. (Cambridge, Mass.: Harvard University Press, 1981), p. 161.
28. CQ, *Regulation*, p. 17.
29. *Ibid.*
30. *Ibid.*, p. 18.
31. Vogel, "'New' Social Regulation," pp. 156–157.
32. *Ibid.*, pp. 161–162.
33. Thomas McCraw, "Regulatory Change, 1960–1979, in Historical Perspective," pp. 1–2, 5, in *Special Study on Economic Change*, vol. 5, *Governmental Regulation: Achieving Social and Economic Balance*, U.S. Congress, Joint Economic Committee, December 8, 1980.
34. Stone, *Regulation*, pp. 184–189.
35. Lilley and Miller, "New 'Social Revolution,'" p. 53.
36. Vogel, "'New' Social Regulation," p. 162.
37. Rabin, "Federal Regulation," p. 1282.
38. *Ibid.*, p. 1283.
39. CQ, *Regulation*, p. 9.
40. Fred Thompson and L. R. Jones, *Regulatory Policy and Practice: Regulating Better and Regulating Less* (New York: Praeger, 1982), p. 67.
41. *Ibid.*, p. 77.
42. Vogel, "'New' Social Regulation," p. 160.
43. *Ibid.*
44. Michael Pertschuk, *Revolt Against Regulation: The Rise and Pause of the Consumer Movement* (Berkeley: University of California Press, 1982), pp. 16–17.
45. Kim McQuaid, "Big Business and Public Policy in Contemporary United States," *Quarterly Review of Economics and Business*, 20, no. 2 (Summer 1980): 61–65.
46. Vogel, "'New' Social Regulation," p. 176.
47. Nina Cornel, Roger Noll, and Barry Weingast, "Safety Regulation," in *Setting National Priorities: The Next Ten Years*, Henry Own and Charles Schultze, eds. (Washington, D.C.: The Brookings Institution, 1976), p. 463.
48. Backman, "The Problem," p. 30, fn. 62.
49. *Ibid.*, p. 243.
50. *Ibid.*, p. 25, fn. 47.
51. *Ibid.*, p. 20.
52. CQ, *Regulation*, pp. 29–30.
53. Walter Gellhorn, "Deregulation: Delight or Delusion?" *St. Louis University Law Journal*, 24 (October 1980): 470.
54. Joan Claybrook, "Crying Wolf," *Regulation*, 2, no. 6 (November/December 1978): 14.
55. CQ, *Regulation*, p. 30.

CHAPTER 3

The Move
to Deregulate

The move to deregulate has had a broad basis of support. Over the past twenty years, Congress has been strongly interested in legislation designed to limit the regulation of trucking and has acted to eliminate oversight of airlines. The judiciary also has flexed its deregulatory muscles, particularly in the area of telecommunications. Regulated industries, in fact, have had their once-protected status diminished by congressional and court actions and even stripped where further pressure came from competing private- and public-interest groups. But of all the assaults against the regulation tradition, presidential actions have had the most significant impact.

Presidents are not legislators; they have the power, however, to issue executive orders. Although not judges, they can appoint agency heads and commissioners who have quasi-judicial powers. Perhaps Richard Neustadt understates the point when he remarks that the president's most important power is the "power to persuade,"[1] for it seems to give the chief executive a *de facto,* if not *de jure,* authority equal to that of the other branches of government.

The presidency has emerged as the most critical force for deregulation, although not the only one. Martha Derthick and Paul Quirk note that regardless of political party, "successive presidents beginning with Ford have made regulatory reform a leading part of their domestic agendas, conceiving of it broadly as a response to the excesses of government or at least of bureaucracy."[2] With respect to the analysis here, we add two thoughts: One, regulatory reform actually began with Ford's predecessor, Richard Nixon, and two, reform efforts have been couched primarily in the context of deregulation.

Presidential administrations have long had a "love–hate" relationship with the federal bureaucracy, the seemingly incomprehensible maze wherein most regulatory authorities are housed. Indeed, virtually every chief executive has struggled to remold the bureaucracy to his vision, only to complain of resistance. Although White House occupants have been unrelenting in condemning an unresponsive bureaucracy, their concern increased greatly in response to the growth of federal regulation during the early 1960s. To establish better control over the bureaucracy, presidents have created innovative management techniques and adopted new regulatory structures. Initially used to manage and reform the process of regulation, these new techniques and structures became the basis of future deregulatory actions.

This chapter reviews the deregulatory initiatives of the last four presidential administrations, which followed surges of regulation during the first two-thirds of the twentieth century. Although experience with regulation had shown benefits, both politicians and the public began to question the wisdom of governmental oversight. And as the economy deteriorated in the late 1970s and early '80s, the price paid for regulation took on even greater importance.

Deregulation: The Early Years

When Ronald Reagan battled Jimmy Carter for the presidency in 1980, he described his candidacy as a radical departure from a series of administrations dedicated to "big government." Reagan's conservatism has definitely distinguished his administration from his predecessors' back to Franklin D. Roosevelt's New Deal. But with respect to deregulation, his values have roots that go back to the late 1960s.

The Nixon Administration

The antecedents of current deregulatory policy can be found in the administration of Richard Nixon, who was dismayed by a federal bureaucracy seemingly beyond presidential control. When Nixon first took office, he asked Roy Ash, president of Litton Industries, to chair the Advisory Council on Executive Management. The council's mission was to recommend new managerial and organizational methods so that the White House could more effectively manage independent regulatory commissions and executive agencies.[3] The council fulfilled its mandate and suggested "more sweeping regulatory reforms than those proposed by any prior official study group."[4] Virtually all of its recommendations, however, received little serious attention.

In July 1970, Congress approved a major plan to reorganize the White House office. A key part of the reorganization was the conversion of the Bureau of the Budget into the Office of Management and Budget (OMB).[5] OMB was established in the executive office of the president as his policy arm. In addition to developing and managing federal-agency budgets, OMB was given additional responsibilities for reviewing the executive branch's management procedures, assisting in interagency cooperation, and developing regulatory reform proposals.[6] The design of OMB was partly intended to give a central focus to regulatory activity under the president's control.

In the early 1970s, concern began to mount about the costs to the private sector imposed by federal regulations, especially as those costs affected inflation. Many business leaders were specifically spurred to action by the numerous regulatory promulgations of the EPA. Alarmed about the potential costs of the agency's requirements, industry appealed to the Department of Commerce for relief. Maurice Stans, then-secretary of the department, urged the EPA to slow its regulatory pace and lobbied for regulatory relief within the White House.[7]

In June 1971, John Ehrlichman, Nixon's chief domestic-policy aide, issued a memorandum establishing a quality-of-life committee, which was to study the desirability of establishing a high-level review of important federal regulations that affected the balance among consumer, environmental, and business interests.[8] Convinced of the need to contain costly regulations and maintain control over regulatory initiatives, President Nixon issued an executive order in October 1971 that, for the first time, established an interagency regulatory review process. OMB was to conduct its own "quality of life" review of regulations and alternatives as proposed by those agencies with jurisdiction over consumer protection, environmental quality, and occupational health and safety.[9]

To facilitate interagency review, the quality-of-life review process required agencies to submit proposed rules to OMB at least thirty days before their publication in the *Federal Register*. In addition, an agency was to submit an analysis of the rule's objectives, possible alternatives, and a comparison of the costs and benefits of the rule and its alternatives. After receiving the agency's analysis, OMB would solicit views from other agencies, review the comments, and return the information to the original agency. Before submitting a final rule, an agency would have to resubmit a draft copy to OMB in advance, facing the possibility of having the interagency-review process repeated.[10]

The quality-of-life review was limited because, in reality, only EPA regulations were considered for review. George Eads and Michael Fix note that this "seemingly arbitrary operation of the review created ill will among environmentalists, their allies in Congress, many of the professional staff at EPA, and former EPA officials. This legacy would haunt all future White House oversight efforts."[11] Such widespread resentment led to the termination of the quality-of-life review process when Jimmy Carter assumed the presidency. Whatever its limitations, the quality-of-life program was important in establishing the OMB as the focal point in controlling and managing regulatory activity; it was also one of the first attempts by a president to develop a "regulatory clearing-house" under executive control.

The Ford Administration

Deregulation under the Ford administration consisted of both statutory and administrative initiatives. On the statutory front, plans were developed to deregulate the airline, trucking, and railroad industries. After several years of debate, variations of these proposals were enacted by Congress during the Carter administration. On the administrative front, Ford tried to moderate regulations and rules issued by executive-branch agencies in Ford's attempt to lower the inflation rate.

Much of the Ford administration's difficulties stemmed from inflation, which was running at an alarming 11 percent a year, stimulated by high energy-price increases. In an effort to cope with this bane to all Americans, Ford got Congress to create the Council on Wage and Price Stability (COWPS). As with Nixon's efforts to centralize control, this agency would be housed in the office of the president.

COWPS had two missions. First, it was charged with monitoring private-sector activities that might increase the inflation rate. Upon finding such activity, however, COWPS was virtually powerless to take action; the council was limited to "jawboning" labor and industry to moderate their price-increase and labor demands.[12] Second, COWPS was instructed to review existing federal programs and activities to determine their inflationary impact, a mandate COWPS interpreted as requiring cost–benefit analysis of major regulatory proposals.[13]

In November 1974, three months after COWPS was created, President Ford issued Executive Order 11,821, which established the Inflation Impact Statement (IIS) program. The order required that "[m]ajor proposals for legislation, and for the promulgation of regulations or rules by any executive branch agency must be accompanied by a statement which certifies that the inflationary impact of the proposal has been evaluated."[14] At first, OMB wanted to delegate authority for overseeing compliance to the actual agencies affected, but COWPS insisted that a meaningful review be conducted. Consequently, OMB and COWPS divided monitoring activity between them with COWPS economists taking the lead in evaluating proposed regulations.[15] Soon COWPS began to issue written statements and detailed studies in an effort to persuade executive agencies to moderate their rule making. Ford's executive order, however, did not require the agencies to follow OMB and COWPS recommendations, although it did direct the agencies to "cooperate" with them. COWPS reviews were advisory only and the council had no power to halt or delay any agency rule that COWPS thought was unjustifiably inflationary.

Another significant problem with the IIS program was the often poor quality of the affected agencies' analyses. Many of the agencies did not have the proper staff to develop credible analyses of the inflationary effects of their proposed rules. The analyses often became little more than after-the-fact justifications of the rules the agencies had already issued. Even when agencies contracted the work to more experienced analysts, they often ignored or were incapable of properly evaluating the finished reports.[16] According to James C. Miller III, then an assistant director of COWPS (later, director of the OMB under President Reagan), the quality of the IIS statements varied greatly by agency. In many cases, agencies tended to develop "good estimates of costs but weak assessments of benefits, and alternatives [to the regulation] were usually ignored."[17] In general, although the executive order forced the agencies to consider the economic effects of their proposed rules, it did little, on balance, to affect the actual decisions of the executive agencies.[18]

The Carter Administration

The deregulation movement gained considerable momentum during the presidency of Jimmy Carter, who cooperated with Congress to bring greater competition to the private sector by enacting changes in a number of areas, all of them economic in focus. Table 3-1 lists the major deregulatory enactments during Carter's term.

It is important to remember that the groundwork for a number of these laws was laid by increased congressional activity during the Ford administration. This allowed Carter and Congress to translate growing disaffection with economic regulation into policy changes.

The Carter administration's attitude toward regulatory reform was inconsistent at best. Movement toward economic deregulation was significant and was in sharp contrast to a more limited effort to scale back social regulation. Social regulatory activity, in fact, actually increased during both the Ford and Carter administrations. New laws included the Resource Conservation and Recovery Act (1976), the Toxic Substances Control Act (1976), the Surface Mining Control and Reclamation Act (1977), and major revisions of the Clean Air Act (1978) that led to substantially broadened coverage.[20]

Much of the Carter administration's inconsistent deregulatory actions stemmed from deep divisions within the executive branch on the need for social deregulation. President Carter personally favored a strong policy of social regulation, especially for environmental quality.[21] His favorable stand on social regulation, in fact, had been strongly supported during the 1976 presidential campaign by organized labor and environmental interests. And once in office, Carter appointed many agency heads who were sympathetic to the goals of social regulation. But at the same time, some of Carter's closest advisors, including Charles Schultze, head of the Council of Economic Advisors, and Robert Strauss, the administration's chief inflation fighter, strongly favored reining in social regulation.[22]

Throughout Carter's term of office, his advisors tangled over the reform of social regulations. His economic specialists advocated eliminating or scaling back costly regulations and using cost–benefit analysis to improve agency rule making. Opposing them were agency heads Douglas Costle of EPA and Eula Bingham of OSHA.[23] Bingham's and Costle's agencies were more clearly tied to the benefits of social regulation, seeing the gains from cleaner air and water and safer workplaces. The economic advisors, however, without a specific con-

Table 3-1.   Major deregulatory acts during the Carter administration, 1977–1981[19]

Affected Industry	Legislation
Surface transportation	Motor Carrier Reform Act, 1980 Staggers Rail Act, 1980 Household Goods Transportation Act, 1980
Air transportation	Airline Deregulation Act, 1978 International Air Transportation Competition Act, 1979
Financial institutions	Depository Institutions Deregulation and Monetary Control Act, 1980
Energy production	Natural Gas Policy Act

stituency, were more sensitive to the general economic effects of regulation.

The Regulatory Analysis Review Group and Executive Order 12,044

To better coordinate and manage federal agency regulations, Carter modified Ford's approach of requiring Inflation Impact Statements. In January 1978, Carter created the Regulatory Analysis Review Group (RARG), composed of members of major executive agencies. RARG was instructed to review and make recommendations on a small, select number of executive-agency proposals—generally, those costing industry $100 million or more per year. To prevent RARG from picking on a particular agency, as the quality-of-life program had with EPA, RARG was to review no more than four rules per agency and was expected to review only a total of ten or twenty rules each year. A four-member executive committee (composed of a member of the Council of Economic Advisors, an OMB representative, and two rotating members) was charged with selecting the proposed regulations to be reviewed.[24]

In March 1978, President Carter issued Executive Order 12,044, which was aimed at the regulatory agencies located in the executive branch. In issuing the order, Carter stated that it "promises to make federal regulations clearer, less burdensome . . . [and] will ensure that federal regulations are cost-effective and impose minimum economic burdens on the private sector. . . . The agencies are to eliminate those [regulations] which are unnecessary and reform others to reduce the burden to the minimum."[25] Carter's executive order seemed to straddle the line between the adversaries within his administration over how best to reform the regulatory process.

In a number of ways, President Carter's approach to regulatory reform significantly departed from the Inflation Impact Statements required during Ford's administration. The key components of Executive Order 12,044 stipulated that:

1. Proposed regulations should be as simple and clear as possible.
2. Meaningful alternatives must be considered and analyzed before an agency could promulgate a regulation.
3. The public should have a meaningful opportunity to participate in the development of agency regulations.
4. Agencies must publish an agenda of significant regulations under development at least twice a year.
5. An economic-impact analysis must be prepared for all significant regulations.
6. Existing regulations must be periodically reviewed to determine whether their objectives were still being met.[26]

The Carter directive expanded upon the relatively narrow focus of the Ford administration in three important ways. First, the executive order expanded the scope of analysis from inflation to economic-impact statements. Second, it emphasized the consideration of lower-cost alternatives. Third, the approach provided for the review of *existing* as well as proposed regulation.

Executive Order 12,044 was an escalation with respect to the concern for regulatory reform. Nevertheless, the directive was limited in that it allowed the individual agencies to determine which of their rules were "significant," thus requiring economic-impact analyses. But the order was unclear about who had final responsibility for resolving conflicts between the agencies promulgating the rules and OMB, the body that performed the review. Although Carter's executive order assigned the OMB the responsibility of ensuring performance and submission of proper regulatory analyses, in reality extensive review of agency analyses was performed only by RARG.[27]

One advantage of the RARG process was that agencies were forced to develop in-house analysis groups. EPA, for example, was just one of several agencies that hired numerous economists in order to more adequately assess the costs of its proposed regulations. The efforts seemed to have had some success. In May 1979, in fact, Charles Schultze concluded that RARG's existence as a monitoring body had led to a general improvement in the quality of agency-generated analyses.[28]

Despite improvements in agencies' analytical abilities, RARG had only limited success in influencing actual agency rule making. In a dispute between an individual agency and RARG, the agency had little if any incentive to cooperate or follow RARG's recommendations to limit or abandon a rule. RARG alone possessed no power: It could not cut appropriations or otherwise discipline a recalcitrant agency. If an agency ignored RARG, there was no mechanism to resolve a dispute without involving the president.

The so-called cotton-dust incident of 1976–1977 (discussed at length in chapter 8) proved a key setback for the RARG process. After several years of study, OSHA had developed a rule that required textile-industry employers to institute engineering controls (generally ventilation equipment) to protect their workers against exposure to hazardous cotton dust. RARG, however, argued that employers should have the option of providing workers with respirators, a much cheaper alternative. After a lengthy struggle that drew considerable media attention, President Carter resolved the situation by siding with OSHA and reversing an earlier commitment he had made to Charles Schultze to support RARG's position.

The cotton-dust case was particularly significant because it affected all subsequent RARG–agency confrontations. Sensing a lack of resolve on Carter's part, agencies became less willing to compromise their regulations, and RARG officials became less likely to seek presidential review.[29] In an analysis of RARG's effectiveness, Robert Litan and William Nordhaus, formerly of the Council of Economic Advisors, concluded that RARG's comments made a difference in changing an agency's original proposal only in the case of the Department of Transportation's equal-access-for-the-handicapped rule.[30]

The Regulatory Council

Aside from RARG, Carter created the Regulatory Council in October 1978 in an effort to provide more deliberate oversight of regulatory policies. The council differed from RARG in both membership and mandates. With representatives from both executive and independent regulatory agencies, the council was charged with coordinating similar policies across agencies to eliminate redundant regulations and prevent any one industry from being unduly burdened with federal requirements. RARG focused on specific rules, but the Regulatory Council encouraged agencies to coordinate policies as they affected particular areas (e.g., cancer-causing substances) or industries (e.g., the auto industry).[31]

The Regulatory Council, like RARG, ultimately proved of limited value. Although the council's regulatory calendar provided a systematic way for the public and other government agencies to preview proposed regulations, the council was unable to reconcile conflicting policies or even coordinate similar ones. One major disappointment for the council was its failure to persuade several agencies that had the power to regulate carcinogens to adopt similar risk-assessment techniques.[32] These failings followed from two drawbacks. First, the council had no power to enforce its decisions; second, the head of the council, Douglas Costle (also head of EPA), was not inclined to impose his views on other agencies. "Naming Doug Costle to chair the Regulatory Council," according to one regulator, "is like putting the fox in charge of the chickens."[33] Although such an analogy may have been overly critical, it does validate the claim that an agency is only as effective as its personnel, irrespective of the legislation that establishes the agency.

Deregulation and President Reagan

At the time that Ronald Reagan became president, a consensus had emerged among many policy makers and economists that something had to be done about the rising tide of federal regulation. During the 1970s, by almost any indicator, federal regulatory activity had increased significantly. Between 1970 and 1979, for example, the annual number of pages in the *Federal Register,* where all proposed federal regulations are first printed, almost tripled, and expenditures for major regulatory agencies quadrupled.[34] Compounding the problems associated with the sheer size of the federal regulatory presence, the public believed that many of these regulations were stifling competition and raising prices. Social regulations were criticized for undue reliance on prescriptive command-and-control requirements and insufficient use of such analytic techniques as cost–benefit analysis. Summing up the dissatisfaction with federal regulations, one former presidential advisor wrote, "Too many rules are needlessly rigid, or are written in legal gobbledegook, or conflict with other rules. . . . Dozens of regulatory horror stories have undermined the legitimacy of regulation as a means of settling policy . . . [and] have created the impression that individual and business initiative is being stifled with red tape."[35] The status quo was no longer acceptable to many people in and out of government.

As a presidential candidate, Ronald Reagan campaigned on the need to reassess federal regulations, which he believed were dragging the economy down. In a September 1980 speech, Reagan declared: "When the real take-home pay of the average American worker is declining steadily and eight million Americans are out of work, we must carefully reexamine our regulatory structure to assess to what degree regulations have contributed to the situation."[36] Reagan strongly believed that most social and economic regulations were unwarranted intrusions into the private sector by the federal government. A preview of his regulatory program was provided by the Republican party platform, which, in part called for deregulation, consolidation of existing agencies, sunset laws, cost–benefit analyses of major proposed regulations, and elimination of redundant, contradictory, and outmoded regulations.[37]

The Reagan deregulation program differed from its predecessors in one important respect: Previous administrations, both Republican and Democratic, had focused on regulatory reform for many agencies, but true deregulation was considered seriously only in the economic arena. In the past, critics had challenged the existence of the CAB but shied away from social agencies like OSHA. But under Reagan, the entire spectrum of regulatory activity was open for examination. For the first time, the often-made claim that economic regulation stifled free enterprise held sway, and there was widespread consideration of substantial cutbacks in the levels of protection offered by social regulation.

The ultimate goal of Reagan's regulatory policy was to provide direct "regulatory relief" to U.S. industry. Reform and repeal of existing regulations as well as a slowdown in the initiation of future regulations were seen primarily as means to aid the interests of business over those of consumers or the public in general. As businesses were freed from unnecessary government interference, the rationale went, the benefits from their lowered costs of production would accrue to the public at large.

Reagan's deregulatory-policy initiatives took a strategy of "shocking" regulatory expectations downward. With his 1980 victory, the president-elect's soon-to-be OMB director, David Stockman, called for a "well-planned and orchestrated series of unilateral administrative actions to defer, revise, or rescind existing and pending regulations where clear legal authority exists."[38] According to Stockman, a substantial and dramatic rescission of regulatory burdens was necessary "for the short-term cash flow relief it will provide to business firms and the long-term signal it will provide for corporate investment planners."[39] Stockman would, in fact, have a significant impact on the new administration's regulatory directives.

To meet his objectives as outlined by Stockman, Reagan accorded a much higher priority to regulatory oversight and reform than had his predecessors. Deregulation became the fourth cornerstone of his economic policy, the others being reducing the budget, cutting taxes, and stabilizing monetary growth.[40] And the president began to act on these elements almost as soon as he set foot in the White House. As the first element of his regulatory relief policy, on January 22, 1981, the new chief executive announced the formation of the Task Force on Regulatory Relief under the leadership of Vice-President George Bush. One week later, on January 29, Reagan put into effect the second element of his relief program by ordering a freeze on a series of "midnight" regulations that had been issued in the Carter administration's final days.

The third major policy commitment came in mid-February, when Reagan signed Executive Order 12,291. Its key provision mandated that executive agencies use cost–benefit analysis to justify future regulations, unless forbidden by statutory mandates. Alfred Kahn, head of the CAB under President Carter, summed up Reagan's early regulatory actions: "They instituted a promising mechanism. They threw out a lot of junk. They had a bold beginning."[41] Where previous administrations had only tinkered with regulatory reform, Ronald Reagan now worked to make it political reality.

One of Reagan's first actions—freezing Carter's "midnight" regulations—clearly indicated the new regulatory mood. In a memorandum to twelve major executive-branch departments and regulatory agencies, Reagan ordered that any regulations that were scheduled to go into effect within the next 60 days were postponed; furthermore, the agencies were not to issue any new rules for the same 60 days.[42] This delay allowed Bush's task force time to "review many of the prior [a]dministration's last-minute decisions that would increase rather than relieve the current burden of restrictive regulation."[43] In reality, Reagan's order exempted, for various reasons, 196 Carter regulations that were to become effective over the next 60 days.[44] Of the 172 regulations actually frozen, 112 were approved without change, 12 underwent major revision, 18 were withdrawn, and 30 were referred back to their agencies for further consideration and refinement.[45]

The Task Force on Regulatory Relief

The Task Force on Regulatory Relief embodied Reagan's regulatory philosophy. By naming George Bush to chair the task force, Reagan sought to give it considerably more political presence and authority than that enjoyed by similar oversight bodies during the Ford and Carter administrations. James C. Miller III, the task force's executive director and former member of the COWPS staff in the Ford administration, noted that "[h]aving the Vice-President leading the task force makes a big difference. . . . If it were just OMB versus the agencies it would be [at] a loggerhead."[46] The political importance of the task force was made clear by its membership: executive branch officers, including several cabinet heads (the Secretaries of Treasury, Commerce, and Labor), the director of the OMB, and Martin Anderson (assistant to the president for policy planning), Richard Williamson (special assistant to the president) as associate director, and C. Boyden Gray (counsel to the vice-president) as counsel to the task force.[47]

According to Vice-President Bush, the task force had three duties: First, to review major proposals issued by executive regulatory agencies; second, to assess existing rules, especially those particularly costly to the economy or key industrial sectors; and third, to oversee legislative proposals to modify the Clean Air Act and other major statutes in an effort to "codify the [p]resident's views on the appropriate role and objectives of regulatory agencies."[48] Compared to previous attempts, the task force had much more comprehensive objectives.

In practice, the task force took aim at those regulations targeted by business leaders as unusually burdensome. After two years of operation, the task force had managed to revise or kill 37 rules out of the 100 it had reviewed.[49] Most notable of these was a set of safety and antipollution regulations covering the auto industry, the rescission of which would purportedly save the industry several billion dollars each year.

Executive Order 12,291

The third element in Reagan's regulatory relief program was Executive Order 12,291, issued in February 1981. Far more comprehensive than Carter's Executive Order 12,044, which it superseded, Executive Order 12,291 set out stringent requirements and detailed guidelines. In the words of President Reagan, the purpose of the directive was to "reduce the burdens of existing and future regulations, increase agency accountability for regulatory actions, provide for presidential oversight of the regulatory process, minimize duplication and conflict of regulations, and insure well-reasoned regulation."[50]

Executive Order 12,291 significantly departed from earlier policy in several important ways. Except where expressly prohibited by law, the order required that all regulations pass a cost–benefit test. In all cases, "among alternative approaches to any given regulatory objective, the alternative involving the least net cost to society shall be chosen."[51] According to George Eads, former member of the Council of Economic Advisors, this was a major change from the Carter administration, which "always took pains to stress that its requirements for regulatory analysis should not be interpreted as subjecting rules to a cost–benefit test."[52] In addition to requiring the use of cost–benefit analysis, the Reagan executive order shifted the burden for proving that a proposed rule was cost-effective from the White House to the sponsoring agency itself.

Executive Order 12,291 also broke with past policies by expanding the scope of regulations to be reviewed. Under the Carter administration, "major" rules were those that would cost industry more than $100 million a year. Under the new directive, this criterion was expanded to include "any rule that is likely to result in . . . a major increase in costs or prices for consumers, individual industries, . . . [or] government agencies . . . [or] significant adverse effects on competition, employment, investment, productivity, [or] innovation."[53]

Equally important was the amount of discretion given to OMB. The authority for determining which rules were "major" was transferred from the individual agencies to the director of the OMB; in addition, the office was given the power to exempt "major" rules from review.

The unprecedented enforcement powers given to the OMB and the task force by Reagan's executive order distinguished the new policy from its predecessors. Previous regulatory-review procedures had relied on the persuasiveness of oversight officials to convince agency heads to modify or rescind regulations. Both Ford and Carter divided review among several agencies, but Reagan's order delegated to OMB and its Office of Information and Regulatory Affairs (OIRA) the responsibility and authority to make sure the mandates of the executive order were carried out. Proposed regulations could not go into effect without OMB clearance. If an agency refused to defer to OMB's judgment, the office could delay a rule's publication until any differences between it and the agency were resolved. A significant amount of OMB's power resulted from its ability to review an agency's proposed major rules not just once, but twice.

Executive Order 12,291 also directed that an agency must have forwarded a copy of a proposed notice of rule making along with a regulatory-impact analysis to OMB sixty days prior to the proposed publication of a rule and thirty days before the final rule was to be published. Even those rules not deemed major were required to be submitted ten days in advance for clearance by OMB.[54]

But even within the OMB, OIRA's power extended even further—to the designation of *existing* rules to be reviewed. Carter had only used the OMB for recommendations, not hard rules or reassessments; furthermore, there had been no formal "sunset" requirements (that is, no automatic expiration of a regulation at a certain date unless it were specifically renewed).[55] Now OMB had the authority to examine *every* regulation issued by an executive agency if it so chose. And by requiring agency heads to submit detailed regulatory-impact analyses to justify their regulations to OMB, the executive order, according to its critics, turned federal agency heads "from policy makers to policy pleaders in a tough, unsympathetic court."[56] In short, the order significantly consolidated regulatory power within the OMB.

In addition to this centralization of authority, Reagan's executive order had the effect of reducing regulatory activity. Douglas Costle noted that Executive Order 12,291 contributed toward less regulation in two ways. First, mandatory OMB review allowed the opponents of a regulation another opportunity to kill or weaken a rule. Administration budget cutters and industry opponents were guaranteed the opportunity to reformulate policy in the heart of the policy-making process. Second, by requiring cost–benefit analysis, the order made it inherently harder to justify a regulation because benefits of a rule are generally much harder to quantify than are its possible costs.[57] In short, Executive Order 12,291 offered a powerful deregulatory tool to contain and rescind federal regulations.

Despite the power given OMB by Reagan's executive order, the reach of the directive was limited to executive agencies; regulations promulgated by independent regulatory commissions were not affected. The administration had decided not to include these independents in the order for two reasons. First, there was a reasonable chance that the Supreme Court would rule such an act as an unconstitutional infringement of the separation-of-powers doctrine. Second, in a memo to the president, the Department of Justice argued that even if the Supreme Court ruled in favor of the administration, such a move would provoke "a confrontation with Congress, which has historically been jealous of its prerogatives with regard to [independent agencies]."[58] To bring the regulatory policies of the independent agencies into line with those of the administration, Reagan instead relied on several recognized management strategies.

Management Strategies as Deregulatory Tools

Among those management strategies used by the Reagan administration were significant cuts in agency budgets and staff, the appointment of new administrators who were philosophically in agreement, and the transfer of federal regulatory duties to states and localities.

Although President Reagan's primary concern was reducing the federal budget, there is little doubt that cuts in independent regulatory commissions were an important part of a strategy to cut their activity. A study by the Center for the Study of American Business at Washington University concluded that in Reagan's first year in office, regulatory agency budgets were cut 8 percent, and agency staffing was trimmed by 10 percent.[59] Budget and staffing cuts directly affect an agency's rule-making authority by making it harder for the agency to conduct the necessary analyses to determine what action, if any, should be taken. Indirectly, too, the fear and lowered morale from such cuts gives an administration considerable control over otherwise independent bureaucrats.[60] The close relationship between budgetary resources and regulations was shown in the 38 percent decrease in proposed rules and the 27 percent decrease in final rules issued in the first year of the Reagan administration as compared to the last year of the Carter administration.[61]

In several cases, the budget decreases for both executive branch and independent regulatory agencies were considerable. Between 1980 and 1984, budget cuts for the EPA, CPSC, and Office of Surface Mining (OSM) matched those of the CAB, which was being phased out of existence by statute.[62] Under the Reagan administration, the CPSC became known as the "Incredible Shrinking Agency," with a proposed 1986 fiscal year budget of $33.7 million (compared to $42 million in 1981) and a staff of 568 (compared to 812 in 1981).[63]

As a result of these budget decreases, the federal regulatory workforce across all agencies declined dramatically. In 1980, there were 90,000 full-time, permanent positions in the major federal regulatory agencies. By 1984, however, that number had declined by 16 percent to 76,000.[64]

De facto deregulation, of course, followed as the enforcement of various statutes and regulations was significantly reduced. At OSHA and EPA, for example, a lack of inspectors and willpower resulted in industry noncompliance with federal regulations. With some laws, including the Clean Water Act and the Resource Conservation and Recovery Act (which deals with hazardous-waste disposal), noncompliance has run as high as 80 percent.[65]

In other situations, agency heads, by reorganizing their departments (ostensibly to improve efficiency) were able to effectively cripple enforcement efforts. OSM, for example, enacted a plan to reorganize itself as a network of twenty-two, rather than forty-four, offices. OSM's workforce was soon cut in half as hundreds of employees resigned or were fired. The end result, in the words of Rep. Patricia Schroeder (D.–Colo.), head of the House Subcommittee on the Post Office and Civil Service, was "total agency chaos and employee panic."[66]

Presidents generally are accorded wide latitude in their appointments. Consequently, there is always some criticism of certain appointees as being unqualified for their jobs, often the result of presidents trying to balance the needs of government with the necessities of patronage. Under the Reagan administration, however, the chorus of criticism has had fuller voice as many of his appointees have been harshly criticized for being unprofessional and unduly partisan. Appointees such as Anne Gorsuch Burford at EPA, Raymond Peck at NHTSA, and Thorne

Auchter at OSHA have been generally viewed as being not only poorly qualified to run their agencies but also interested primarily in helping industry at the expense of the public.

But Reagan's appointees have also achieved more notoriety than did other presidents' appointees (such as Nixon's or Ford's) because the power of government to regulate is significantly greater now than it was ten to fifteen years ago; there are more laws, more agencies, and more regulations. And government is more willing to use that power for political purposes.

Reagan's ability to appoint the heads of both executive-branch and independent regulatory agencies has been of crucial importance in his push to deregulate. Most of these appointees have adhered to his antiregulatory philosophy. Reagan has reshaped regulatory policy by putting free-market advocates in charge of the FCC, FTC, and other independent agencies. In fact, by 1987, he had managed to appoint all sixty-three members of fifteen key independent agencies, thus assuring the chief executive of complete control of the independent regulatory apparatus.[67] This development is important because these officials will hold their positions long after the president's departure.

The actions of EPA head Lee Thomas show how a new agency administrator can change the policy flow in short order. Under the Comprehensive Environmental Response, Compensation, and Liability Act (more commonly known as Superfund), EPA was assigned to clean up abandoned toxic-waste dumps. In 1985, the act was up for renewal and a fierce battle was waged over the level of funding EPA should receive to carry out its mandate. The agency had cleaned up only six of more than 2,000 sites since 1980, yet Thomas argued that EPA should receive only $1 billion a year to finish the clean-up job, a position rejected by both independent studies and senior EPA officials in all ten of the agency's regional offices. The Sierra Club's project director, Carl Pope, charged that Thomas's position on Superfund financing was "obviously a conclusion he came to after consulting OMB, not his own staff."[68]

OMB and Cost–Benefit Analysis

The OMB provided the focal point for Reagan's efforts to manage the regulatory process. Executive Order 12,291 restored the OMB as the preeminent regulatory oversight body, a position it had not held since Nixon's quality-of-life review program. It is hard to overstate the actual and potential impact OMB would have on regulatory policy as a result of this directive both during and after the Reagan administration.

Under the Reagan order, as we have seen, OIRA had the power to decide which rules were major and delay any proposed rule if unjustified by an agency's regulatory analysis. And an unfavorable OIRA ruling could be appealed only to the Bush task force.[69] James C. Miller III, former OIRA head, reports that agencies did not often buck OIRA's decisions. "I'd just say, I'm meeting with the Vice-President this afternoon. I'll raise this with him if you like, but he's real busy." The result, according to Miller, was that "accommodation occurs real fast."[70]

OMB statistics indicate that agencies took the probability of OMB review into consideration *before* issuing any rules. As a result, only those rules that were capable of passing muster tended to be submitted. In fact, after two years of review, OMB had rejected only 2 percent of the 5,346 regulatory proposals it had screened, and only 1 percent had been withdrawn.[71] These statistics, however, significantly underestimate OMB's impact on agency rule making. Perhaps hundreds of regulations were dropped *before* the preliminary proposal stage because the agencies anticipated their rejection by OMB.

Much of the OMB's newfound clout came with its adoption of cost–benefit analysis to determine the worth of existing or proposed regulations. Cost–benefit analysis was originally designed to assess efficiency in the allocation of resources in the private sector. Viewing this tool as applicable in other areas, the Reagan administration made it the litmus test for evaluating public-policy commitments as determined by the regulatory process. In addition, the OMB utilized cost–benefit analysis in a context previously not considered within its original domain. Traditionally, economists have refrained from using the method to evaluate social programs and economic policies because of the difficulties in ascertaining the relationship of *all* gains and costs.[72] But Executive Order 12,291 allowed cost–benefit analysis a broader application.

Aside from its controversial use of cost–benefit analysis, OMB was roundly criticized by Congress, agency heads, and environmentalists through Reagan's first term of office. The office was described by some as a "backdoor" conduit through which business leaders could influence regulations. The Alliance for Justice, a group of public-interest lawyers and lobbyists, charged in an October 1982 report that OMB review had "opened the way for unprecedented interference by special interests in the federal regulatory process and created the potential for corruption."[73] These charges were given currency because OMB was not required to and generally avoided putting anything in writing. The office did not keep a formal record of its criticisms of a regulation; neither did it keep written records of conversations its officials had when meeting with agency representatives or industry leaders. According to a General Accounting Office study, "[t]he result of this non-documented approach to rule making is that the public cannot determine at whose initiative a rule was issued . . . or on what basis it was made."[74] After studying OMB's procedures, Rep. Albert Gore (D.–Tenn.), later a member of the Senate, reached the "inescapable conclusion" that OMB "just sits over there and acts as a back door channel to let affected corporations hot wire the regulatory process to get what they want."[75] Even if OMB's actions were entirely above board, imprudent comments by OMB officials as well as a general insensitivity of regulatory officials toward appearances reinforced the perception of OMB as a politicized agency.[76]

OMB has also been heavily criticized for ignoring the "benefit" part of cost–benefit analysis. For example, OMB's guidelines urged agencies to include indirect adverse effects of a regulation, such as "reductions in competition, innovative activity, or productive growth"; the guidelines, however, failed to require the inclusion of the indirect benefits of regulation.[77] Some critics have argued, in short, that OMB uses the cost–benefit tests as a means to kill off rules it does not like. Hearings before the House Oversight and Investigations Subcommittee disclosed that the forms used by OMB to review proposed rules contained no space to list a rule's benefits but had two spaces to list costs—one for the private sector and one for government.[78]

But perhaps the biggest criticism of OMB's use of cost–benefit analysis has been the agency's overuse and application of the method to areas in which, according to some critics, it will not work. To fulfill the purely economic objective of determining efficiency, a student of cost–benefit analysis "must ignore considerations of which particular people are made better off or worse [off] as resource allocation alternatives are considered."[79] Whereas some observers view such calculations as pure and simple, others lament that this approach depersonalizes government as well as the people whom government serves.

OMB's willingness to selectively deregulate has not escaped the attention of Congress. According to Rep. John Dingell, (D.–Mich.), chair of the House Energy and Commerce Committee, the OMB "has attempted to influence agency [rule] making on philosophical or political grounds without regard for the cost, the basic statutes, and more importantly, the benefits of the regulations."[80] One example was OMB's decision to rescind and delay thirty-four regulations that "cost" the auto industry and consumers approximately $15 billion each year. In testimony before Congress, however, OMB officials were forced to admit that they could provide no estimate of the benefits of these regulations. In fact, one OMB official acknowledged that the benefits of some of the rules exceeded their costs.[81] The OMB was thus charged with favoring business interests by the GAO, which found that the cost–benefit analysis requirement was waived for twenty-one of forty-three regulations classified as "major" by the OMB.[82]

Even if an agency was convinced that a proposed regulation would result in net benefits, it could not always stand firm against the veiled threat of OMB retaliation. In one instance, according to a former EPA chief of staff, EPA Secretary Anne Gorsuch Burford signed a regulatory package without OMB approval. The chief of staff reports that he was told by James Tozzi, the OMB deputy administrator for information and regulatory affairs, that "there was a price to pay for doing what we'd done and we hadn't begun to pay."[83]

As we can see, the Reagan administration worked hard to deregulate and did so in a highly politicized environment. The OMB, in fact, rode "shotgun" on the administration's "Deregulation Express."

The Failed Promise?

At a press conference in August 1983, vice-presidential counsel C. Boyden Gray reported that the Task Force on Regulatory Relief would be disbanded. The reason, according to Gray, was that the task force's work was done. Gray's assessment was news to most people. Hank Cox of the U.S. Chamber of Commerce interpreted the demise of the task force to mean that the administration was placing deregulation in cold storage. Added another observer, "We're at the end of an era of deregulation."[84] According to Lester Lave, a regulatory expert at Carnegie–Mellon University, the administration "took a lesson from the Vietnam war: declare victory and pull out."[85] Clearly, the Reagan administration's declaration was in sharp contrast to the views of leading observers in and out of government service.

Supporting the administration's claim of victory in the fight against needless and wasteful regulation, the Bush task force issued a report that claimed credit for generating $150 billion in regulatory cost "savings" without reducing regulatory benefits.[86] These estimates of savings, however, are highly speculative, if not specious, for four reasons.

First, the task force accepted credit for savings that accrued from deregulatory actions taken by previous administrations or by Congress. Second, the estimates included savings from the "repeal" of regulations that had only been *proposed,* not adopted. There is no evidence that these regulations would have been issued if the task force had not existed. Third, the task force included savings that in reality were nothing more than transfers from one segment of society to another. The postponement of emission standards for auto-industry paint shops provides an example of these cost shifts. Although it was true that this requirement would have been costly to the auto industry, postponing it would have resulted in costs greater to other industries than those the auto industry would have saved.[87]

Finally, the task force included savings from the elimination of standards that were later reinstated by the federal courts. Overall, the benefits of the administration's regulatory relief program were considerably overstated.

The signal failing of the Reagan administration's deregulatory policy was its inability to enact many significant changes in the legislative statutes that established the government's regulatory framework. Rather than attempt to deregulate regulatory statutes (e.g., the Clean Air Act, Clean Water Act, Delaney Amendments to the Food, Drug, and Cosmetic Act), Reagan chose instead to change the administrative regulations that interpreted and implemented those laws.[88]

Several of Reagan's key economic aides were disappointed; they argued that a meaningful deregulatory program must include revision of existing regulatory statutes. These laws must be altered, they argued, to free the regulatory agencies from rigid requirements in general and from specific prohibitions against considering the potential costs of any regulation. Statutory changes are preferred because administrative changes, while desirable, are temporary, and can easily be reversed by the next administration. The inability of the Reagan administration to make any permanent regulatory changes was highlighted by a memo written by OIRA head Christopher DeMuth. In the first three years of the administration, DeMuth declared, "we have not advanced a single detailed proposal of our own for reform of any of the major health, safety, or environmental statutes."[89]

Several reasons exist for Reagan's inability to effect any substantive statutory revisions. First, of Reagan's four economic "cornerstones," regulatory reform was given the lowest priority. Much of Reagan's difficulty stemmed from his administration's unwillingness to expend valuable political capital that it needed in other policy struggles in an effort to change regulatory statutes. Jerry Jasinowski, former assistant secretary for policy at the U.S. Chamber of Commerce, writes that, "When senior members of the White House staff were asked when there would be a big push in a specific area of regulatory legislation, the reply was invariably, 'After we finish the tax and budget issues.' The tax and budget agenda never ended, and the administration never seemed to learn how to walk and chew gum at the same time."[90] With regulatory reform thus given relatively low priority in the executive branch, Congress had little incentive to undertake such reform on its own.

By the time the Reagan administration had finally assembled a social deregulatory package, it was too late. The atmosphere of trust and cooperation the administration needed in dealing with Congress and the public had been irrevocably poisoned by the activities and policies of some of Reagan's political appointees. Sensing a basic unfairness in both administration policies and their implementation by agency heads, many members of Congress now viewed any statutory changes favored by the administration with suspicion.

In March 1983, EPA Secretary Anne Gorsuch Burford and most of her management team were forced to resign amid charges of mismanagement and malfeasance. Reagan's appointment of outspoken probusiness regulators to many federal positions had already raised suspicion among many in Congress and around the country that regulatory protections were vanishing. Secretary of the Interior James Watt's fulminations had already caused a stampede of new members to a broad range of environmental groups. Civil rights positions had been filled by people believed to be unsympathetic to women and minorities. And some criticized the Department of Labor as antilabor, in reality little more than a second Department of Commerce. In this environment, the scandal that resulted in the imprisonment of a high-ranking EPA official, Rita Lavelle, was the last straw.

In his assessment of the Reagan administration's regulatory program, Murray Weidenbaum wrote that in the wake of the scandals at EPA, any White House initiative on the environment was immediately suspect in Congress. "Just try to change a comma in the Clean Air Act and you lay yourself open to charges that you want to 'gut' environmental protection."[91] The EPA scandals unleashed a growing backlash within Congress that resulted in a number of reverses of the administration's deregulatory agenda. This was partly the administration's own fault, since many of its appointees were unfamiliar with the intricacies of the laws governing their agencies. Consequently, in their rush to deregulate, these agency heads often ran afoul of complex administrative requirements and found their decisions reversed by the courts.

Toward the end of Reagan's first term, the administration seemed to lose interest in deregulation. In fact, the debate over regulatory change was muted as the 1984 election drew near. To counter charges that Reagan was anticonsumer and antienvironment, a number of agencies even stepped up their rule-making and enforcement campaigns.[92]

During Reagan's second term, deregulation has not received any more attention than it had during his first term. It has been just as difficult, if not more so, to convince Congress of the desirability of revising social-regulatory statutes. The same domestic and foreign-policy issues that Reagan gave a higher priority in his first term—taxes, the budget deficit, and the military buildup—have continued to dominate the political agenda in his second term. Moreover, the knowledge that the Reagan presidency will end in 1989 has given members of Congress a special advantage in his last term, enhanced by the Democratic capture of the Senate in the 1986 midterm elections. According to James C. Miller III, "the President is just going to let the glue dry on deregulation."[93]

In the final analysis, one cannot term Reagan's deregulatory agenda a failure, yet it is clearly not the success sought by the administration. The Reagan team has certainly affected many specific regulations and would-be regulations, but it has left virtually untouched the country's statutory regulatory structure. In part, this has been due to the unwillingness of Congress to tamper with social legislative enactments, but in larger part the blame must be assigned to the Reagan administration's inadequacy in developing and advocating alternative proposals.

The one area where the administration has made its presence strongly felt is presidential control over the rule-making process, specifically by Executive Order 12,291. Although this will allow Reagan or a successor of like philosophy to reduce regulatory burdens, it has also institutionalized a process that presidents with different regulatory views can use to their own advantage.[94]

The shift from congressional and agency power to presidential power in regulation cannot be properly termed deregulation. Perhaps Reagan leaves behind a more flexible structure that seeks the difficult balance between governmental protection and market efficiency. True deregulation will require a careful reexamination of the laws that built the federal regulatory agencies, and the desirability of dismantling these statutes is very debatable. It is ironic that an administration so dedicated to private enterprise has perhaps presided over a reaffirmation of the basic need for social, if not economic, regulation.

Notes

1. Richard E. Neustadt, *Presidential Power,* 2d ed. (New York: Wiley, 1980), p. 28.
2. Martha Derthick and Paul J. Quirk, *The Politics of Deregulation* (Washington, D.C.: The Brookings Institution, 1985), p. 29.
3. Howard Ball, *Controlling Regulatory Sprawl: Presidential Strategies from Nixon to Reagan* (Westport, Conn.: Greenwood Press, 1984), p. 50.
4. Alan Stone, *Regulation and Its Alternatives* (Washington, D.C.: Congressional Quarterly Press, 1982), p. 247.
5. Ball, *Regulatory Sprawl,* pp. 50–51.
6. Office of the Federal Register, National Archives and Records Service, General Services Administration, *The United States Government Manual,* 1984/5, pp. 82–83.
7. George C. Eads and Michael Fix, *Relief or Reform? Reagan's Regulatory Dilemma* (Washington, D.C.: Urban Institute, 1984), pp. 46–47.
8. *Ibid.,* pp. 47–48.
9. Ball, *Regulatory Sprawl,* p. 51.
10. Eads and Fix, *Relief,* p. 51.
11. *Ibid.,* p. 50.
12. *Ibid.,* p. 51.
13. Ball, *Regulatory Sprawl,* p. 52.
14. Executive Order 11821, 39 Fed. Reg. 41501 (November 29, 1974).
15. Eads and Fix, *Relief,* p. 51.
16. Robert E. Litan and William D. Nordhaus, *Reforming Federal Regulation* (New Haven, Conn.: Yale University Press, 1983), p. 69.
17. James C. Miller III, quoted in Ball, *Regulatory Sprawl,* p. 53.
18. Litan and Nordhaus, *Reforming,* p. 68.
19. Eads and Fix, *Relief,* p. 70.
20. *Ibid.,* p. 80.
21. Jimmy Carter, *Keeping Faith* (New York: Bantam Books, 1982), p. 74.
22. Eads and Fix, *Relief,* p. 54.
23. *Ibid.,* p. 88; and Litan and Nordhaus, *Reforming,* pp. 68–69.

24. Litan and Nordhaus, *Reforming,* pp. 69–70.
25. "Deregulation HQ," *Regulation,* 5, no. 2 (March–April 1981): 15.
26. Executive Order 12,044, 3 CFR 152–156 (1979).
27. Susan J. Tolchin, "Presidential Power and the Politics of the RARG," *Regulation,* 3, no. 4 (July–August 1979): 44–49.
28. *Ibid.,* p. 45.
29. Christopher C. DeMuth, "The White House Review Programs," *Regulation,* 4, no. 1 (January–February 1980): 20.
30. Litan and Nordhaus, *Reforming,* p. 71.
31. Ball, *Regulatory Sprawl,* p. 59.
32. Litan and Nordhaus, *Reforming,* pp. 77–78.
33. "A Flawed Program to Curb Regulators," *Business Week,* no. 2561 (November 20, 1978): 37.
34. Kevin Whitney, "Capitalizing on a Congressional Void: Executive Order 12,291," *American University Law Review,* 31, no. 614, fn. 6.
35. Richard M. Neustadt, "The Administration's Regulatory Reform Program: An Overview," *Administrative Law Review,* 32, no. 2 (September 1980): 130–132.
36. Quoted in Dick Kirschten, "President Reagan After Two Years—Bold Actions but Uncertain Results," *National Journal,* 15 (January 1, 1983): 7.
37. Ball, *Regulatory Sprawl,* pp. 65–66.
38. David Stockman, quoted in Litan and Nordhaus, *Reforming,* p. 121.
39. Michael Fix and George C. Eads, "The Prospects for Regulatory Reform: The Legacy of Reagan's First Term," *Yale Journal of Regulation,* 2, no. 2 (1985): 298.
40. Walter Guzzardi, Jr., "Reagan's Reluctant Deregulators," *Fortune,* 105, no. 5 (March 8, 1982): 35.
41. *Ibid.,* p. 35.
42. 46 Fed. Reg. 11,227 (February 6, 1981).
43. *Ibid.*
44. Murray L. Weidenbaum, "Regulatory Reform Under the Reagan Administration," in *The Reagan Regulatory Strategy,* George Eads and Michael Fix, eds. (Washington, D.C.: Urban Institute Press, 1984), p. 23.
45. Kirschten, "President Reagan," p. 10.
46. Ball, *Regulatory Sprawl,* pp. 67–68.
47. Whitney, "Capitalizing," p. 620.
48. Timothy B. Clark, "OMB to Keep Its Regulatory Powers in Reserve in Case Agencies Lag," *National Journal,* 13 (March 14, 1981): 428.
49. Michael Wines, "Reagan's Reforms Are Full of Sound and Fury, But What Do They Signify?" *National Journal,* 14 (January 16, 1982): 96–97.
50. Executive Order 12,291, 3 CFR 127-28 (1982).
51. *Ibid.,* p. 128.
52. Timothy B. Clark, "Do the Benefits Justify the Costs? Prove It, Says the Administration," *National Journal,* 13 (August 1, 1981): 1383.
53. Executive Order 12,291.
54. *Ibid.,* p. 129.
55. George Eads, "Harnessing Regulation: The Evolving Role of White House Oversight," *Regulation* 5 (May–June 1981): 19–21.
56. Ball, *Regulatory Sprawl,* p. 71.
57. Douglas M. Castle, "Environmental Regulation and Regulatory Reform," *Washington Law Review,* 57 (July 1982): 418.
58. Office of the Legal Counsel, U.S. Department of Justice, memorandum of February 12, 1981, quoted in Whitney, "Capitalizing," p. 614.
59. Ann Cooper, "Reagan Has Tamed the Regulatory Beast, But Not Permanently Broken Its Grip," *National Journal,* 16 (December 1, 1984): 2284.
60. Eads and Fix, *Relief,* p. 148.

61. Ball, *Regulatory Sprawl,* pp. 78–79.
62. Fix and Eads, "Prospects," p. 303.
63. "Reagan's Regulators," *National Journal,* 17, no. 20 (May 18, 1985): 1189.
64. Weidenbaum, "Regulatory Reform," pp. 34–35.
65. *Environment Reporter,* March 16, 1984, p. 2050.
66. Eads and Fix, *Relief,* p. 159.
67. "Reagan's Regulators," p. 1188.
68. *Environment Reporter,* July 5, 1985, p. 356.
69. Eads, "Harnessing Regulation," pp. 20–21.
70. Guzzardi, "Reluctant Deregulators," p. 35.
71. Weidenbaum, "Regulatory Reform," p. 24.
72. For a thorough treatment of traditional cost–benefit analysis as it applies to the private and public sectors, see Robert H. Haveman and Burton A. Weisbrod, "Defining Benefits of Public Programs: Some Guidance for Policy Analysis," in *Public Expenditure and Policy Analysis,* 2d ed., Robert H. Haveman and Julius Morgolis, eds. (Chicago: Rand McNally, 1977), pp. 135–160.
73. Wines, "Reagan's Reforms," p. 93.
74. Eads and Fix, *Relief,* p. 124.
75. *Environment Reporter,* September 30, 1983, p. 928.
76. Eads and Fix, *Relief,* p. 128.
77. "Reagan's Regulators," p. 420.
78. Wines, "Reagan's Reforms," p. 98.
79. Haveman and Weisbrod, "Defining Benefits," p. 137.
80. *Environment Reporter,* September 30, 1983, p. 927.
81. *Ibid.*
82. Kirschten, "President Reagan," p. 10.
83. *Environment Reporter,* September 30, 1983, p. 928.
84. "A Farewell to Deregulation," *Fortune,* 18, no. 6 (September 19, 1983): 49.
85. *Ibid.*
86. Eads and Fix, eds. *The Reagan Regulatory Strategy* (Washington, D.C.: Urban Institute Press, 1984), pp. 2–3.
87. Eads and Fix, *Relief,* p. 242.
88. *Ibid.,* pp. 163–164.
89. Fix and Eads, "Prospects," p. 316.
90. Jerry Jasinowski, "Comments," in Fix and Eads, *Regulatory Strategy,* p. 45.
91. Cooper, "Regulatory Beast," p. 2287.
92. "Deregulation Takes a Holiday," *Business Week,* July 16, 1984, p. 159.
93. In Peter Bernstein, "Ronald Reagan's Second Term Agenda," *Fortune,* 110, no. 7 (October 1, 1984): 30.
94. Eads and Fix, *Relief,* p. 242.

CHAPTER 4

Theories of
Regulation and Deregulation

The debate over deregulation is a microcosm of the contradictions inherent in American politics. On the one hand, society has come to depend on government for protection from a variety of threats. Toxic waste, polluted water, unsafe work conditions, and a risky banking system are among the more worrisome concerns for the public, and government has responded through the creation of various regulatory agencies. On the other hand, Americans have a history of resistance to governmental interference in the private domain. Such concerns were expressed long ago with the Bill of Rights, which, through its addition to the U.S. Constitution, guaranteed the protection of individualism in American political thought and law.

Regulation, of course, means interference with an otherwise unencumbered condition or circumstance. At minimum, regulation places artificial constraints on areas of activity previously with few or no governmental limitations. Explaining the bases of regulatory activities is the job of regulation theory.

Theories of regulation are important because they help us to understand the functions of regulation, predict situations where it is most likely to be effective, and evaluate the outcomes of regulatory policies. A good theory should explain each stage in the regulation process, from the time a potential regulation is proposed, through its adoption, implementation, and enforcement.[1] The theory must be able to account for the success of some regulatory proposals and the failure of others to work their way through the policy process. The theory must also include past regulatory accomplishments and explain the trend to deregulation: how and why policies are changed or eliminated. Finally, a theory needs to be appreciated for its values as well as any claim of fact.

Regulation theory was once limited to simple descriptions of desirable regulatory policies. But as the role of government in society expanded, so did the clamor among academics and policy makers for better theoretical explanations of that increased involvement. Recent questions about the wisdom and effectiveness of regulation have only exacerbated the pressures for rigor as well as for accountability.

Although regulation has come to be a significant element of the U.S. economy, we still have a very limited understanding about why regulatory agencies act as they do. Until recently, there were few obvious connections between theoretical designs and policy outcomes. Social scientists seemed to accept this incomplete linkage as a "given" of the discipline, and one that did not necessarily hamper the process. In fact, according to Eugene Bardach and Robert A. Kagan, "the absence of a strong theory about what regulatory strategy works best under what conditions need not impede policy planning and political action."[2] Yet, the search for a comprehensive framework of explanation continues. Presently, a well-developed theory of regulation remains more goal than reality. This does not mean, however, that present regulatory descriptions are bereft of theory. The current methods of examination provide a starting point for regulatory explanations. No single comprehensive theory may cover all issues and responses, yet we can still identify specific theories that explain areas within the regulatory environment.

This chapter examines four regulatory theories: public-interest, capture, bureaucratic, and economic. These theories are valuable for their abilities to predict and explain aspects of governmental behavior through the use of observation and logic. In this chapter, we will discuss the application of these theories to the phenomenon of deregulation.

Public-Interest Theory

Public-interest theory emphasizes that government is the guarantor of the public good. Ideally, this is achieved as government regulates private functions to maximize public welfare. As we have seen, the goal of equality has often been the justification for governmental intervention in both the economic and social sectors. Economic regulation developed as a way to control a market system that was perceived to be unfair to both consumers and producers.[3] Monopolistic power structures, harmful business practices, and general economic abuses of the public thus necessitated governmental protection through regulation. Similarly, social regulation was initiated to protect workers and consumers from unsafe workplaces, dangerous products, and life-threatening environments.

The assumptions of public-interest theory have focused on the desirability of regulatory agencies, specifically, their structure, organization, and operation.[4] Proponents of regulatory agencies have called for the protection of society from unwanted or abusive market mechanisms and living conditions, arguing that only government is strong enough to correct these inequities. The assertion that these actions are necessary for a "good" society means that the public-interest approach is inherently prescriptive.

Justification of Public-Interest Theory

Whether the problem is economic or social, proponents of public-interest theory contend that the public at large has little control over its own fate. Those in power—business, economic, and political elites—make decisions not with society in mind, but for their own well-being; moreover, their power is omnipotent. As G. William Domhoff notes, "[r]uling-class domination of government can be seen most directly in the workings of lobbyists, backroom superlawyers, trade associations and advisory committees to governmental departments and agencies."[5] The economic elite, according to the theory, dictates what goes into and comes out of the governmental process. As a result, public policies are responses to narrow private needs. Significantly, whenever members of the working class have organized to oppose ruling-class power, their "challenges either have been beaten back by a united power elite or accommodated by the compromising efforts of the ruling-class moderates."[6] In the latter instance, policy changes tend to foster only token equality.

Assuming a lack of accountability among those who manage society, public-interest theory advocates call for the expansion of government control. In claiming that "the fundamental issue no longer relates to the problem of production or distribution but to the problem of power,"[7] Peter Bachrach suggests that such power be shifted from private elites to the hands of government managers. Bachrach's indictment of modern corporations as oligarchical and self-serving has set the tone for regulation as a minimal alternative to outright public ownership, or nationalization of selected industries, which he also considers.[8]

Public-interest theorists have reasoned that regulation would greatly benefit society. Pursuing a cautious course, they have generally viewed the independent regulatory commission as a more desirable means of control than outright nationalization. Looking first into the economic arena, advocates of public-interest theory have attempted to define ways to minimize outrageous business behavior. Thus, at various times, regulation has been sought that would control business excesses, eliminate harmful effects of cutthroat competition, and tame monopoly power. For example, the ICC would set fair rates for transportation, and the CAB would ensure fair airline prices and guarantee that routes were developed for the public's benefit. In general, cooperation among businesses, guided by government, would provide a stable, growing economy that would be freed from abuse by a few unethical businesses.[9]

Purposeful and yet limited in the scope of their intent, early public-interest theorists stressed the technical aspects of regulation. Issues related to food quality or monetary-system stability were far too critical and specialized to be left to traditional political practices. It was an acceptable ritual for Congress and organized interests to bargain over farm supports, minimum wage, or foreign aid, matters whose resolutions were associated with compromise. But some areas were too controversial for negotiation. Freight rates, for example, seemed to cut one way or the other; the railroads' successes almost certainly meant great suffering for corporations and thousands of customers. In such areas of critical importance, the public good could best be guaranteed through the creation of a government body that would oversee national economic activities in an atmosphere free from political influence—in short, an independent regulatory commission.[10]

Many of the concerns that led to economic regulation in the late 1800s and early 1900s eventually encompassed social problems as well. Once again, industry scandals often hastened the call for social regulation. For example, in the mid-1930s, 107 people died from sulfanilamide, an antibiotic drug that had never been tested for safety; public outrage led to the passage of food and drug reforms in 1935.[11] And numerous tragedies from poor working conditions—collapsed tunnels, methane gas explosions, and black lung disease—led to the federal Coal Mine Safety and Health Act of 1969.[12] More recently, criminal behavior by some individual led to a rash of deaths from cyanide-poisoned Tylenol capsules, thus prompting protective-packaging legislation for over-the-counter medicines.[13] The inability of a free market to provide safe goods and workplaces justified the claims for social regulation, according to the proponents of the public-interest theory.

As demands for a healthier, safer society gained momentum from the 1930s through 1970s, elected officials expanded their definitions of the "public interest." Many nationwide problems that had not been addressed for years were added to the public agenda; and the government acted. Pollution, for example, had been a problem long before creation of the EPA, but increased awareness and concern in the late 1960s and 1970s stimulated government action.[14] Such new pressures for protection and equality fostered government growth in two ways: "[T]he first in a quantum increase in social programs, the second in a spate of new regulations" and regulatory agencies.[15] Thus, by the early 1970s, public-interest theory advocates had staked their claims to two prominent areas of control: economic and social regulation.

Criticism of Public-Interest Theory

Opponents of public-interest theory expressed their reservations about government involvement from the theory's inception. But events overruled their objections. The successive crises that led to the Progressive Era and the New Deal led to more than sixty years of government expansion and regulation. Yet, by the mid-1960s, critics of public-interest theory had concluded that application of theory had proved naive and idealistic, if not completely wrong. The belief that regulation served the public rather than private interests was contradicted by analyses of regulatory activity in the governmental process. One such assessment concluded that high-level corporate and government leaders had essentially the same values and goals. Thus, Michael Parenti argued, "[t]he interests common to the entire business class become the interests of the state, specifically maintaining high profits, shifting production and taxation costs to the public, making public resources accessible to private exploitation, and limiting and repressing the demands of the working class and the poor."[16] With government and business elites holding such similar objectives, regulation favorable to private interests seemed unavoidable.

Some analysts have strongly stressed that regulation has protected the private sector from instability and unsatisfactorily low profits, benefits that provide powerful incentives for business and status quo–oriented elites to control the regulatory process. Under these circumstances, the regulated find it in their best interest to court their regulators. The extent that such influence is successful blunts any suggestion that regulators are concerned with the public interest. As James Q. Wilson notes, "it is difficult to be certain about the relationship between campaign contributions, electoral success and bureaucratic policy . . . . That there has been an incentive for regulated industries to supply campaign contributions, however, is beyond dispute."[17]

Critics charge that the inability of public interest theory to be predictive has permitted an unchecked concentration of power in the hands of those who, ironically, have caused the most harm to society.[18] Put another way, the public interest is hard to define and even more difficult to make function on any consistent basis.[19] The most skillfully drafted and organized regulatory policy may not benefit all segments of society equally. Given these drawbacks, public-interest theory seems to have limited utility.

Capture Theory

A second school of regulatory thought dismisses the public interest as the focal point of regulation policy. Instead, this school holds that regulation serves the interests of the regulated—interests that have decidedly different objectives from those of the public.[20] Yet another element separates the public-interest and capture theories: The former is normative, while the latter purports to be empirical. Although public-interest theory might describe the way regulation should work, capture theory describes actual agency behavior.

Capture theory itself holds two views. One, the *capture-at-origin* view, argues that regulation is adopted at the behest of business to protect its needs. The other view, that of *co-opting,* contends that although regulatory agencies were originally formed to serve the public interest, they have been co-opted over time by those they were meant to regulate.[21] Through either method of capture, the relationship between the regulated and the regulator is similar to that of the fox and the henhouse: The client firms come to guard and enjoy the rewards of beneficial public-agency policies.

Justification of Capture Theories

Capture-at-origin theorists argue that regulation was never intended to serve the public; rather, it was promulgated to serve business. Businesses might prefer regulation to competition for many reasons. Regulation can reduce a firm's risk and help to ameliorate inefficiencies within a company.[22] It can also protect existing firms from market entry and competition by new business as well as protect and increase profits. Business thus can have very strong motives to seek regulation as a security blanket.

One proponent of the capture-at-origin viewpoint, Gabriel Kolko, traces this regulatory development back to the beginning of the twentieth century, documenting the strong and pervasive influence of industries from the first proposals of regulation, through drafting and adoption of legislation, to the implementation of policy by the new regulatory agency. It was business, not the public, Kolko concludes, that solidified control over the economy through regulation. As a result, the rise of regulation during the Progressive Era was a "triumph of conservatism."[23]

Some recent accounts of the evolution of capitalism in the United States have also tended to support the capture-at-origin theory, pointing to government regulation as a mechanism for assisting private power rather than controlling it. Foremost among these observers is Theodore J. Lowi, who writes of the dangers connected with "interest-group liberalism."[24] Lowi stresses that modern government is intimately connected with the rise and success of private power. Moreover, the practices of rule making and administration have changed greatly over the course of the twentieth century. Whereas government once set rigid rules for all of society to follow, modern use of authority has become increasingly discretionary. In the process, government has all but lost its independence from the private sector. Major policy areas once managed by Congress have been delegated to regulatory agencies and cabinet departments that often accede to the pressure of powerful interests in a new era of discretionary policy making. Consequently, interest-group liberalism permits government to "parcel out to private parties the power to make public policy."[25] The fact that private interests dominate government allows the perpetuation of privilege over equality.

Given easy access to government, businesses can increase their control over regulatory agencies in many ways. Occasionally, public officials are bribed, although such gross persuasion is seldom necessary. Business representatives usually rely on subtler, more indirect means. More often, the parallel interests of regulators and businesses are exploited through mutual memberships in professional associations. Inasmuch as considerable regulation relies upon voluntary compliance and reporting of data, businesses often enjoy a monopoly of available information. The outcome, according to capture theorists, is inevitable. In the words of G. William Domhoff, "the constituent groups—the industries of the American business aristocracy that the agencies supposedly regulate—control the regulatory agencies."[26] Such an argument is the heart of capture theory.

Many case studies claim to provide evidence for the co-opt view of capture theory. The ICC is considered a classical example of an agency that has come to identify with the industry it was designed to regulate. Such was the determination of a 325-page study sponsored by Ralph

Nader; the report concluded that the "ICC is now primarily a forum at which private transportation interests settle their disputes."[27] Other agencies have been similarly described. The FTC, for example, was designed to protect consumers, but increasingly protected businesses over the years. This primarily occurred as the commission stressed the enforcement of false-advertising charges brought by competing businesses rather than by the prosecution of those businesses whose practices hurt consumers the most.[28]

Although not as frequently condemned as have been economic agencies, social regulatory agencies have also been accused of being captured. For example, the FDA's early standards regarding pure foods often favored established industries over those that provided cheaper substitutes, even when the substitutes were found to be safe. Laws favoring butter over margarine serve as a case in point.[29]

Capture theory is very much a part of American political discourse. Every time a regulatory agency issues a controversial decision or rule, its opponents are ready to accuse the agency of capture by those it is supposed to regulate.

Criticism of Capture Theory

Although either view of capture theory often better explains observed regulatory behavior than does the public-interest theory, critics still argue that both views are one-dimensional. Most regulatory agencies, they contend, are designed to represent a variety of constituents, the public as well as the regulated. That the agencies are "public" means that through a variety of procedures—i.e., hearings and investigations—public opinion will be considered or incorporated in the decision-making process. An agency like NHTSA, for example, must deal with Congress, the president, the courts, insurance companies, and the auto industry as well as with consumer-interest groups. Such interaction suggests that capture theory as a whole fails to consider the diversity of interest groups represented in the regulatory process.[30]

Multiple interests not only affect agencies but also each other. Opponents of capture theory thus point to the diversity within American society as a guard against abuse. The domination of government by powerful economic groups should not be feared because these groups are checked in the marketplace. More than three decades ago, John Kenneth Galbraith wrote that "power on one side of a market creates both the need for, and the prospect of reward to, the exercise of countervailing power from the other side. This means that, as a common rule, we can rely on countervailing power to appear as a curb on economic power."[31] For the most part, various forces offset one another, thereby minimizing the likelihood of any one narrow interest controlling either the marketplace or government.

Some empirical examinations of industries and their governing public agencies have suggested an openness of government that militates against the capture-theory models. In their recent study of regulatory activities, Martha Derthick and Paul J. Quirk studied the airlines, telecommunications, and trucking industries along with their respective government agencies. In each case, they note, regulatory body responsibilities were diluted in the face of strong opposition from management and organized labor: "When surrounding institutions began to encourage procompetitive reform, nothing in the commissions' relations with industry blocked or significantly slowed it."[32] Derthick and Quirk found that an array of actors—presidents, public-interest groups, and rival political forces— managed to effect change contrary to the wishes of the regulated interests, an outcome contrary to capture theory. Finally, just as there is seldom one "public interest," there is seldom one business interest. Neither consumers nor producers are a homogeneous group. In fact, regulations can benefit some firms more than others within an industry. For example, although the financial-services industry is still highly regulated, the interests of a small, rural savings-and-loan association are quite different from those of a huge money-center bank. To add to the confusion, many of the regulators themselves are involved in this industry. Thus, it is apparent that simple capture theory does not explain how differing industry needs are satisfied.

Bureaucratic Theory

Another way to explain regulatory activity is by examining regulation as an independent variable. This approach departs from the two theories already presented. With respect to public-interest theory, a normative claim for regulatory agencies attempts to be responsive to the public will; in the case of capture theory, agencies respond to the demands of vested interests. Of importance here is that in both instances, regulation depends on stimuli external to the agencies.

Bureaucratic theory sees the sequence of events and outcomes as occurring in reverse. Specifically, the flow of power begins inside the regulatory bodies. As Guy Benveniste succinctly states, "[o]rganizations create authority rights."[33] With this framework as a source of legitimate activity, agencies create rules for others to obey.

Justification of Bureaucratic Theory

The main assumption of bureaucratic theory holds that the life of the organization is an entity in itself. In effect, the agency itself assumes responsibility for appropriate regulatory activity. Decisions are based largely on the experience that comes with evolution and growth. Such development allows policy makers to develop procedures based on internal reason and logic rather than in reaction to outside pressure. To quote Charles Perrow, a well-known scholar on the subject, "[a] 'natural history' implies natural forces: organizations as living entities grow in natural ways. The discovery of these forces . . . will yield understanding."[34] From understanding comes independent and dispassionate regulation.

According to bureaucratic theory, public agencies mature as they develop. Because of this maturation, agencies may or may not identify with the objectives of those they regulate over the course of time. Marver H. Bernstein discusses this evolution in the context of the "life cycle." He argues that all independent regulatory commissions undergo roughly similar periods of growth, maturity, and decline. "These common experiences can be generalized into a rhythm of regulation whose repetition suggests that there is a natural life cycle for an independent commission."[35] Initially, these agencies seek to serve the public with aggressive rule making. Toward the end of their life cycles, agencies adopt policies that parallel the aspirations of those they regulate. Worn down from years of battle with those in and out of government, the regulators retreat to a more static, conservative position, an outcome radically different from the early years of almost frenetic zeal.

At first glance, the evolution of agency behavior might lead one to interpret such change as another illustration of capture theory. But this would be superficial. Because bureaucratic theory postulates that agency decision making comes from within, the development of attitudes sympathetic to those of the regulated interests is likely to come from experience rather than from outside pressure.

Bureaucratic theory focuses on the management techniques that develop within public organizations, including regulatory agencies, which are assumed to have a number of goals. First and foremost, they seek to survive and grow.[36] Second, they attempt to carry out the mandates they are assigned; EPA workers, for instance, want to help clean up the environment, and federal bank examiners want to ensure stability and safety in banking.[37] Third, agencies want to promulgate rules that are not overturned in Congress or by the courts. Fourth and finally, they want the industries they regulate to remain healthy.[38]

Analysis of the types of people who work in regulatory agencies supports the bureaucratic theory. James Q. Wilson describes three categories of agency employees, most of whom have an underlying conservative bent that ultimately promotes cautious behavior. The first category consists of *careerists,* employees who associate their careers with agency longevity. Members of the second category, *politicians,* see themselves as using successful agency management as a stepping stone to elective office. *Professionals,* the third category, depend on the approval of colleagues in similar positions outside their own agencies for status and self-esteem. This combination of managers makes for increasingly quiet, passive behavior over the life of the agency. No wonder that Wilson describes government regulatory bodies as "more risk averse than imperialistic. They prefer security to rapid growth, autonomy to competition, stability to change."[39] The caution that characterizes the long careers of agency managers also accounts for their agencies' low profiles.

Even among bureaucrats, differing motivations and actions are apparent. In his dissection of agency employees, Barry Mitnick identifies six groups: *climbers,* who want to maximize power, income, and prestige; *conservers,* self-interested protectors of the benefits they already receive; *zealots,* who care about specific, usually narrow goals in addition to their own self-interests; *advocates,* who are concerned with both themselves and the general goals and concerns of the agency for which they work; *statesmen,* who seek not only to better themselves but also society as a whole; and *loyalists,* who work for the goals of a specific leader in addition to their own goals.[40] This diversity alone can increase the difficulties in predicting agency behavior.

Depending on the assumption of basic agency motives, different cases can be made to explain regulation. Such motives are not always easy to ascertain inasmuch as the agency personnel may not share consistent policy goals. The relationship between agency heads and bureaucrats is one example. An agency head is usually appointed for a limited amount of time and may be tied to a political position. His or her motives will differ from those of a career worker in the regulatory agency.[41] An agency director will be concerned about future prospects beyond the agency appointment, while a career bureaucrat will have a greater interest in the long-term survival of the agency.

Regulatory agencies undoubtedly often begin as bastions of vision and reform. The more compelling issue, however, focuses on the impact of their activities over time.

Criticism of Bureaucratic Theory

Those who fault bureaucratic theory point to long-term behavior as evidence of the failure of both agency and theory. The life-cycle outline not only describes an agency's origin but also its probable demise. The relatively quiet death of the CAB serves as a case in point. Its last administrator, Alfred Kahn, was appointed primarily because he had opposed the agency's existence. Significantly, few middle-management employees opposed Kahn's work once he took over his position.

Critics of bureaucratic theory stress a direct cause-and-effect relationship between early agency activities and subsequent hostility from those impacted by regulatory decisions. As the agency increases its vigilance and areas of interest, resentment and hostility develop among those feeling the pressures of agency rule. This private-sector resistance often begins with the reluctance of the regulated to be cooperative—i.e., to provide routine data to government bodies. The lack of voluntary compliance further undermines the legitimacy and success of the agency. Increasingly unsure of their authority, regulators retreat to a "minimalist attitude," leaving them unresponsive to more serious problems that demand effective action.[42] From such caution, ineffectual governance develops.

Although some critics of bureaucratic theory condemn regulatory agencies for waning effectiveness as they age, others attack the agencies for making unrealistic demands. Actually, this second line of criticism is quite compatible with the first. In their efforts to be fair and thorough, regulators require tremendous amounts of information from the private sector. Not only are such zealous efforts part of the regulator's undoing, but also such requirements place a terrible burden on the regulated community. Murray Weidenbaum, formerly a member of the Council of Economic Advisors, provides a firsthand insight into the dilemma, noting that "the major source of government intrusion is the paperwork burden imposed by the many agencies of federal, state and local governments . . . . [The] burden is primarily the result of federal regulation."[43] The exhaustive demands made by regulatory agencies ultimately interfere with their abilities to make and implement policy.

Economic Theories

Almost all theories of regulation include some informal economic analysis, but not all can be considered to be *economic theories* of regulation. These parallel the bureaucratic theory in that they usually recognize that many public actors with complex motives participate in the regulatory process. But economic theories also acknowledge the costs and benefits of regulation, outcomes of the process that are likely to be spread among a number of groups. Unlike the public-interest and capture theories, economic theories use standard economic assumptions and tools to assess the effectiveness of regulation.

Justification of Economic Theories

Early economic theories of regulation focused on the conditions of market failure, instances where the lack of genuine competition led to unequal and potentially harmful relationships between producers and consumers. In examining the problems of "natural monopolies," for example, economic-theory advocates argued for regulation as a mechanism for setting efficient prices or levels of production. These proponents explained that in an appropriate nonpolitical environment, an agency would be able to establish effective regulatory policies as long as it enjoyed access to information and other necessary resources.

Economic theories took an important step forward in 1971 with George Stigler's article on the theory of regulation. According to Stigler, an industry often has more to gain by seeking regulation than avoiding it. Through the regulation of entry, price floors, and other protections, an industry can achieve large gains that it otherwise could not secure in an unregulated setting. There is a valuable relationship between government, the supplier of regulation, and producers, who demand government benefits. Stigler finds that smaller groups with concentrated interests are more likely to dominate larger groups whose higher organizational costs lower benefits to each member.[44] Such an analysis suggests that regulation is likely to be conferred on those who are best able to secure it.

Stigler's work is also important because it stated relevant political questions in familiar economic terms. The concepts of "supply and demand" and "costs and benefits" gave seemingly quantifiable answers to otherwise nebulous assumptions; in other words, this approach quantified theoretical questions. When considered in this basic economic framework, regulatory policies could be studied with the standard tools of economic analysis. Moreover, the economic approach appeared to many observers as a logical extension of well-grounded political analysis. But in his work on interest groups and organizations, Mancur Olson challenged the school of thought that suggested an "equilibrium"—that is, a balanced relationship between all groups, large and small, organized and unorganized.[45] With "selective incentives," wrote Olson, such as discount cards and retirement benefits, some groups naturally would be more powerful and successful than others.[46] The political premise that some groups enjoyed radically different levels of success than did others not only suggested inequality but also justified governmental regulation.

Another recent treatment of regulation has focused on the fluid political and economic relationships between business and government. For example, in his supply-and-demand model of regulation, Sam Peltzman contends that the purpose of the regulatory process is to transfer wealth. Such movement, he asserts, takes place in a dynamic, everchanging environment. Even though regulators attempt to maximize a "political power function," interest groups bid for the benefits of regulation by providing "votes" for regulators. Agency officials not only seek to help impacted groups, but also use part of the gains from regulation to pay off "losers" in order to keep the largest possible power base.[47] Not to be lost is the fact that regulators use economic means to satisfy political objectives.

Criticism of Economic Theories

Most defenders of economic theory argue that the complex nature of modern society makes it almost impossible for a true free-market economy to exist. Hence, government regulation has become necessary as a means of preventing unfair manipulation of the market or its consumers. Critics, however, suggest that the increase of government regulation has occurred without much regard for the consequences. One observer of the entire regulatory process argues that the involvement of government as a distributive agent of benefits has done more harm than good. In his review of a variety of economic and social regulations, Paul MacAvoy concludes that they have resulted in performance declines: "Beyond regulatory lag and inefficiency, the poor results reflect the inevitable end product of the present administrative procedures."[48] Government tinkering, he laments, reduces private revenues and increases private costs. Moreover, the adjustments rarely have any positive impact on social conditions.

Critics of economic theory argue that determining the "right" amount of regulation should not come from whimsical outside political pressure but from an economic test of efficiency. To do so means finding a way to hold outside factors constant; it also assumes that nonquantifiable variables can be controlled. Neither of these is likely in the real world. Moreover, when such tests are applied, the results may warrant less regulation than under current conditions.[49]

Ironically, size and influence, essential elements in economic theory, are also used by its detractors. We may recall Stigler's argument that smaller, better organized groups leave large, more dispersed groups at a disadvantage, thus requiring intervention in the name of fairness by government. Yet, critics respond, the opposite occurs "because large, bureaucratic firms may find it easier to comply with complex forms and regulations than do their small or medium-sized rivals."[50] Regulation may redistribute benefits but not necessarily as the reformers intended.

From a larger perspective, critics of economic theory often are not at odds with the concept as much as they are with the motive assumptions behind the concept. These observers agree that there may be examples of market failure or monopoly, and that there may be instances of inefficient prices or poor production. But whatever problems may exist, they argue, government intrusion may make the result considerably more expensive, and thus more harmful, to consumers than necessary. Where such conditions prevail, the cure may be worse than the disease.

Environmental Considerations in Regulation Theory

The four theories discussed above offer justifications for and criticisms of the values that are inherent in the struggle over regulation. In addition to the general approaches, however, a number of environmental factors play important roles in determining the outcomes of the regulatory process.

Structures of regulatory agencies vary; some are headed by commissions, others by single administrators. Agencies may also be independent or housed in the executive branch. Although there has been much speculation on the importance of these factors, there has been little systematic analysis of the effects from different agency structures.[51] The differences in organization may indeed have an impact on susceptibility to external pressures, internal values, and policy outputs.

The occupational composition of regulatory agencies has also been postulated to affect regulatory performance. The influence of lawyers, in particular, has been held to be important in the forms of regulation that develop. For example, the EPA's early strategy was partially determined by the strong influence exerted by lawyers on the choice of standards and the enforcement taken.[52] In contrast, agencies composed primarily of scientists might emphasize different goals than might those that depend on economists or engineers for technical support.[53]

The impact of *specific individuals* in the regulatory process has also been informally studied. Alfred Kahn at the CAB, Anne Gorsuch Burford at EPA, and Michael Pertshuk at FTC each brought significant change to their agency. Strong leadership or the suggestion of scandal can influence the work of bureaucrats within the agency and the success that the agency finds in the political arena. The relative importance of individuals, as opposed to regulatory structures, is another area requiring continued research.

The importance of the *agency mandate* may also have significant influence. Some agencies have a wide range of discretionary powers, while others are given highly specific goals and timetables. One hypothesis contends that the more discretion an agency has, the more likely that industry capture will occur. On the other hand, extremely detailed mandates may lead to inflexibility and inefficient regulation.

The Limits of Theory

The four theories presented in this chapter represent the most commonly held views and defenses of regulation. In each instance, political theorists have justified government involvement as a benefit for bureaucrats, narrow groups, or the public interest. Various claims of its proponents notwithstanding, each major regulatory theory has been criticized for inaccuracy, distortion, or cost–benefit inefficiency.

Perhaps the major problem with regulatory thought is that the theories seem to simultaneously concur, conflict, and overlap. Concurrence exists with the general defense of some governmental action. Conflict becomes apparent when fixing blame for the economic or social dysfunctions that lead to the call for regulatory activity. Overlap occurs with respect to the ways in which the theories address issues of inequity and the poor distribution of resources.

Finally, the multitude of social and economic ills and the unique responses to each make it difficult to embrace the recommendations of any single theory as the means of solving all problems. As James Q. Wilson concludes, " 'regulatory politics' is not an especially useful category of analysis because it encompasses forms of political action that have little in common other than the fact that some agency issues or applies a rule. A single-explanation theory of regulatory politics is about as helpful as a single explanation of politics generally, or of disease."[54] Does this discourage the use of theory? No, although it does suggest potential problems in application and prediction.

A well-founded theory of regulation should not only explain the conditions leading to regulation but also the consequences following such activity. Here again, past and present developments do not mesh particularly well with extant theories. Furthermore, deregulation—the lessening of governmental control over the private sector—has assumed a new importance in American political life.

The change in climate cannot be denied, although assessing the surge of deregulatory pressure may be as difficult as accounting for the rise of regulation itself. Nevertheless, in the chapters that follow, we will examine several cases of regulatory activity and attempt to explain the reasons and bases for deregulatory change.

Notes

1. Barry M. Mitnick, *The Political Economy of Regulation: Creating, Designing, and Removing Regulatory Forms* (New York: Columbia University Press, 1980), p. 155.
2. Eugene Bardach and Robert A. Kagan, *Going by the Book: The Problem of Regulatory Unreasonableness* (Philadelphia: Temple University Press, 1982), p. 303.
3. Richard A. Posner, "Theories of Economic Regulation," *Bell Journal of Economics and Management Science,* 5, no. 2 (Autumn 1974): 335.
4. Mitnick, *Political Economy,* p. 97.
5. G. William Domhoff, *The Powers That Be* (New York: Vintage Books, 1979), p. 25.
6. *Ibid.,* p. 199.
7. Peter Bachrach, *The Theory of Democratic Elitism* (Boston: Little, Brown, 1967), p. 105.
8. *Ibid.,* p. 104.
9. Alfred E. Kahn, *The Economics of Regulation: Principles and Institutions,* vol. 1, *Economic Principles* (New York: Wiley, 1970), pp. 9–10.
10. Marver H. Bernstein, *Regulating Business by Independent Commission* (Princeton, N.J.: Princeton University Press, 1955), p. 62.
11. Mark V. Nadel, *The Politics of Consumer Protection* (Indianapolis: Bobbs–Merrill, 1971), p. 18.
12. Susan Tolchin and Martin Tolchin, *Dismantling America: The Rush to Deregulate* (New York: Oxford University Press, 1983), p. 74.
13. *San Francisco Chronicle,* February 20, 1986, p. 34.
14. James Q. Wilson, *The Politics of Regulation* (New York: Basic Books, 1980), p. 384.

15. Charles O. Jones, *An Introduction to the Study of Public Policy*, 3d ed. (Monterey, Calif.: Brooks/Cole Publishing Co., 1984), p. 19.
16. Michael Parenti, *Power and the Powerless* (New York: St. Martin's Press, 1978), p. 189.
17. Wilson, *Politics*, p. 387.
18. Posner, "Theories," p. 336.
19. Kenneth J. Meier, *Regulation: Politics, Bureaucracy, and Economics* (New York: St. Martin's Press, 1985), p. 9.
20. Sam Peltzman, "Current Developments in the Economics of Regulation," in *Studies in Public Regulation*, ed. Gary Fromm (Cambridge, Mass.: MIT Press, 1981), pp. 371–372.
21. Paul H. Weaver, "Regulation, Social Policy, and Class Conflict," in *Regulating Business: The Search for an Optimum*, ed. Chris Argyris (San Francisco: Institute of Contemporary Studies, 1978), p. 195.
22. Don L. Worrell and Edmund Gray, "Uncle Remus Meets Regulatory Reform: The Briar-Patch Phenomenon," *Business Horizons*, 28, no. 4 (July–August 1985): 64–65.
23. Gabriel Kolko, *The Triumph of Conservatism: A Reinterpretation of American History, 1900–1916*, 1968, p. 2.
24. Theodore J. Lowi, *The End of Liberalism* (New York: Norton, 1969).
25. *Ibid.*, p. 58.
26. G. William Domhoff, *Who Rules America?* (Englewood Cliffs, N.J.: Prentice–Hall, 1967), p. 107.
27. Robert Fellmeth, *The Interstate Commerce Omission* (New York: Grossman, 1970), p. 311.
28. Nadel, *Consumer Protection*, pp. 24–27.
29. *Ibid.*, p. 8.
30. Sam Peltzman, "Toward a More General Theory of Regulation," *Journal of Law and Economics*, 19, no. 2 (August 1976): 217.
31. John Kenneth Galbraith, *American Capitalism* (Boston: Houghton Mifflin, 1952), p. 113.
32. Martha Derthick and Paul J. Quirk, *The Politics of Deregulation* (Washington, D.C.: The Brookings Institution, 1985), p. 92.
33. Guy Benveniste, *Bureaucracy* (San Francisco: Boyd and Fraser, 1977), p. 31.
34. Charles Perrow, *Complex Organizations*, 2d ed. (Glenview, Ill.: Scott, Foresman, 1979), p. 1979.
35. Bernstein, *Regulating Business*, p. 74.
36. Mitnick, *Political Economy*, p. 133.
37. Meier, *Regulation*, p. 9.
38. Roger G. Noll, "The Economics and Politics of Regulation," *Virginia Law Review*, 57, no. 6 (September 1971): 1029–1030.
39. Wilson, *Politics*, p. 376.
40. Mitnick, *Political Economy*, p. 443.
41. Jack Hirshleifer, "Comment," *Journal of Law and Economics*, 19, no. 2 (August 1976): 242.
42. Bardach and Kagan, *Going By the Book*, p. 108.
43. Murray Weidenbaum, *Business, Government, and the Public*, 2d ed. (Englewood Cliffs, N.J.: Prentice–Hall, 1981), p. 197.
44. George J. Stigler, "The Theory of Economic Regulation," *Bell Journal of Economics and Management Science*, 2 (Winter 1971): 3.
45. The major proponents of the equilibrium school included Arthur F. Bentley, *The Process of Government* (Chicago: University of Chicago Press, 1908), and David B. Truman, *The Governmental Process* (New York: Knopf, 1951).
46. See Mancur Olson, *The Logic of Collective Action* (New York: Schocken Books, 1968). Olson writes that small groups "have not only economic incentives, but also

perhaps social incentives, that lead their members to work toward the achievement of the collective good. The large, 'latent' group, on the other hand, always contains more people than could possibly know each other, and is not likely to develop social pressures that would help it satisfy its interest in a collective good."

47. Peltzman, "General Theory," pp. 211–240.
48. Paul W. MacAvoy, *The Regulated Industries and the Economy* (New York: Norton, 1979), pp. 121–122.
49. Robert C. Puth, *American Economic History* (New York: The Dryden Press, 1982), p. 471.
50. Paul L. Joskow and Roger C. Woll, "Regulation in Theory and Practice: An Overview," in *Studies in Public Regulation,* ed. Gary From, p. 40.
51. Wilson, *Politics,* p. 381.
52. David McCaffrey, "New Issues in the Study of Regulation," *Polity,* 15, no. 3 (Spring 1985): 466.
53. Wilson, *Politics,* p. 393.
54. *Ibid.,* p. 387.

PART TWO

Case Studies
in Deregulation

CHAPTER 5

The Airline Industry

The airline industry in the United States has been blessed with a history of safe service and a forty-year period of stable growth. Until recently, the rest of the world's airlines regarded the U.S. industry as a model of efficiency and profit. Indeed, the growth of airline service has been nothing short of phenomenal. In 1938, when passenger service was still limited to those who had money and a sense of adventure, domestic airlines served about 1.5 million passengers.[1] Less than fifty years later, air travel was available to almost everyone; in 1983, for example, the twenty-five largest airports in America served 440 million passengers.[2] And for most of this period of expansion, airlines were heavily regulated by the federal government.

As the availability of air service expanded, even those less well off were able to take advantage of changing air-fare structures. Until the early 1950s, all passengers flew first-class, forced to pay expensive fares. The government first allowed "tourist" fares in 1952; six years later, "economy" fares were introduced to the traveling public.[3] In the 1980s, luxury service is still available, but so are low-service prices. When Congress passed the Air Transport Deregulation Act of 1978, it opened up air travel to a whole new group of travelers on tighter budgets. These passengers on no-frills airlines pay for tickets on the plane and, perhaps, selectively for combinations of other conveniences ranging from baggage checks to coffee. But as a trade-off, they usually pay significantly less for a ticket.[4]

Deregulation has significantly changed the way airlines do business. Some critics argue, however, that these changes have not all been for the better. In addition to offering a variety of new fare classes, for example, airlines are now permitted to determine where to fly. As a result, some communities once served because of the requirements of regulation are no longer considered profitable enough as airlines search for the most lucrative routes.

Because of these benefits and drawbacks, the airline industry provides an excellent case study of deregulation. The industry has made a dramatic adjustment from substantial regulation to a competitive environment. Enough time has passed since deregulation first began to reasonably evaluate its success. This chapter will thus look at the original purposes of airline regulation, the fight to deregulate the industry, and the results of that deregulation.

The Rise of Regulation

When the industry first began, revenues from passengers and cargo were not enough to keep the young airlines profitable. They found their survival by obtaining federal airmail contracts, granted in 1925 when Congress transferred primary responsibility for carrying airmail from the

Army to the commercial airlines. Thus, for an air company, a government mail contract meant success.[5] In fact, with so much at stake, in the early 1930s some of the larger airlines colluded with the U.S. Post Office in the awarding of contracts. A highly publicized investigation by Sen. Hugo Black (D.–Ala.) exposed the system of collusion in 1934.[6] The mail contracts were cancelled, and the Army again replaced the airlines as airmail carriers—with disastrous results.

Flying with little experience and the wrong equipment under unfamiliar conditions, a dozen Army pilots were killed and many more injured in less than three months. Outcries from the public and government leaders alike forced Congress to reassess the arrangement. Consequently, the Airmail Act of 1934 placed the airline industry under the control of several government agencies. The Post Office was given basic authority over entry into the airline industry when it was allowed to award contracts and determine routes and schedules for airmail. The ICC set the rate of pay for mail transport, and the Bureau of Air Commerce took charge of safety.[7]

Within the industry, major airline companies united both to fight off competition and to bargain with the government, forming the Air Transport Association in 1936. The association lobbied for increased federal aid and protection from "excessive competition," which, they warned, would ruin the industry—the established airlines feared that new entrants would drive prices down. Congress responded with the Civil Aeronautics Act of 1938. This new legislation consolidated airline regulation under one federal agency, a predecessor of the CAB.[8] Now under federal protection, the major airlines saw hope for stability and profitability.

The Airline Industry under Regulation

Between 1938 and 1978, the CAB regulated the airline industry. The period was marked by remarkable stability. Few groups demanded reform, and when complaints occasionally arose about the lack of competition, they were rarely taken seriously. The CAB found favor with both Congress and the executive branch; it seldom advocated domestic policies that would conflict with those of other agencies. The CAB was "dictator" of the skies,[9] but for the most part, major airlines found the dictatorship to be benevolent.

The CAB controlled almost every aspect of domestic air transport, although it shared jurisdiction with the Department of State for international routes. An airline had to convince the CAB that it met standards of public convenience and necessity in order to fly a particular route. The CAB decided which airlines entered the market, the routes they flew, and the fares they charged.[10] The board's policies discouraged the "excessive competition" that the airlines and Congress had feared when passing the 1938 Act, for the CAB policies seldom allowed true price competition. Instead, airlines competed with service. Frequent flights were scheduled on their regulated routes to give passengers a wide selection of departure times and uncrowded planes.[11] Drinks and meals were free, and airlines tried to attract customers by offering fast ground service and lavish in-flight amenities. For those who could afford it, air travel was easy and comfortable. The CAB approved (with antitrust immunity) multiairline agreements for ticketing, baggage handling, and the maintenance and servicing of aircraft, among other things.[12] The industry ran smoothly almost as a government-sanctioned oligopoly, rather than as a competitive venture.

After twenty years, technological development and growth led Congress, airlines, and the CAB to modify the regulatory structure to separate concerns for safety from economic regulation. The 1938 act was revised by the 1958 Federal Aviation Act. A new agency, the Federal Aviation Administration (FAA), was established to control the industry's technical aspects—safety, airport development, and air-traffic control. As the FAA took responsibility for safety issues, the CAB became more strictly an economic regulator.[13] Part of the CAB's mandate was to protect the air industry, and the board took great interest in preserving the economic health of the airline companies for which it had responsibility.

In the course of the airline industry's growth, various types of scheduled passenger service developed. The first category was that of *trunk airlines,* which carry the bulk of air traffic. United, American, Delta, TWA, and Eastern are examples. These major airlines carry passengers long distances and to many destinations. *Local-service airlines* form the second category. These companies developed, with federal aid, to bring air service to small cities not previously reached by trunk carriers. Before deregulation, Ozark, Allegheny, and Hughes Airwest provided local service. Finally, *commuter airlines* constitute a third category. These companies fly small planes (currently less than sixty seats) to small towns. Their importance has grown as local-service carriers have purchased jets and changed the focus of their markets.[14] The commuter airlines were never included in the CAB's economic regulation system.

Shortly after its creation in 1938, CAB granted "grandfather" licenses to sixteen major airlines. Although the number had dwindled through merger to ten by 1978,[15] the CAB had not allowed any new trunk airlines to enter the market during its forty years of regulation. The board did approve operating privileges for a few new airlines, but these could only serve small communities or markets that the trunk airlines did not want, such as Alaska. Although many companies wanted to begin trunk-airline service, the CAB thought that new trunks might hurt the established airlines, which the board was supposed to protect. Between 1938 and

1976, more than 230 applications were filed with the CAB. But after 1950, the board did not even allow hearings for 95 percent of the applicants.[16]

Although the CAB protected the established airlines, it also assigned the carriers unsolicited responsibilities. For example, in order to receive a favored route, an airline sometimes had to accept a less desirable city as well. The CAB thus encouraged airlines to use the profits from long, popular hauls to subsidize small-town service; i.e., passengers from major cities subsidized small-town travelers, and, in general, long-haul passengers helped to pay for those who took shorter trips.

Whenever airline costs increased, company managers applied to the CAB for fare increases. The CAB usually granted these, although often after lengthy delay. Relatively little management skill was needed to run an airline: The major business decisions—where to fly, how much to charge—were made by the CAB.

Regulation Reconsidered

Although the system of air regulation had no serious problems, its merits were debated from time to time. In the late 1960s and early '70s, several economists began to question the efficiency of regulation. A number of studies concluded that regulated prices were higher than they would be if true competition existed.[17]

Several other CAB policies also caused a reevaluation of airline regulation. In 1970, the CAB instituted a route moratorium for domestic airlines; that is, no new competitive routes were authorized for any airline. Regulation critics were annoyed not only by the decision, but also by the way it was handled. The route moratorium meant that a new route request would not receive a formal hearing. The CAB's critics believed that each new request deserved a chance to be heard, regardless of the outcome. The assumption that *no* new routes might be desirable was considered somewhat presumptuous, an affront to would-be carriers.[18] The moratorium lasted until 1976.

The CAB began to take criticism from other quarters as well. Decisions on fare regulation brought complaints from several passenger groups, who were already displeased with route regulation. The CAB had authorized discount youth fares in the late 1960s, but in 1972, the agency abruptly cancelled this popular discount program. Students protested and received significant press coverage in the process.[19] The CAB was also criticized because of questionable price structures; fares between pairs of cities an equal distance apart were sometimes significantly different. Although these disparities could sometimes be justified by differing operating costs, the public seldom understood.[20] What had been occasional complaints about the CAB now became increasingly common.

The Push for Deregulation

The movement to deregulate the airline industry caught fire in 1975. In February, a presidential economic report detailed the problems of regulation in general, and that of airlines in particular. New president Gerald Ford placed deregulation as a key item on his agenda. Now the issue was no longer the exclusive property of academic journals. Over the following months, newspapers and popular magazines questioned CAB policy. Airline regulation became the topic of studies, conferences, and speeches. In effect, the issue once restricted to the industry had become public. In October, Ford proposed the Aviation Act of 1975, the first serious attempt to change airline regulation since 1958.[21]

The bill did not call for total deregulation, but it did provide for flexibility in setting fares and allowing entry of new carriers. Faced with unpredictable patterns, the established airlines were alarmed. Spokespersons claimed the bill would "tear apart a national transportation system recognized as the finest in the world."[22] Because of the industry's opposition, the proposed aviation act died in the Senate. In 1976, Sen. Howard Cannon (D.–Nev.) tried to initiate a less-ambitious set of changes. Although his bill was not seriously considered, it served to keep the issue before Congress as well as to keep interest in airline deregulation high.[23]

The Interest Groups Line Up

In 1977, advocates of deregulation found their position stronger than it had been in recent years. CAB chair John Robson publicly lobbied for a much more limited role for his agency. Another Senate critic, Edward Kennedy (D.–Mass.) joined Cannon to work for one bill to change airline regulation.

Ironically, Ford, the original champion of deregulation, was defeated by Jimmy Carter in 1976. But deregulation remained on the public agenda, and newly elected President Carter decided to make airline deregulation the key element of his plan to reduce government intervention in business.[24] With the president and key congressional leaders on the same side, the airline deregulation movement had solid backing.

One of the most diverse sets of groups ever to come together to lobby for legislation supported the Kennedy–Cannon bill. Naturally enough, the American Conservative Union and the National Taxpayers Union supported the bill, but so did the liberal groups Americans for Democratic Action and Common Cause.[25] At a time when frequent presidential transitions brought disharmony, both the outgoing Ford and incoming Carter administrations expressed interest in the bill. Even members of the CAB, individuals who had authority over airline regulation, lobbied to decrease their board's power.[26]

Neither liberals nor conservatives, however, could claim airline deregulation as their own issue, and not all liberals or all conservatives favored the bill. For example, in the Senate, George McGovern (D.–S. Dak.) and Barry Goldwater (R.–Ariz.) cosponsored an amendment to weaken the bill. The amendment would have seriously limited the bill's automatic-entry provisions. (Essentially, automatic entry meant that during the transition to deregulation airlines would be allowed to enter a limited number of routes of their own choosing, which the CAB would automatically approve. Beyond that number, route requests were to be subject to normal CAB approval.)

But those groups who had long benefited from regulation were the bill's primary opponents. Every union that represented employees of trunk airlines perceived the bill to be a threat to their members' jobs. Many airline executives not only feared lost jobs, but also that the industry would be wracked by instability. Not all executives, however, opposed the bill. In a move that made it the black sheep of the industry, United Airlines supported substantial deregulation. Although United's president, Richard Ferris, claimed this made him "as popular as a skunk at a lawn party,"[27] he believed United's support was important in fashioning a bill that would benefit the industry. But most other airlines were outraged; denied an "industry position" at the hearings, they claimed that United wanted to use deregulation to dominate the industry.[28] One of Eastern Airlines' senior vice-presidents, Morton Ehrlich, contended that the "United position is designed to maximize United's market share. It is extremely self-serving."[29] Despite these statements, it is doubtful that a unified stand by the airline industry could have prevented passage of the Kennedy–Cannon deregulation bill; the emergent broad consensus in Congress and the high priority given the bill by the Carter administration made airline deregulation a foregone conclusion.

The Case for Deregulation

Deregulation advocates cited efficiency as the primary reason for change. Under the regulated system, they argued, consumers were offered too much service at too high a price. With more freedom in entry and in setting fares as they desired, airlines could compete in both price and service, and consumers would be free to choose the sort of air travel that best met their needs.[30] In addition, the airlines would be given incentives to be innovative and more productive. Why should an airline work hard to lower costs if these savings could not be passed on to passengers, the airline benefiting from increased business? With regulated fares, price competition was impossible; CAB pricing policies prevented the market from rewarding the innovative and efficient at the expense of the passenger.[31]

Several studies supported the contention that airline prices could be significantly lower than under CAB regulation. If consumers were able to choose the combination of fares and services they preferred, the studies showed, many would select lower prices and fewer services.[32] The General Accounting Office figured that airline passengers paid $1.4 billion more than necessary because of government regulation of trunk airlines.[33]

Two states provided perhaps even more persuasive evidence that passengers would benefit from an increase in competition. California and Texas were each large enough to support substantial intrastate air traffic, which fell outside of the CAB's jurisdiction. Left on their own to choose prices and routes, the airlines charged significantly lower instrastate fares than they did for interstate flights of equal distance. Studies of the industries in California and Texas concluded that competition had not ruined the airlines in either state.[34] These success stories made it difficult for the trunk-line executives to claim that competition would be the "beginning of the end."

The arguments for deregulation seemed to reflect the public's increasing agitation with excessive government. And the CAB already had evidence that lowered fares would benefit both airlines and passengers: In the 1960s, the board had allowed the industry to offer student stand-by fares; basically, the airlines were allowed to offer nonguaranteed seats at lower prices—students benefited from these and the airlines from the increase in business. This limited experiment also convinced industry critics that airline deregulation would provide all travelers with direct benefits.[35] Such possibilities fit well with the contention that an overly protective bureaucracy had led to a government insensitive to the public's needs. Many began to question the assumption that the nation actually needed a CAB, commentators and policy makers alike demanding that the CAB (and a host of similar agencies) justify its existence. In general, supporters of regulation thus found themselves on the defensive.

The case for deregulation was not complicated. The product of the airline industry was clearly defined—scheduled passenger service. The producers were clearly identified. But one question remained to dominate the discussion: Was the price of the product needlessly high? Supporters of airline deregulation had impressive evidence that it was and that the time for change had come.

The Defense of Regulation

Supporters of the status quo argued that the system worked well. Indeed, none of the Kennedy–Cannon bill's supporters had argued that regulation had no benefits; almost everyone agreed that it had provided a safe and stable industry. Those who favored government controls believed the benefits outweighed the harm from high prices. After all, air fares were not exorbitant in a comparative context. While the consumer price index increased 146 percent from 1948 to 1977, air fares rose only 24 percent over the same period. According to the defenders of regulation, the industry performance should have been applauded, not criticized. Moreover, such performance could not have occurred without regulation.

Proregulators directly attacked the argument that deregulation would lead to lower fares. Although most agreed that competition might lead to lower prices in the short run, they also believed that fares would be even higher under deregulation in the long run. Excessive competition in the wake of deregulation, they said, would drive many of the existing airlines out of business. The result, they argued, would be control of the airline industry by just a few successful carriers with enormous power and high prices for consumers, the opposite of the goal of deregulation.[36] Proregulators argued that the key determinant of ticket prices, airline operating costs, would not go down as a result of deregulation. Variables other than regulation were more critical to airline costs and thus ticket prices. As long as fuel costs increased, airline employees demanded higher wages, and airports charged ever higher fees, the price of airline tickets would have to rise as well.[37]

Airline executives argued that whatever the result of the debate over price, regulation had provided a stable, reliable system of air transport. Business and vacation plans could be made with confidence that the routes and airlines would not change without notice. But under deregulation, travelers would have little advance warning of changes in fares or schedules, and decreased efficiency would result from canceled plans. As one commentator wrote, "[c]haos, confusion, and uncertainty are poor substitutes for orderliness, regularity, and continuity."[38] The basic theme of the proregulation contingent was to "leave well enough alone."

Those senators and congressional representatives with constituencies in small towns also opposed the bill, at least initially. If airlines were free to choose the markets they served, they would abandon smaller cities in favor of more profitable routes between large cities. Advocates for small towns argued that all citizens had benefited from the ability to fly to most American cities. Although the argument was rarely made, small cities also feared the reduced status attendant to loss of air service.[39]

Labor unions believed deregulation would significantly weaken their powers, and many argued that the real purpose of the bill was to undermine union contracts. Some of the intrastate airlines that offered inexpensive fares did so by hiring nonunion labor at significantly lower wages. New entrants under deregulation might also use lower-paid workers, and union pay scales would be lowered as older airlines tried to compete with new entrants. Labor leaders also argued that the failure of many airlines, sure to follow deregulation, would leave thousands unemployed. Unionized airline workers clearly stood to lose if airlines were forced to compete.[40]

Opponents of deregulation conceded that not all CAB policies were rational. Delays in CAB rulings were cited as needing improvement. Problems with the board, however, did not imply a need to deregulate, only for the CAB to move more quickly, perhaps even to allow more innovation and experimentation. It was not the structure of regulation that was unsound, but only an occasional policy resulting from that structure that needed to be changed.[41]

The Deregulators Respond

After three years of extensive debate, the backers of the Kennedy–Cannon bill made a final push for deregulation. Proponents challenged the argument that an oligopoly would result. Small and large carriers were both successful; larger size did not automatically give an airline an advantage. Many airlines that specialized in just a few routes were quite profitable. Furthermore, without CAB restrictions, the airline industry would not be as difficult for new carriers to enter. If existing airline prices were too high, a new airline could enter the market, offer lower prices, and grab a large share of the business. A lack of competition would not be a problem.

Although a deregulated industry would not necessarily be as stable as it had been under the CAB, the bill's supporters did not believe that chaos would result. Airlines without reliable service would not survive, thus self-interest on the part of airline executives would preserve reasonable order. As former CAB chair Alfred Kahn noted, "there seems to be a general belief among defenders of the present regulatory regime that . . . once the CAB removes its body from the threshold, they (airline executives) will rush into markets [pell-mell], like lemmings, without regard to the size of each, how many sellers it can sustain, and how many others may be entering [at] the same time."[42] In other words, advocates of a reduced governmental role were confident that the airlines could make reasonable marketing decisions and successfully perform other management tasks.

Deregulators also argued that there was no demonstrable relationship between regulation and the airline industry's health. Contrary to popular belief, the industry was not very profitable. Excess revenues generated by high ticket prices were lost through high service cost and excess capacity. In the ten years prior to the beginning of the deregulation debate, an airline typically had well below average return on equity (the value of the company), and the return on investment was far less than the CAB recommended.[43] Furthermore, during the 1980s, the airlines would have to replace their older jet fleets with new, more fuel-efficient models. Under regulation, the airlines might have serious trouble raising the capital for modernized fleets.[44]

The Safety Issue

Safety was one of the most important considerations to everyone debating the Kennedy–Cannon bill. Many opponents contended that deregulation would inevitably lead to a decline in airline-maintenance standards. As competition drove airlines to seek the lowest possible costs, mechanics would be encouraged to cut corners. Older aircraft would remain in service for longer periods of time. With easy entry into and exit from the business, an airline would tend to employ inexperienced pilots and ground crews, who could easily make mistakes. Finally, both opponents and proponents recognized that commuter airlines would play a critical role in deregulation, but that these airlines could not come close to the impressive safety records of the trunk carriers.[45]

The proposed bill did not directly affect the FAA, which regulated safety, and the supporters of deregulation challenged the contention that competition would hurt safety. The costs inherent in flying and in flying safely were substantially equal, and the publicity following an air disaster would ruin any airline that was revealed to have cut corners on safety. Moreover, the FAA had always done a good job of overseeing air safety, leaving no reason to believe that it would be less effective under deregulation. If necessary, the FAA staff could be increased to allow more frequent and detailed inspections. Although safety was critical, most observers viewed economic regulation and safety regulation as reasonably separate issues.[46]

Other Questions

Deregulation supporters did not deal directly with the fears of small towns and unions. In order to ensure passage of the bill, amendments were included to protect both groups. The Essential Air Service provision directed the CAB to determine the needed level of service for small communities and to provide subsidies where needed to guarantee that small towns would not be victimized by deregulation. The program was scheduled to last ten years.[47] This provision allowed proponents to argue that small towns would be better served under deregulation; in fact, they said, small cities had no service guarantee under regulation, and that from 1960 to 1977, 180 towns had lost certified air carrier service.[48] The provision effectively ended most small-town complaints.

Even many of the bill's supporters realized that the transition to deregulation might impose significant burdens on airline workers. In order to help those workers who might be unemployed as a result of the Kennedy–Cannon bill, it also provided that workers who were laid off following bankruptcy or major contraction of the industry would be compensated. This provision made it more difficult for the unions to oppose the bill, robbing them of one of their most effective arguments against deregulation. The bill provided no long-term assurances to unions, however. Labor leaders did not think that this provision completely addressed their concerns, but as it seemed clear that the bill would pass, they considered it better than nothing.[49]

To those who argued that the CAB just needed to work better, deregulation proponents responded that old answers would not solve new questions. Even the two most recent CAB administrators had concluded that something had to be done to open up the industry. Without deregulation, they argued, a change in attitude of an administrator was all that was needed to derail innovation. Finally, to those who believed that it was not worth the risk to change a system that worked, the bill's supporters responded that the system no longer worked, at least not very well, and for all the reasons discussed above.

Airline Deregulation Becomes Law

The deregulators won the debate. Once the labor-protection provision was added, the Senate passed its version of airline deregulation on April 19, 1978, by a vote of 83 to 9. The House passed its version, 363 to 8, on September 21. Less than a month later, the two houses reconciled their differences and passed the Air Transportation Deregulation Act of 1978. President Carter signed the bill on October 24, 1978, noting that, "[f]or the first time in decades, we have actually deregulated a major industry."[50]

Carter was right—deregulation of an entire industry is indeed a rare event. Almost every regulatory agency faces continual criticism, but they seem to survive rather well. What made the airlines a special case? Given the arguments of proponents and opponents alike, of potential winners and losers, how could these differences be reconciled by law?

The proposal seemed to gain support because many believed that the benefits to the "winners"—the public—would be much more than the costs to the "losers"—airline companies and personnel—although the losers might disagree. The airline passenger—especially the lower-income traveler who might have previously been priced out of the airline market—was clearly the biggest winner. The losers were not groups usually considered powerless: travelers who wanted luxury service, airline workers, and the airline industry itself. Although labor unions were not without influence in Congress, airline workers did not garner much sympathy. For example, a captain belonging to the Air Line Pilots Association (ALPA) earned, *on average,* $103,000 in 1985.[51] Compared to people with similar skills in other industries, salaries were even high for flight attendants and airline mechanics. These workers did not seem oppressed by any measure.

The potential losers from deregulation are often groups that Congress has protected in the past. Many felt that the industry, once young and vulnerable, could now make it on its own. The idea found acceptance on both sides of the political spectrum. Liberals wanted to open up the skies to more passengers, and conservatives preferred a free market over regulation. Thus, a broad-based coalition was not only possible but also successful.

Provisions of the Act

The act provided for a six-year transition to deregulation. For the first three years, each airline was allowed to enter one new route without CAB approval. Each was also allowed to "protect" one route by declaring it ineligible to entry by other airlines. Dormant routes were open to any airline that could prove itself ready and able to offer service.

Airline fares were deregulated in stages. During the transition, fares could be raised by 5 percent or lowered by as much as 50 percent without CAB approval. All entry control was eliminated on December 31, 1981, and fares were completely deregulated one year later. Finally, the CAB itself would cease to exist on December 31, 1984.[52] Republicans and Democrats alike congratulated themselves on the reduction in big government and the expected increase in competition. Even as the bill passed, however, problems began to develop for the airline industry. Many of the difficulties would worsen in the deregulated environment.

Airlines under Deregulation

For airline executives, the deregulated society was an abrupt change from the comfortable past. Even if the future was more uncertain, however, the challenge was more exciting. Designation of markets and determination of prices, decisions that most executives are accustomed to making, were new to people in the airline industry. Despite the opposition to deregulation of most carriers, they quickly moved to take advantage of its benefits. The CAB promised to assign new routes on a first-come, first-serve basis, and the airlines were anxious to take advantage of potential bonanzas. Four days before President Carter signed the bill, perhaps one of the most bizarre deregulation scenes was played out. Airline representatives lined up outside CAB offices, like music fans waiting for coveted concert tickets. They brought sleeping bags and thermoses and had airline catering trucks bringing food and amenities. The Eastern representative was first in line, but lost his place to United's representative when he needed relief and could find no replacement to stand in line for him.[53]

Five months after the act was passed, 3,189 new routes were granted, and some 7,000-plus awaited approval.[54] New airlines were also soon born. Some completely new trunk airlines entered the market, some former charter airlines began to offer scheduled service, and commuter airlines grew as well. Many intrastate airlines began service to other states. Proving true the argument that the market would support lower service at lower fares, "no-frills" airlines soon began flying. Customers proved more than willing to give up meals and movies for cheaper tickets. These airlines brought new passengers to the industry as a whole, although the market share of trunk airlines fell significantly.[55]

Deregulation required an entirely new outlook in the airline industry. Executives had to become much more cost-conscious, aggressive, and attuned to the needs of the customer. Similarly, managers needed to learn different ways of thinking. As they quickly tried to increase market shares, most airlines copied Delta Airlines' "hub-and-spokes" system, whereby passengers arrived at a central airport from outlying areas with many points of departure and were then carried to their final destinations. Some airlines tried to expand quickly, while others worked to consolidate their strongest routes and protect them from competition. But all in all, in the early going most airlines were disturbed, if not frightened, by deregulation.

The Early Results

In retrospect, deregulation came at a time when the U.S. economy was in trouble. Almost immediately, the nation entered a serious recession, the cost of jet fuel skyrocketed, and the government's own air-traffic controllers went on a strike that broke their union and cost the country a significant number of invaluable federal employees. It is almost impossible to tell how well airlines would have coped with deregulation under less troubled economic conditions. The combination of events led the airlines to some of their worst years ever. Passenger traffic declined in 1980 and 1981, both in numbers boarded and miles flown.[56] Members of the Air Transport Association lost $222 million in 1980 and $421 million the following year (see Figure 5-1).[57] Profit margins improved in the mid–1980s, however, providing further evidence of industry volatility.

Experts have debated the extent to which deregulation contributed to the industry's uncertainty. As a share of operating expenses, jet fuel increased from 11 percent in 1970 to 30 percent in 1980.[58] The air-traffic controllers' strike forced serious reductions in the numbers of departures and landings at major airports.

But the onset of the recession itself posed the most serious problems for the industry, making competitive strategies difficult to develop. Continental vice-president Charles A. Bucks described the situation: "Everyone is still jockeying for position. The real fight hasn't started yet. We are all trying to determine which routes we want to become deeply entrenched in and fight for."[59] Ironically, Continental became an early loser in the deregulation struggle. These decisions were much more difficult

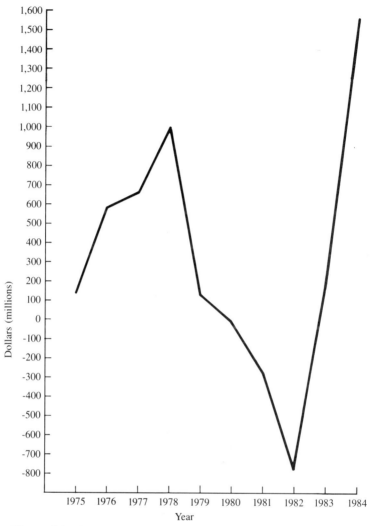

Figure 5-1. Net operating income (revenue less expenses for certified route passenger/cargo air carriers)
Source: *Statistical Abstract of the United States, 1984, Table 1098.*

when the recession kept passengers at home. Airlines also found that some changes were difficult to make. Although fares and routes were easily adjustable, airlines that had very high labor costs and the wrong mix of aircraft found these problems hard to face and slow to solve. It is almost impossible to answer the critical question: How would the industry have faced such poor conditions under regulation?

Some problems have resulted more directly from deregulation. One has been delay. The hub-and-spokes system, for example, requires that flights arrive at and depart from an airport close enough together in time and space to allow passengers to make easy connections. But without CAB control over scheduling, nothing has prevented airlines from scheduling large numbers of flights, all of which depart or land at the same time. Even though airports cannot handle so many flights at once, no airline wants to give up a flight at a popular time. As a result, long delays have become commonplace.[60]

The airline industry has certainly been more volatile since deregulation. The number of airline companies has significantly increased: 100 carriers provided certified service in 1984, up from 36 before deregulation.[61] Including commuter airlines in the same period, the number providing service rose from 219 to 419.[62] The rise of new airlines, however, was only one part of the story. Between the beginning of deregulation in 1978 and the end of 1984, approximately 120 airlines either went bankrupt and reorganized or closed down entirely.[63] Although few of these were trunk airlines, the failure rate seems high given the size and former stability of the industry. But in 1983, as the economy improved, so did airline profits. Even though a deregulated market meant that good times did not ensure survival for all, those airlines with strong management were able to thrive. Nevertheless, the Air Transportation Deregulation Act had brought instability to a once-stable system of carriers.

The Deregulation Debate in Retrospect

Even the advocates of airline deregulation knew that the transition from a highly structured, government-controlled industry to a market-oriented, competitive one would not be easy. Indeed, the airlines have gone through a difficult period of adjustment, one that was compounded by a poor economy. But the transition is nearly complete. The CAB no longer exists, and each airline has had time to find its niche in the new competitive environment. But looking back to the debate over deregulation, the questions linger. Who has benefited? Have the costs been excessive? Has deregulation worked well for society and the industry alike?

New Fare Structures

The key hope for deregulation was that of lower airline fares. There is more competition for routes between more pairs of cities. Routes served by just one airline have declined.[64] The larger airlines do not appear to be able to use market power to force up fares, and the average fares in the first years of deregulation declined.[65] Prices came closer to reflecting actual costs, so previously subsidized passengers paid significantly higher fares, whereas passengers on long-haul, popular routes found lower fares.[66]

Prices have risen since 1978, but most observers agree that the fares are lower than they would have been under deregulation. Fares under deregulation have, on average, increased less than the consumer price index.[67] One study estimated that if regulation had continued, consumers would have paid an extra \$6 billion in air fares in 1982.[68] Even if the actual figure had been significantly lower, the average consumer would still seem to have been saving money under deregulation (see Figure 5-2).

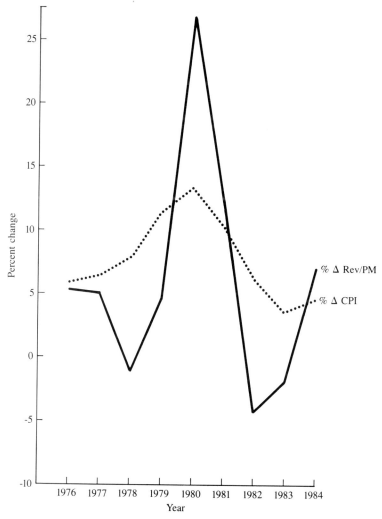

Figure 5-2. Airline Fare increase versus CPI increase
%Δ Rev/PM (solid line): Percent change in revenue per passenger mile–airline fares per mile (amount airlines receive from passengers)
%Δ (dotted line): Percent change in Consumer Price Index
Sources: CPI, Bureau of Labor Statistics; airline fares, Air Transport Association of America, 1985

Critics of the CAB had argued that high fares were coupled with excessive service. In the short run, however, business travelers paid much of the cost of deregulation. Although average fares may be lower, these figures reflect special discount fares available to discretionary travelers. Basic air fares have significantly increased. Business travelers found that service was reduced, schedules were often less convenient, and the cost was higher.[69] But because business travel accounts for a significant portion of air travel, it would have been surprising if, in the long run, airlines chose not to compete for business passengers.

American Airlines found one way to lure business travelers, a frequent-flyer program. Passengers receive credit for travel on American's flights through bonuses for accumulated miles. First-class upgrades and free tickets are the most common rewards. Other airlines quickly followed with similar programs of their own. Many developed "business class" service with wider seats, better meals, and free drinks. Because the bonuses go to the individual passenger, and not to the company for which he or she works, the business traveler has been happier, although his or her company has paid the price.

Deregulation has provided a range of fares and levels of service that give the consumer more choice. Flights that offer large, leather-upholstered seats and gourmet meals are available, as are flights that seem like cattle cars in the sky. Airlines now compete with both price and service, the goal of the deregulators.

Although fears of an airline oligopoly seemed remote in the first years following deregulation, events during 1986 raised questions about the industry's changing structure. People Express purchased Frontier Airlines, and then Texas Air bought People Express. Delta purchased Western, USAir took over PSA, American bought Air Cal, and Northwest acquired Republic.[70] These are only a few of the mergers and acquisitions that have sharply decreased the number of major airlines. The consolidations of 1986, in fact, have raised new fears that a few powerful airlines will come to control the market.

Few observers expected that all new entrants would survive in the new airline market. As the industry settled down, some mergers were inevitable; this does not mean that deregulation has been a failure. The level of competition from five or six trunk airlines in combination with the remaining regional and commuter airlines may provide enough competition to keep fares low. If prices do rise, new airlines may once again enter the market to force prices down. If any small group of airlines finds itself with too much market power, antitrust laws may come into play.[71]

Service under Deregulation

When the market took over from the CAB, opponents of deregulation predicted chaos. As we have discussed, the problem of delay is one that the airlines must resolve. And some passengers have been stranded when they were left holding tickets on airlines that declared bankruptcy without warning.

As a result of overexpansion in an unfavorable market, Braniff, one of the original trunk airlines, went bankrupt in 1982, leaving some passengers with unhappy memories. With reorganization, it began flying again, but with a radically reduced system of routes. Continental also filed for bankruptcy in 1982. When it reorganized, airline personnel were rehired at drastically reduced wages, leading to charges of union hostility. Such major changes in the industry have meant that travelers must consider the financial health of an airline before buying a ticket. Airlines, on the other hand, must worry about a loss of confidence that might decrease ticket sales and make consumer fears of an airline's failure a self-fulfilling prophecy.[72]

Even if the industry is less stable than it once was, that does not mean that chaos has resulted. Although consumers face more choices in the types of service available, most reach their destinations without difficulty. Nevertheless, price and route alterations now often occur on rather short notice, making it difficult at times for the traveler to believe that his or her flight will remain as scheduled. More than ever, the airline traveler shops for the best deal; air travel has become like other consumer products. The options have become almost limitless.

Small Towns under Deregulation

Not every small town has been happy with deregulation, even though wide-scale loss of service has not resulted. As expected, commuter airlines have usually moved in when larger airlines have departed. Although certainly not true in all cases, one study found that small-community residents paid lower fares, on average, on the commuters.[73] The number of one-airline towns has decreased, and many small towns are now served by more flights.

Some small towns did more than complain about the loss of services. Many actively campaigned to bring regional- or local-service airlines to their communities. Fresno, California, attempted to solve its air-service problems with an innovative approach: The city invested $2 million to help start a Fresno-based carrier, Far West.[74] Unfortunately, the airline collapsed because of a lack of operating capital before its first flight.

Just as airlines have learned to attract passengers, smaller cities are learning how to attract airlines. Often they have worked out arrangements with the leading carriers to bring in service through new airline-subsidized feeder lines. For example, American Airlines has developed American Eagle and TWA has formed TWX.

But the quality of the service has often declined, especially during the transition period, when the smaller commuter airlines proved to be undependable replacements where major airlines were lost. Although never economical, the departure of jet service left many small cities unhappy. As Senator Kennedy noted, "[l]ocal residents might have liked having a 707 all to themselves, but it was no way to run an airline."[75] The argument that service to small towns serves socially desirable goals may be valid, but it is difficult to argue that such service should be provided by heavily subsidized, near-empty jets.

The quality of commuter airlines has recently improved, quieting much of the initial complaint from small towns. In 1972, CAB rules effectively limited commuter airlines to nineteen or fewer passenger planes. Now the limit is sixty seats, which allows commuter lines to use larger planes, which are more comfortable and more acceptable to travelers.[76] Many of the commuter lines received government loan guarantees through the Essential Air Service (EAS) program to help buy the larger planes. The importance of the EAS program probably cannot be accurately assessed until after its funding ends in the next few years.

Both sides of the debate were right about service to small towns. Small communities did, in many cases, lose the subsidized jet service they had enjoyed under regulation. The commuter airlines, however, have filled the gap to the satisfaction of many passengers. The service is certainly more rational, with prices more closely reflecting cost, and more appropriate aircraft are used.

Safety under Deregulation

Nobody wanted to deregulate safety. Several commentators have concluded that a substantial decrease in safety would be the most likely reason that regulation of the airline industry would be reconsidered.[77] This concern has been emphasized by the ALPA, which has maintained that increased flying time and airline cost-cutting measures have reduced the level of safety in the 1980s.[78] Others have argued that new pilots on new routes in the fast-changing deregulated environment have jeopardized, or at least compromised, safety considerations.[79]

The increased role of commuter airlines has also raised questions about their safety. Recognizing their poorer safety record, the deregulation act called for higher safety standards for commuters, to which the FAA complied. Although commuter airlines are more dangerous than the trunk lines, they still offer a safe means of travel. Even by the least favorable calculations, accident statistics indicate that the commuter lines are as safe as cars.[80] And the better commuters have safety records approaching those of the major airlines.

Deregulation has been cited by some observers as contributing to at least one crash. In January 1982, an Air Florida plane crashed into the Potomac River in Washington, D.C., killing seventy-eight passengers. The stark image of the Air Florida logo on the plane's tail, which jutted out of the river, may have had much to do with the airline's eventual bankruptcy.[81] Prior to deregulation, Air Florida had been an intrastate carrier. Under deregulation, the airline expanded to fly interstate routes, but its hasty growth may have cost it dearly: The crash investigation indicated that the pilots' unfamiliarity with the poor weather conditions in Washington had contributed to the crash.[82]

Fears persist that the newer airlines, having no long tradition of safety, will not keep the same high standards as the older trunks. Under regulation, many airlines held to safety routines beyond those required by FAA rules. According to John Mazor, ALPA spokesperson, "We didn't get the tremendous safety record we have just by meeting FAA minimums."[83] Some observers believe that the erosion of safety will not be noticed immediately, but is instead a problem that will grow quietly over time.

Recent evidence indicates that these fears may be well-founded. An investigation into airline safety by *Los Angeles Times* reporters Richard Meyer and Ralph Vartabedian revealed significant decreases in expenditures on airline safety. The number of mechanics employed by the major airlines decreased by 2,000 from 1974 to 1984, while the number of airliners in service dramatically increased. At the same time, the average airplane in service is aging.[84] Airlines, however, contend that they maintain their planes at a more than adequate level and that the skies are still safe. There has been no rash of airline accidents caused by poorly maintained aircraft, but the *Los Angeles Times* report and others like it have done little to reassure critics.

Two other factors have complicated the safety question. Although the responsibility of the FAA increased under deregulation, the Reagan administration decreased the number of FAA field inspectors by 23 percent from 1981 to 1984 while 1,700 more planes were brought into service. Many in Congress were concerned that fewer inspections would send the wrong message to the airlines, and argued that the FAA should have increased, not decreased, inspections.[85] The air-traffic controllers strike in August 1981 also brought lasting safety questions. After members of the Professional Air Traffic Controllers Organization (PATCO) went on strike, President Reagan ordered them fired if they did not return to work. Subsequently, 11,300 controllers lost their jobs.[86] Significant efforts were made to hire and train new workers, but in 1984, 20 percent fewer controllers were handling 6 percent more air traffic. On average, these controllers are less experienced than were the fired PATCO members.[87] Furthermore, these new air-traffic controllers have voiced concerns about large numbers of mandatory overtime hours required in an already highly stressful job; ironically, these were the very complaints that led PATCO members to strike. Consequently, safety must still be given top priority to prevent the sort of air disasters that would bring back stricter regulation.

Given the numerous concerns about deregulation, most safety questions seem to have been adequately answered, at least for now. In 1984, the major U.S. airlines had their best accident rate in ten years, suffering only twelve accidents.[88] But on August 31, 1986, a mid-air collision between an Aeromexico jet and a small private plane in Southern California killed eighty-one people and raised new safety concerns.[89] Flying is still the safest way to travel, and postderegulation statistics have demonstrated, on average, better industry performance than in 1978. As with the preregulation period, major air disasters remain rare. If this is to continue, the FAA cannot allow safety to play a secondary role to profits.

Wages under Deregulation

Union leaders had argued that labor would bear the brunt of any savings derived by the airlines from deregulation. Certainly, labor costs have been critical to the airline industry. Salaries under regulation were high: Mechanics averaged as much as $30,000 per year and had substantial benefits.[90] Labor is the largest controllable cost in an airline budget. In 1983, the major unionized airlines, for instance, paid between 33 and 37 percent of their total operating costs in labor, whereas their newer, nonunion competitors paid only 19 to 27 percent.[91] This difference has provided a significant problem for older airlines in price competition with the upstarts.

The nonunion carriers forced older airlines to significantly change the way they dealt with their unions. Since increased labor costs were usually passed on to consumers as part of CAB-regulated fares, management had no real incentives to hold costs down. So, when deregulation arrived, the older airlines were left with expensive labor contracts. Management had to learn tough bargaining, and unions had to accept the economic realities of the deregulated industry.

The older airlines adopted a number of strategies to cope with labor costs. Some set up nonunion subsidiaries to compete with the nonunion carriers. Every airline asked its workers for concessions, and almost every union had to accept wage cuts and deferrals. American convinced its union to accept a two-tiered wage scale that provided high pay for current employees but reduced starting salaries for new hires by almost 50 percent. Other airlines have sought to follow suit.[92] To allow airlines more flexibility in scheduling their employees, unions have also agreed to significant alterations in work rules. Two of the most important of these have been the increased pilot and flight-attendant flight hours, and the decrease of the pilot crew from three to two on some aircraft.[93]

In return for their concessions, union employees often received some form of increased control over airline management. Eastern employees, for example, were rewarded with about 25 percent ownership of the company and were allowed to select four of the twenty-one members on Eastern's board of directors.[94] Other airlines arrived at similar agreements with their workers. Although many were skeptical at first, the increased involvement of union employees in management has worked better than most managers and union officials expected.

The means of lowering labor costs chosen by a few airlines has been considerably more controversial. When Braniff resumed flying after bankruptcy, it rehired many of its former workers; the union, however, had to accept significantly lower wages. On September 24, 1983, when Continental declared bankruptcy, chair Francisco Lorenzo cited inadequate labor concessions as the most important reason for the company's straits. By declaring bankruptcy, Continental sought to wipe out previous labor contracts and resume operations in two days with lower fares and greatly reduced salaries for its former employees.[95] Continental workers were outraged, and some of the airline's pilots went on strike. Enough of the pilots crossed picket lines, however, to allow the restructured airline to continue at reduced service. Just a few days after the Continental move, Eastern announced its intention to declare bankruptcy unless its workers accepted a 15 percent pay cut and changes in work rules. Eastern's president, Frank Borman, eventually backed down, and after concessions by both sides, Eastern continued to fly without declaring bankruptcy.

As the economy improved, airlines became less likely to use the threat of bankruptcy to force worker concessions, but it still hangs over the heads of union workers as a viable, albeit drastic, airline strategy during troubled times. Legal redress may not avail the unions. The courts have been reluctant to allow bankruptcy to proceed solely to abrogate collective-bargaining agreements, for it is difficult to tell when this move is absolutely necessary. The courts may, in fact, take years to finally decide the legality of the bankruptcy strategy.[96]

The unions have wondered where the concessions will end. In early 1985, Eastern was once again in trouble, and bankruptcy was imminent. Again, the unions were asked to help bail out the company. Eastern employees, now owning 25 percent of the company, were more cooperative than they had been in earlier negotiations.[97] Even at that, Eastern ceased as an independent entity in 1986 when it was absorbed by Texas Air.

But the resulting agreements left unions wondering how long the adjustments to deregulation would last. Furthermore, one of the recent rounds of mergers has cost airline workers thousands of jobs. In 1986, for example, the merger of Northwest and Republic alone forced out 800 workers.[98] In 1987, Delta's acquisition of Western eliminated a similar number of jobs.

The federal program to help laid-off airline workers has offered little help to the industry's employees. The CAB's early interpretation of the trigger mechanism effectively blocked the use of the program.[99] When it still existed, the CAB ruled that workers would be eligible for assistance only if they could prove deregulation to be the cause of their unemployment. Given the rise in fuel prices, the serious recession, and other economic factors, workers have found it almost impossible to demonstrate a clear deregulation–unemployment relationship.[100] Consequently, unions have expected that their members will receive little, if any, benefit from this provision of the deregulation act.

Not everyone has felt sympathy for airline workers. "The purpose of competition is to make things tough for people who are fat," stated Alfred Kahn.[101] For many years, wage increases were expected by both labor and management, but this trend has now been totally reversed. Some experts expect that the pay scale for some airline jobs will slide by some 40 percent over the next five years.[102] In effect, deregulation has radically changed the way airlines and unions do business.

Union leaders are understandably bitter about deregulation. Total employment in the airline industry is down, and salaries are significantly lower for employees. Unions have lobbied for new regulation, but they hold little hope for victory. The implicit government subsidy for airline labor, paid for by the high fares forced upon consumers, was probably not justified, but airline workers who have felt significant decreases in their standard of living are not comforted by this fact. The adjustment to deregulation for airline workers was and continues to be painful.

The airline unions have not been alone in their loss of power. Unions in most sectors of the economy are facing declining membership and tougher negotiations with management. Deregulation has certainly increased problems for airline unions, but most unions are facing difficult times.

Regulation Theory Applied to Airlines

The regulation and deregulation of the airline industry is a good example of how the economic theory of regulation has been applied. Although the CAB was an advocate for the established airlines from the board's beginning, it would be hard to call this an example of capture; support of the industry was part of its congressional mandate. But with the increased general interest in deregulation in the 1970s, the costs and benefits of airline regulation became open for discussion.

One strength of the economic theory is that it can help explain the shift from regulation to deregulation. When the costs and benefits of regulation change, or are perceived to change, economic theory predicts that the regulatory structure will change as well. In this instance, as new information became available (such as the lower fares offered by intrastate carriers in Texas and California), groups that had been harmed by regulation used that information to push for deregulation.

The airline case study also shows the importance that one person can play in the regulatory process. Without the strong support of Alfred Kahn at the CAB, it is uncertain whether airlines would have been deregulated as quickly or as completely. Both human and economic elements were thus important in the airline-deregulation story.

Assessing the Future of the "Friendly Skies"

The airline industry has undergone substantial change in the transition to deregulation, but it has survived, settling into more stable arrangements. New airlines have grown and prospered. Texas Air has become the nation's largest airline, buying Eastern, People Express, Frontier, Continental, and New York Air.[103] Meanwhile, several other established carriers solidified their positions in 1986 through new acquisitions.

In some cases, the carriers that faced significant problems with the new, deregulated environment have done better as well. In early 1987, a leaner Continental announced record low fares of $89 on one-way, coast-to-coast flights with the provision that such tickets were not refundable once purchased. Continental's competitors reluctantly matched the new fare. Not all airlines, however, have found solid ground. Braniff reentered the market as a high-service airline catering to business travelers, but found that this has been a hard market in which to compete. Now a no-frills airline, Braniff still struggles to find its niche in the market.[104]

The differences between the union and nonunion airlines are beginning to diminish, and the upstarts are slowly losing their cost advantages. As a result of work-rule changes, productivity at union airlines is increasing. As a whole, the airline industry is providing 19 percent more output with less than 1 percent more employees.[105] The wage structures at union and nonunion airlines are also more comparable. As American Airlines' senior vice-president Carty noted, "[f]or awhile it was easy [for nonunion airlines] to blow United and American out of the market based on cost. But it isn't that easy any more."[106]

Airline executives did not react to competition as well as many deregulators had hoped. After years of working in a regulated environment, many executives made serious mistakes, and both workers and passengers suffered. But the transition period seems to be over, and the industry has proved itself viable under deregulation.

Several problems, however, still remain as barriers to effective competition among airlines. At the busiest airports, the inadequate numbers of available slots for the best flight times do not come close to the demands created by airlines and passengers. Many concerned airline officials are now advocating a market solution to the problem: allow the sale of air landing rights, that is, the arrival and departure gates at terminals. Prices for the most popular times would be high, and this added cost would be reflected in peak-time ticket prices. Travelers who were willing to fly at less popular times, when airlines have less trouble landing, would pay less for their flights.[107] The major question to be resolved is, Who gains most from the sale of landing rights—airports, older airlines flying from popular airports now, or someone else? Aside from this proposal, airlines have recognized delay to be a significant problem and are seriously considering other ways to improve their scheduling. The situation appeared to improve in early 1987 when the FAA absolved the scheduled airlines of potential antitrust violations and ordered the carriers to work out mutually compatible schedules.

On December 31, 1984, the CAB ceased to exist. The Department of Transportation took over the CAB's few remaining chores. Problems with smoking on flights, damaged baggage, and bumping of passengers are now handled by the DOT.[108] In many ways, the phase-out of the CAB was probably less traumatic for its workers than the contraction of a private company would have been. Long before the agency was gone, most CAB employees had left. They retired, shifted to jobs in other government agencies, or left for private firms.[109] Although the highest-level executives at the CAB favored deregulation, many of the board's career workers did not, and they have been as unhappy with deregulation as have the airlines' union employees.[110] Some had believed that it would never happen, but a major government agency had been successfully shut down.

A Look Back

On balance, the supporters of deregulation have demonstrated that airlines can function without governmental oversight. Most who have analyzed the industry since the 1978 act agree that even though the transition was not smooth, the dire predictions of the bill's opponents have not materialized. As long as the industry continues along its present lines, it is unlikely that it will be regulated again. The airlines themselves have come to support deregulation, and very few want to see the return of an agency such as the CAB. After spending years in trying to convince policy makers that deregulation would be a disaster, Frank Borman of Eastern declared, "We much prefer to be in control of our own destiny."[111] Most airline executives, having learned to compete, agree with him. But not all destinies are necessarily fortuitous. Borman himself learned as much when, in the wake of Eastern's acquisition by Texas Air, he lost his job.

Aside from unions, the FAA has been the only other major force to push for more government control. This concern has stemmed from the difficulties of air-traffic management. If airlines are unable to cope with scheduling problems and the difficulties they create for air-traffic control, the FAA may try to do it for them.[112] In general, however, when the federal government allowed several airlines to declare bankruptcy and did not try to save them, it was clear to deregulation's opponents that the government and the public were willing to accept the risks that competition entailed and that deregulation had come to stay.

Lessons for Other Industries

The experience with airline deregulation provides some lessons for those who advocate less governmental oversight and control of other industries. Hard choices must be faced when policy is decided. Economic regulation grants significant benefits to specific groups, but there are costs as well. In the long run, deregulation may have many benefits, but in the short run, some groups may suffer substantially. The most important task of would-be deregulators is to assess both the credits and debits on the deregulation ledger. There are always winners and losers in any change, be it social, political, economic, or a combination of the three. For the airline industry, deregulation seems, on balance, to have provided more benefits than costs.

Other industries are less likely to be as completely deregulated as the airlines, at least not for the same reasons. The issues were more clearly defined in the airline debate than they are for many other deregulation debates; supporters and opponents of deregulation did not substantially disagree in identifying the critical issues. Were the potential costs worth the potential benefits? The answer to this major question was easier to find under these circumstances.

The risks of deregulation in the airline industry were, in many ways, less severe than the risks of deregulation in other areas. In two other industries heavily involved in the deregulation debate, telecommunications and financial services, policy makers are concerned that at least minimal service be available to almost everyone at a reasonable cost. The fear that low-income and elderly people will find themselves without access to telephone service is of far more concern to Congress than the fear that these same people will not have convenient airline service. Air service, to some degree, has always been a luxury, and acceptable substitutes for powerless groups have usually been considered to be available.

Airline deregulation can be considered to be a success for now, but one writer has summarized its likely impact on further deregulation: "The CAB shutdown could be a dusty memory before the federal government takes the politically sensitive step of executing another sizable agency."[113]

Notes

1. Michael E. Levine, "Is Regulation Necessary? California Air Transportation and National Regulatory Policy," *Yale Law Journal,* 74 (1965): 1416.
2. *Information Please Almanac, 1985* (Boston: Houghton Mifflin, 1985), p. 532.
3. Umberto Nordio, "Airline Industry: The Shock of Reaching Maturity," *Congressional Record,* 129, no. 159 (November 16, 1983): E5610.
4. Peter Nulty, "A Champ of Cheap Airlines," *Fortune,* 105, no. 6 (March 22, 1982): 130.
5. Levine, "Regulation Necessary?" p. 1417.
6. *Ibid.,* pp. 1417–1418.
7. Dorothy Diane Sandell, "Deregulation: Has It Finally Arrived?," *Journal of Air Law and Commerce,* 44 (1979): 800.
8. James P. Rakowski and James C. Johnson, "Airline Deregulation: Problems and Prospects," *Quarterly Review of Economics and Business,* 19, no. 4 (Winter 1979): 67.

9. Robert L. Thornton, "Deregulation: The CAB and Its Critics," *Journal of Air Law and Commerce,* 43 (1977): 641, 644.
10. *The United States Government Manual,* Office of the Federal Register, National Archives and Records Service. General Services Administration. (Washington, D.C.: U.S. Government Printing Office, May 1, 1984), p. 471.
11. Rakowski and Johnson, "Airline Deregulation," p. 68.
12. W. Glen Harlan, "Airline Deregulation—Antitrust and Safety Considerations," *Forum,* 14 (Summer 1979): 106.
13. Levine, "Regulation Necessary?" pp. 1420–1421.
14. Marvin S. Cohen, "New Service and Deregulation: A Study in Transition," *Journal of Air Law and Commerce,* 44 (1979): 696.
15. Alfred E. Kahn, "Applications of Economics to an Imperfect World," Richard T. Ely Lecture, *American Economic Review,* 69, no. 2 (May 1979): 10.
16. Rakowski and Johnson, "Airline Deregulation," p. 68.
17. See studies by Theodore Keeler, James Douglas, and others.
18. Thornton, "The CAB and Its Critics," pp. 645–646.
19. *Ibid.,* p. 643.
20. *Ibid.,* p. 645.
21. David A. Hemsfeld, "Deregulation of Air Transportation under the Aviation Act of 1975," *Akron Law Review,* 9, no. 4 (Spring 1976): 643.
22. Rakowski and Johnson, "Airline Deregulation," p. 72.
23. *Ibid.*
24. "The Odds Look Good for Less Airline Regulation," *Business Week,* no. 2475 (March 21, 1977): 156.
25. Sen. Edward Kennedy, *Congressional Record,* 124 (April 19, 1978): 10659.
26. Sen. Howard Cannon, *Congressional Record,* 124 (April 19, 1978): 10648.
27. Richard J. Ferris, "Playing the Game After the Rules Change," *Congressional Record,* 130, no. 16 (February 21, 1984): S1377.
28. Sen. George McGovern, *Congressional Record,* 124 (April 19, 1978): 10660.
29. "The Odds Look Good," *Business Week,* March 21, 1977, p. 158.
30. Anthony P. Ellison, "The Structural Change of the Airline Industry Following Deregulation," *Transportation Journal,* 21, no. 3 (Spring 1982): 58.
31. Daniel P. Kaplan and David R. Graham, "Airline Deregulation *Is* Working," *Regulation,* 6, no. 3 (May–June 1982): 27.
32. Vincent C. Olson and John M. Trampani, III, "Who Has Benefited from Regulation of the Airline Industry," *Journal of Law and Economics,* 24, no. 1 (April 1981): 76.
33. Sen. Charles Percy, *Congressional Record,* 124 (April 19, 1978): 10653.
34. Michael E. Levine, "Revisionism Revised? Airline Deregulation and the Public Interest," *Law and Contemporary Problems,* 44, no. 1 (Winter 1981): 194.
35. *The Politics of Regulation,* ed. James Q. Wilson (New York: Basic Books, 1980), p. 118.
36. "Delta's Flying Money Machine," *Business Week,* no. 2482, (May 9, 1977): 89.
37. James E. Landry, "Some Plain Talk About Airlines and Regulation," *Akron Law Review,* 9, no. 4 (Spring 1976): 640.
38. Warren Rose, "Three Years After Airline Passenger Deregulation in the United States: A Report on Trunkline Carriers," *Transportation Journal,* 21, no. 2 (Winter 1981): 56.
39. Cohen, "New Service," p. 700.
40. Frederick C. Thayer, "And Now the Deregulators: When Will They Learn?," *Journal of Air Law and Commerce,* 43 (1977): 676.
41. Thornton, "The CAB and Its Critics," p. 659.
42. Kahn, "Applications of Economics," p. 7.
43. Thornton, "The CAB and Its Critics," p. 649.
44. "The Odds Look Good," *Business Week,* March 21, 1977, p. 156.

45. Harlan, "Airline Deregulation," p. 1029.
46. *Ibid.*, pp. 1027–1028.
47. Ellison, "Structural Change," p. 62.
48. Sen. Harrison Schmitt, *Congressional Record,* 124 (April 19, 1978): 10652.
49. "Airline Employees Pressing for Special Layoff Benefits," *National Journal,* 16, no. 19 (May 12, 1984): 944.
50. Rakowski and Johnson, "Airline Deregulation," pp. 74–76.
51. Sara Rimmer, "People Express," *San Francisco Chronicle,* January 27, 1985, p. W14.
52. Rakowski and Johnson, "Airline Deregulation," pp. 74–75.
53. "The Line Forms Here for Air Routes," *Business Week,* no. 2559 (November 6, 1978): 66.
54. Elizabeth E. Bailey and John C. Panzar, "The Contestability of Airline Markets during the Transition to Deregulation," *Law and Contemporary Problems,* 44, no. 1 (Winter 1981): 130.
55. Kaplan and Graham, "Deregulation *Is* Working," p. 27.
56. Richard C. Schroeder, "Troubled Air Transport Industry," *Editorial Research Reports,* 2, no. 20 (November 26, 1982): 873.
57. *Ibid.*, p. 871.
58. William N. Leonard, "Airline Deregulation: Grand Design or Gross Debacle?," *Journal of Economic Issues,* 17, no. 2 (June 1983): 455.
59. "One Year After Deregulation: The Airlines Hit a Downdraft," *Business Week,* no. 2610 (November 5, 1979): 104.
60. Kenneth Labich, "How to Cure Those #?*&! Airline Delays," *Fortune,* 110, no. 7 (October 1, 1984): 34.
61. Ann Cooper, "Free-wheeling Airline Competition is Apparently Here to Stay," *National Journal,* 16, no. 22 (June 2, 1984): 1086.
62. Donald D. Engen, *Congressional Record,* 130, no. 7 (January 31, 1984): E187.
63. Lucia Mouat, "Nation's Airlines Compete for a Piece of the Sky," *Christian Science Monitor,* February 8, 1985, p. 22.
64. Frederick J. Stephenson and Frederick J. Beier, "The Effects of Airline Deregulation on Air Service to Small Communities," *Transportation Journal,* 20, no. 4 (Summer 1981): 60.
65. Ellison, "Structural Change," p. 63.
66. Rose, "Three Years After," p. 52.
67. Cooper, "Free-wheeling Airline Competition," p. 1090.
68. Sen. Edward Kennedy, *Congressional Record,* 129, no. 145 (October 29, 1983): S14925.
69. Leonard, "Grand Design," p. 457.
70. W. John Moore, "Airline Mergers Creating Strife," *National Journal,* September 20, 1986, p. 2260.
71. Nathanial Nash, "Is Oligopoly a Legacy of Airline Deregulation?" *New York Times* (national ed.), October 5, 1986, 4:4.
72. John V. Janonius and Kenneth E. Broughton, "Coping with Deregulation: Reduction of Labor Costs in the Airline Industry," *Journal of Air Law and Commerce,* 49, no. 3 (1984): 523.
73. Stephenson and Beier, "Effects of Airline Deregulation," p. 60.
74. "How Deregulation Puts Competition Back in Business," *U.S. News and World Report,* November 26, 1984, p. 52.
75. Kennedy, *Congressional Record* (October 29, 1983): S14925.
76. Clinton V. Oster, Jr., and Kurt C. Zorn, "Deregulation and Commuter Airline Safety," *Journal of Air Law and Commerce,* 49, no. 2 (1984): 318.
77. Harlan, "Airline Deregulation," pp. 1027–1028.
78. Cooper, "Free-wheeling Airline Competition," p. 1088.

79. Robert M. Kaus, "Cheap Seats and White Knuckles," *Washington Monthly,* 15, no. 9 (December 1983): 46. Similar concerns were also expressed by a member of the National Transportation Safety Board during airline deregulation hearings.

80. Oster and Zorn, "Commuter Airline Safety," p. 325.

81. "Behind the Rise and Fall of Air Florida," *Business Week,* no. 2852 (July 23, 1984): 123.

82. Cooper, "Free-wheeling Airline Competition," p. 1088.

83. Lucia Mouat, "Intense Fare Battles May Result in Cutting Some Corners on Safety, Experts Say," *Christian Science Monitor,* February 8, 1985, p. 23.

84. Richard E. Meyer and Ralph Vartabedian, "Aircraft Safety: Cracks Begin to Show in the System," *Los Angeles Times,* March 30, 1986, p. 1.

85. Rep. Norman Mineta, *Congressional Record,* 130, no. 7 (January 31, 1984): E187.

86. Reggi Ann Dubin, "The Air Traffic Jam Could Bring Back Regulation," *Business Week,* no. 2861 (September 24, 1984): 80.

87. Labich, "How to Cure," pp. 36–37.

88. *San Francisco Examiner,* January 11, 1985, p. A10. See also Marc Leepson, "Safety in the Air," *Editorial Research Reports,* 2, no. 15 (October 19, 1984): 779.

89. Richard Witkin, "FAA Seeks to Require Airlines to Install Anti-Collision Devices," *New York Times* (national ed.), September 20, 1986, p. 1.

90. Cooper, "Free-wheeling Airline Competition," p. 1088.

91. "Airlines in Turmoil," *Business Week,* no. 2811 (October 10, 1983): 99.

92. Cooper, "Free-wheeling Airline Competition," pp. 1088–1089.

93. Jansonius and Broughton, "Coping with Deregulation," pp. 532–533.

94. *Ibid.,* p. 546.

95. "Airlines in Turmoil," *Business Week,* October 10, 1983, p. 98.

96. Jansonius and Broughton, "Coping with Deregulation," p. 531.

97. "A Union Deal Pulls Eastern Back From Default," *Business Week,* no. 2882 (February 25, 1985): 32.

98. "Northwest Air Layoffs Are Set," *New York Times* (national ed.), September 19, 1986, p. 35.

99. For an explanation of trigger mechanisms, see Larry N. Gerston, *Making Public Policy: From Conflict to Resolution* (Glenview, Ill.: Scott, Foresman, 1983): pp. 32–49.

100. "Airline Employees," *National Journal,* May 12, 1984, p. 944.

101. Cooper, "Free-wheeling Airline Competition," p. 1089.

102. "Airline Wages Set for a Long Slide," *Business Week,* no. 2837 (April 9, 1984): 127.

103. Nathaniel Nash, "Texas Air's Eastern Bid Approved," *New York Times* (national ed.), September 19, 1986, p. 33.

104. "Why So Many Airlines Are Dropping Out of the Friendly Skies," *Business Week* (December 17, 1984): 76.

105. "A Painful Transition for the Transportation Industry," *Business Week,* no. 2818 (November 28, 1983): 86.

106. "A Pact That Will Help American Become a Low-Cost Airline," *Business Week,* no. 2818 (November 28, 1983): 41.

107. Labich, "How to Cure," p. 36.

108. *Congressional Quarterly Weekly Report,* 42, no. 38 (September 22, 1984): 2303.

109. Ann Cooper, "The CAB Is Shutting Down, But Will It Set an Example for Other Agencies?" *National Journal,* 16, no. 39 (September 29, 1984): 1822–1823.

110. *Ibid.,* p. 1821.

111. "One Year After Deregulation," *Business Week* (November 5, 1979): 105.

112. Dubin, "The Air Traffic Jam," p. 80.

113. Cooper, "CAB Is Shutting Down," p. 1820.

Financial Services

Not too long ago, banking and other financial services were relatively easy to understand. As recently as the mid-1970s, most consumers divided the financial marketplace into two neat categories: Banks offered checking and savings accounts and made loans, and savings and loan associations offered savings accounts and made home mortgages. Strict federal regulations made it unnecessary to shop around for the best interest rates on savings—each institution paid the rate *allowed* by the government. A financial transaction occurred as a customer went to a bank (preferably an imposing structure) and negotiated with a teller. Beyond that, stocks were purchased through stockbrokers and insurance through neighborhood insurance agents. Sears was a place to buy refrigerators.

Over the past decade, the nature of financial services has undergone a revolutionary transformation. Today, consumers are faced with an almost overwhelming array of financial choices. Savers often find it difficult to understand the multitude of terms and rates offered by just one bank, let alone compare and evaluate the differences between banks. And out-of-state offers for insurance policies and bank credit cards now flood the mail.

Most people are aware that the financial marketplace has changed significantly, but few are really aware of the causes and effects of this transformation. Deregulation is an important part of the story, but changes in both technology and the economy have brought most of the restructuring of the new financial services industry. Regulators and government officials have struggled to keep up with the quickly changing markets as much as have the industry's executives.

This chapter examines financial regulation, how it has developed, and how deregulatory pressures have forced change. The deregulatory process has just begun, and many of the critical issues that will determine the future structure of the industry are yet to be decided. Vast amounts of money have been staked in one of the largest battles ever to take place in Congress and in the marketplace.

Identifying the Players

In today's world, many different types of businesses offer financial services. Depository institutions, such as banks, savings and loan associations (S&L's), mutual savings banks, and credit unions compete for checking and savings accounts and for loans. Related industries include securities brokerages, investment banks, real estate firms, insurance companies, and mutual funds. Each of the contemporary depository institutions mentioned has developed to meet needs that were not being met by the traditional financial businesses. Although some competition historically existed among different types of institutions, specialization within the industry was strong. In contrast, deregulation of the financial industry has facilitated a new level of competition that was almost unimaginable a decade ago. Nevertheless, governmental oversight remains important.

Industry Structure

The financial services industry is a large and vital part of the American economy. With the large number of banks, S&L's, and credit unions, consumers have a wide variety of choices when selecting a financial institution; still, there are powerful leaders in each industry.

In 1984, American commercial banks had $2.15 trillion in assets.[1] In England, Germany, France, and other countries, a handful of banks control the banking industry, but in the United States financial institutions are relatively dispersed. In 1983, for example, there were 14,960 banks with 40,380 branches.[2] Still, the top 100 banks control about 60 percent of the banking assets in this country, leading smaller, independent banks to worry that deregulation may cause larger banks to become even more dominant than they have been.[3]

Savings and loans are significant in the United States. In 1984, there were 3,391 S&L's, but that was nearly 2,000 fewer than in 1970.[4] Inasmuch as the largest 10 percent of these S&L's control more than 65 percent of assets, economic power is concentrated in the hands of just a few.[5]

Depository institutions are strongly regulated, particularly by federal agencies, this despite a decade of deregulation. Substantial control still exists and is likely to remain. Each kind of institution must adhere to its own particular rules and regulators from the complicated and overlapping regulatory structure. This situation developed almost by accident, not by design. As needs arose, new laws, agencies, and regulators were added, leaving a structure of many layers.[6]

The Bank Regulators

Commercial banks face substantial governmental oversight at both the national and state levels. A bank can receive its *charter,* or right to operate, from either authority. The Comptroller of Currency oversees all federally chartered banks. The comptroller's office is the oldest of the federal bank regulators, created in 1863 as part of the federal banking system. This office approves the organization of new national banks.[7] Among states, there is no single counterpart, leading to a variety of rules among the fifty governments. Regardless of agency responsibility, commercial banks at either level perform the same basic function: they take demand deposits (checking accounts), savings deposits, and make loans for both individuals and businesses.

All national banks must be members of the Federal Reserve System, commonly called the Fed. Membership is optional for state banks; however, those that join are subject to Fed supervision in addition to state regulation. All national banks are required to belong to the Federal Deposit Insurance Corporation (FDIC), a government agency that guarantees bank deposits to a maximum of $100,000 per account. The Fed also requires FDIC insurance for state bank members. State banks not belonging to the Fed may also choose federal insurance. In such an instance, the bank is regulated by both the state and the FDIC.[8]

This complicated regulatory structure forces many strategic decisions for a bank. In a state with liberal banking rules, state charters may be popular, but where state laws are restrictive, federal charters will predominate. A bank will choose the charter that gives it the regulatory structure best suiting its needs. Sometimes the bank may switch charters if its officers feel the institution can get a better deal under one or the other government. This became common in the late 1970s and early '80s, when a sudden burst of inflation caused some financial institutions to trade their state charters for national charters that allowed more flexible treatment of their portfolios.

Other Financial Regulators

Savings and loan associations were developed to provide low- and middle-income workers a place to save relatively small amounts of money and to finance the purchase of homes. S&L's face a somewhat less complicated regulatory structure than do banks. They also can carry a state or federal charter. The Federal Home Loan Bank Board (FHLBB) oversees all nationally chartered S&L's, and all national S&L's must join the Federal Savings and Loan Insurance Corporation (FSLIC), the FDIC's counterpart for S&L's. At their option, state-chartered S&L's may choose federal insurance, which also leads to regulation by the FSLIC.[9] Mutual savings banks are also regulated by the FHLBB.

In addition to S&L's, other banklike organizations exist. Credit unions are associations of limited membership, often covering an employer or organization, such as a labor union. A credit union can usually offer consumers a good deal because the members are known to the institution, and such knowledge is thought to imply lower risk. As with banks and S&L's, a credit union can be either federally or state chartered. The National Credit Union Administration regulates federal and federally insured associations, while state agencies cover the remaining institutions. Table 6-1 outlines the size and regulatory structure of the most common types of depository institutions.

Table 6-1.   The financial services industry

	Assets ($ billion)	Number	Primary regulators	Traditional responsibilities
Banks	2,147,651	15,489	FDIC FRB Comptroller of Currency State agencies	Consumer savings Consumer checking Consumer loans Business checking and savings Business loans
S&L's	902.4	3,391	FSLIC FHLBB State agencies	Consumer savings Home mortgage loans
Credit unions	99.0	15,144	National Credit Union Administration State agencies	Member savings Member (nonmort- gage) loans
Mutual savings banks	135.6	267	FHLBB FSLIC FOIC State agencies	Consumer savings Mortgage loans Other personal loans

Source: *Statistical Abstract of the United States, 1986.* All figures for 1984.

Nondepository Institutions

The other players in the financial services industry also face both federal and state regulations. The federal Securities and Exchange Commission (SEC) regulates securities (stock) offerings. Insurance companies are regulated by the states. When the list of federal agencies that deal with some type of financial service is added—the Commodity Futures Trading Commission, the Farm Credit Administration, the Government National Mortgage Corporation, the Student Loan Marketing Association, and others—the scope of governmental intervention in the financial services marketplace is quite extensive.

Development of Financial Services Regulation

The United States traditionally showed great reluctance to developing a national banking structure. Banks were regulated exclusively by the states for almost 100 years. There was no national currency such as the Federal Reserve notes we use today. Each bank issued its own bank notes, redeemable for gold or other coins. Banks did not keep all of their gold or other assets in a vault; instead, they kept a fraction of these assets in ready reserve for customers who wished to exchange their bank notes for coins. Because it was unlikely that every bank customer would claim his or her money on any one day (or week or month), banks used the remainder of their assets for loans and other investments.[10]

Confidence was, and is, the cornerstone of banking. As long as customers believed that a bank would be able to redeem its notes, the notes were accepted as money and used to buy goods and services. But if for some reason customers lost confidence in a bank, a disastrous run might begin. This happened several times during the 1880s and early 1900s. Believing that a bank was not financially sound, customers would rush to redeem their bank notes for coins. They had to act very quickly, for only the earliest to make their claims would receive coins for notes. Usually, bank reserves were unable to cover a sudden demand for cash because they could not call in their loans on such short notice. As a result, the bank often failed.

The loss of confidence in a bank was not necessarily related to its true financial health. Even the strongest bank could not provide all of its customers with cash in a short period of time; no bank kept 100 percent of its assets as cash in a vault. It takes time for a bank to convert even the worthiest of its loans to cash. On the other hand, a weak bank could survive almost indefinitely as long as its customers *believed* that the bank was sound. Rumors and negative perceptions were all it took to close a bank.

A panic often occurred when a run on one bank spread to the banking system in general. In the Panic of 1857, for example, banks were unable to redeem their notes, and the need for a system to provide more stability in banking became clear. In an attempt to prevent systemwide failures, Congress passed the National Bank Act in 1863, establishing national bank charters and mandatory reserve requirements for banks as means of providing some level of safety.[11] This did not stop panics, however, and every few years serious bank runs occurred in the United States. When depositors sensed that the financial institutions were in jeopardy, they still claimed their savings. After their fears were quieted, the depositors usually restored their accounts, although not always with the same banks.

The Panic of 1907 convinced Congress to establish a commission that would investigate ways for the government to bring stability to banking. The commission's efforts resulted in the Glass–Owens Act, which established the Federal Reserve Board and the country's first central bank.[12] The federal role in banking had significantly increased.

The Depression Brings Further Regulation

Even after the passage of the Federal Reserve Act, banking remained relatively unrestricted. A bank often acted in the interests of a particular business by helping it issue stock; at the same time, the bank loaned money to investors to purchase the stock. This conflict of interest led to many poor business decisions. The stocks were often of poor value. This did not seem critical until the stock market collapsed in 1929, and customers defaulted en masse on their loans for securities. The banks had insufficient reserves to cover the runs that followed.[13]

More than 1,000 banks each year failed from 1930 to 1932, and more than 4,000 banks closed their doors in 1933.[14] The country's financial institutions were in total disarray. Responding to this crisis, national legislation in the '30s sought to restore stability and confidence through two changes in the banking structure. First, Congress narrowed the range of activities allowed to each institution. Second, Congress created deposit insurance to increase consumer confidence in banks and S&L's.

Limits on Bank Power

Several laws were passed during the Great Depression to increase the soundness of the nation's financial institutions. Under the 1933 Glass–Steagall Act, banks were not allowed to deal in or own many types of securities; on the other hand, stock brokerages were forbidden to act like banks by taking deposits.[15] By separating financial functions, Congress hoped to eliminate excessive interdependence and conflict of interest among financial institutions. Additional legislation further restricted the activities of banks.

Savings and loan associations of the 1930s were usually very small, often open only one or two days of the week, and staffed by volunteer members. Most S&L's did not want to expand far beyond their role as mortgage providers, so restrictive S&L regulation simply codified existing practices. Only the largest and most aggressive S&L's wanted significantly greater power.

Even before the depression, fear of economic concentration and a desire to let smaller states set their own bank policies had led to the 1927 passage of the McFadden Act, which prohibited interstate banking. But with the economic collapse of the 1930s, state banking regulation tightened, and the probability of banks operating across state lines became even more remote.

Deposit Insurance Restores Confidence

Federal involvement in banking had not been popular with everyone, but after the early '30s, "federal" was associated with "stability" in the minds of most people. The concept of deposit insurance, funded by member banks and S&L's, pleased the public. If a bank failed, customers would not have to rush to be among the first lucky few who got their money back; the insurance fund would pay off all deposits. Because consumers would know that they could not lose their money, rumors would not be likely to start a panic. In an industry where perceptions are critical, ending the *fear* of bank runs would almost certainly end the reality of panics as well. A three-way partnership thus emerged among the government, financial institutions, and depositors. The federal government became the key provider of confidence, and thus stability, to banking.

Thirty Years of Stability

The late 1930s brought improvement to the economy and prosperity to financial institutions. Now secure, banks sometimes felt unnecessarily restricted by regulation. They periodically tested the limits of regulation, and Congress responded by adopting regulations that prohibited those practices it found unsound and encouraged those it believed to be safe.[16] Although often important to the financial institutions involved, bank regulation of the 1940s and '50s was not a burning concern for the general public. Financial institutions were strong, and deposit insurance kept the rare failure from causing alarm.

As providers of home mortgages, savings and loan associations also prospered. In order to promote a national goal of home ownership, Congress granted tax and other types of advantages to S&L's. The combination of protected market limits on the maximum rate of interest paid on savings accounts (as legislated during the 1960s) kept the industry profitable.[17]

Banks and S&L's had always been rivals in a sense, but their competition in the late 1960s intensified. Banks questioned the reliability of the regulatory structure created almost forty years earlier. As the economy became more volatile, the housing industry in particular suffered more dramatic swings. With banks and S&L's the traditional mortgage agents, old market structures were less reliable than they had been in the past.

By 1975, signs of these changes were clearly evident. Banks complained that S&L's received government protection at a time when banks were subject to an increasingly unpredictable economy. Congress had long prevented banks from encroaching on S&L territory, a situation that only heightened anxieties. Every time a new crisis in housing developed, the assault on the S&L industry was renewed. Predictably, the two industries' lobbies would converge on Congress asking for regulation favorable to their particular interests. Eventually, Congress tired of the frequent crises, and when the S&L–housing link began to weaken, the prospects for change were improved.[18]

Regulation Breaks Down

While some banks had worked for change, others had thrived in their restricted environment. It did not take exceptional management skill to run a bank, and even less was needed to run an S&L. Innovators may have felt constrained, but much of the banking industry was conservative and content with the general, if not the specific, goals of regulation. Ultimately, in the late 1970s, this dispute within the financial community became academic, for banks and S&L's ended up with little choice. Earlier fights had been primarily territorial squabbles between the two kinds of financial institutions, but now outside forces brought most of the pressure for change for two reasons: technological and economic.

Technological Pressures for Change

Bank regulation was anachronistic to the technology of the 1980s. Geographic restraints and product restrictions were more easily enforced when financial institutions had depended on the carefully handwritten record of bankers rather than on high-speed computer programs.

The regulators themselves saw technological change outstripping their ability to regulate. In 1982, FDIC chair William Issac noted that "(banking industry) protections are now quickly falling by the wayside, not so much because of government action, . . . but because of what is occurring in the marketplace, because of technology—the airplane, the telephone, the computer. These barriers simply are no longer effective."[19] Issac argued that much regulation in such an environment was simply not feasible. For example, both money and information can now be instantly transmitted across a city or around the world, twenty-four hours a day. For many customers, especially the largest and most financially sophisticated, the actual location of the financial institution has become a minor consideration.[20]

Changing technology also blurred the lines between various financial services. With access to a computer, it was much easier for banks to expand into new product lines, such as credit cards, money market accounts, or insurance sales.[21] S&L's were less enthusiastic about change, but had no real choice in the matter. As FHLBB chair Richard Pratt stated, "I think the thing that is driving all of this blurring of distinction is the technological revolution. . . . Telecommunications and computer technology are the driving forces to restructure the financial markets of this country."[22] Yet, like any change, the technological revolution created a highly uncertain environment.

The new technology made specialization unnecessary; financial institutions now had incentives to offer a wide range of products. Detailed profiles of consumers could be developed, and specific kinds of accounts could be targeted to specific groups of customers. Many institutions sought to become "one-stop" financial stores for their customers.

Although banks and other depository institutions were critically affected by modern technology, they were much slower to adopt innovations than were other financial businesses. Again, outside forces intervened. New competitors in the industry (most notably Sears, Merrill

Lynch, and other multifaceted financial businesses) brought with them the technology to develop new kinds of accounts and services and to market them effectively. Banks could not compete unless they automated as well. But banks and S&L's still have a long way to go to catch up. One research firm estimates that to remain competitive, banks will have to spend a minimum of $45 billion on automation and new data systems over the mid- to late-1980s.[23]

Economic Pressure for Change

Consumers did not worry too much about financial services competition when interest rates ran about 5 percent and inflation was even lower. The cost of putting small amounts of money in the wrong place for the wrong amount of time was seldom significant. The economic climate of the late 1970s, however, ended consumer complacency. Because of double-digit inflation, interest rates rose much higher and became more volatile than in previous years. In 1980, the prime rate (the rate charged by banks for loans to their most favored customers) fluctuated between 11 and 21.5 percent; it changed forty-two times.[24] This had a direct impact on the interest available, particularly for accounts not carried in traditional banks or S&L's. Because inflation decreases the value of money (a dollar is worth only eighty cents in real terms after a year of 20 percent inflation), the savings in a bank passbook account paying 5 percent interest was not about to generate enough money to offset high inflation.

As new and varied opportunities became available in the economic climate of the 1980s, account holders large and small reconsidered the functions of financial institutions. Consumers withdrew their money from traditional depository institutions and placed their funds by the billions in such alternatives as money market accounts, which paid higher interest. In 1977, Merrill Lynch created the Cash Management Account, which offered many of the conveniences of a checking account but with the higher interest rate of a money market account. In other words, depositors could write checks, a traditional bank function, while receiving high rates of interest, a nonbank benefit. Other institutions soon copied this successful formula. By the end of 1982, such accounts had reached more than $230 billion in assets.[25] Consumers also proved to be remarkably volatile in their choices of financial institutions. As competition increased, it was high interest that attracted depositors, not free toasters.

Finally, depository institutions themselves were in poor condition, ranging from the just-surviving to the outright failure. S&L's were particularly hard-hit, because they primarily held long-term, fixed-rate mortgages that were issued when interest rates were single-digit. The thirty-year, 5 percent mortgage so highly valued by people who bought homes in the 1950s and '60s proved to be the downfall of many S&L's in the 1980s. As a result, they were locked into unprofitable portfolios of assets. Many S&L's found that the income they received from these mortgages was too low to keep them in the black, and their failures increased. The worst years for the industry, the early 1980s, have passed, but S&L failures continue to be high. Government-assisted mergers, another sign of industry weakness, also remain high (See Figure 6-1).

Depository institutions found competition with new entrants such as Merrill Lynch difficult. These "nonbank banks" were not encumbered by the complicated and restrictive regulatory structure that limited the banks and S&L's, legally defined as institutions that take deposits and make commercial loans. A nonbank bank, or limited-service bank, could provide a wide range of services to consumers not legally possible through a regular bank, although they could not offer commercial loans. And the nonbank banks were not stuck with old, low-paying portfolios.

In a rapidly changing environment, the ability to respond quickly to new situations was critical. Even with sympathetic regulators, unrestricted competitors could adapt more quickly to each change than could the heavily regulated banks and S&L's. In particular, the ability to escape interest-rate ceilings was perhaps the most important advantage that limited-service banks had in the 1970s. With inflation at 10 to 15 percent, customers wanted more than a 5 percent return on their savings.

Congressional Reaction

By this time, representatives of the traditional banking institutions claimed that their economic lives were at risk. They argued that unless government agencies granted them the ability to compete, the depository institutions would succumb to the unchecked power of unregulated entrants. Rather than allow nontraditional financial firms to dominate financial services, Congress acted to increase the powers of the regulated institutions. In 1978, banks and S&L's were given the right to offer one kind of account at market rates.[26] Although still highly restrictive, it was

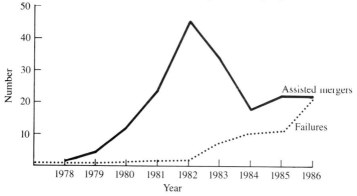

Figure 6-1. Savings-and-loan-failures and
FSLIC-assisted mergers, 1977–1986
Source: FSLIC, FHLBB.
Note: 1986 figures extrapolated from data as of October 2, 1986

a first step toward replacing government-mandated interest rates with those dictated by the economy.

More substantial deregulation occurred with the Depository Institutions Deregulation and Monetary Control Act (DIDMCA) of 1980. Congress passed the DIDMCA quickly. S&L's were in serious trouble as their nonregulated competitors grew at astounding rates. Facing their most serious crisis since the Great Depression, the differences between S&L's and banks seemed less important to the financial services industry than did the need to find a better regulatory structure.

The act gave such thrift institutions as S&L's expanded asset powers, including the ability to offer credit cards, make consumer (nonmortgage) loans, and offer adjustable-rate mortgages. These new products did have significant limits, but they gave S&L's some badly needed flexibility. Perhaps most important, interest-rate ceilings for both banks and S&L's were to be gradually lifted. After a six-year phase-in, banks and S&L's would be able to set the interest rates on savings that they thought best.[27] By 1986, interest-rate setting had become an entirely deregulated activity, and S&L's were finding parity with the newer institutions.

The relief provided by DIDMCA was short-lived. By 1982, it was clear that more would have to be done to keep depository institutions competitive, so Congress passed the Garn–St Germain Depository Institutions Act that year. Among its other provisions, the act allowed banks and S&L's to pay market interest on certain kinds of checking accounts. S&L's also received temporary aid in the hope that their financial condition would thus improve.[28]

In retrospect, neither act completely solved the major problems in financial services regulation. Although banks and S&L's can now choose the interest rate they pay on deposits, they still face significant limits on the kinds of loans and investments they can make and the types of products they can offer. As Richard Pratt of the FHLBB noted, "the financial structure is totally out of tune with the present situation. It is similar to the dinosaurs coming into the Ice Age. . . . Unless the organic structure of these institutions can be changed, I don't see that they have much of a future."[29] Even with these changes, the regulated depository institutions and their unregulated competitors have not yet reached parity. To that end, the traditional institutions have prodded Congress and regulatory agencies alike for further easements in their regulated world.

Financial Services Today

In the late 1980s, the structure of the financial services industry is in a state of transition. The present system is a combination of old laws, exploitation of loopholes in these laws, and partial reforms. Technological and economic pressures for change still exist, and substantial opportunity for competition continues.

The State of the Industry

With respect to financial services, it has become much more difficult to talk about the health of the banking and S&L industries as such. As banks offer different products, and competitors establish different prices for similar products, some banks succeed while others do not. Moreover, the services offered by nonbank banks have taken away some of the business of traditional banks, a once-stable industry.

Although the economy grew slowly and without serious recession during the mid-1980s, some sectors, such as energy and agriculture, still remained quite weak. Banks that depend on loans in these sectors have thus been vulnerable to losses.[30] Banks in Texas and Oklahoma, in particular, have suffered from these problems. Banks in agricultural communities lend money to farmers each year to plant crops, and are repaid in the fall after harvest. But if many of these farmers have been crippled by low prices for their crops, they go bankrupt, and the banks are then in trouble. We will examine the serious problems inherent in energy loans in the Continental Bank case in a few pages.

In other instances, banks may be sitting on potential disasters because of loans to unstable Third World countries, a situation known to plague the Bank of America, the nation's second largest bank.[31] Problem areas such as these affect more than a bank and its employees; they have a rippling effect throughout the nation. Encouraged by the federal government, many of the country's largest banks have extended billions of dollars to these developing countries. These loans have recently been rescheduled when the borrowers have been unable to make payments, but economic or political pressures may force some countries to default outright.

As we have shown, compared to previous decades, banking has become unstable in the 1980s. The cost to banks of poor loans is very high; competition and the economy give them little opportunity to recover from mistakes. Savings and loan associations face similar problems. Some new S&L's are quite profitable, not being burdened with low-interest mortgage portfolios from the past; but many S&L's are still in distress. This spread between the most profitable and most troubled institutions is increasing. The *Wall Street Journal* estimates that the top third of the industry is thriving, the middle third is muddling through, and the bottom third is in serious trouble.[32]

When an S&L fails, the deposit insurance created during the Great Depression protects its depositors. But the FSLIC attempts to find other solutions before it closes a sick S&L and pays insurance to its depositors. In some cases, the FHLBB and FSLIC have been unable to avoid a bankruptcy by finding a buyer for the troubled S&L. Under these circumstances, a failing S&L may be just what a healthy bank needs. Because buyers need not be based in the same state as the weak institution, some banks have purchased troubled out-of-state S&L's as a way to prepare for interstate banking. As more liberal rules regarding interstate banking give banks other alternatives, however, fewer of them will find buying a distressed S&L is the best way to expand.

For both the financial institutions and the public, deregulation has been a mixed blessing, for not all developments in the industry have been troublesome. For example, the new flexibility has brought great benefit to many consumers. The convenience of one-stop financial-service shopping and the variety of products now available offer the public a wide range of options. Savers who are dependent on interest income are no longer forced to accept artificially low rates while the very largest investors receive higher market rates of return.

The Threat of Deregulation

After the bank runs and bank holidays of the Great Depression, the reestablishment of stability and confidence were the primary goals of financial services regulation. Regulators, Congress, and members of the business community all believed that the failure of a bank or S&L was to be prevented at almost any cost. Over the past several years, however, banks and S&L's have failed with increasing regularity (see Figure 6-2).

In the summer of 1982, Penn Square, an Oklahoma City bank with a large portfolio of energy loans, failed.[33] The effects were widespread. Many other banks had purchased part of the loans held by Penn Square, and when it failed, they suffered significant losses. One such bank was Continental of Illinois, the eighth largest in the United States. Experts

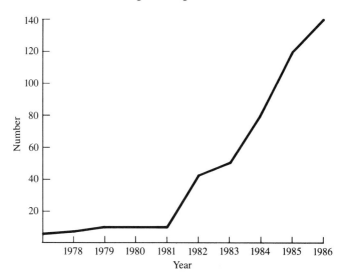

Figure 6.2. Bank failures, 1977–1986
Source: FDIC
Note: 1986 Figure extrapolated from data as of October 2, 1986

have debated whether regulators should have acted sooner, but by May 1984 the need for action was clear.

Rumors of serious problems at Continental caused a run by foreign and then American investors. Despite efforts by regulators to alleviate the crisis, the run continued.[34] FDIC insurance is limited to $100,000 per deposit, but in the past, the FDIC had compensated all investors, regardless of size. Some regulators now believed that large depositors should take losses from Continental to teach the market a lesson: Uninsured deposits were not as safe as FDIC- (or FSLIC-) guaranteed funds. Others argued that the loss in confidence from such an event would be a disaster for U.S. banking. It took a $4.5 billion plan to stop the run, a move many said led to the *de facto* nationalization of the bank. The federal government assumed $3.5 billion in delinquent Continental loans and retained the ability to fire the bank's board of directors and veto its policies. The most frightening implication to many was that the government had proved unable to stop a bank run. Confidence in U.S. banking had been seriously eroded.[35]

In one respect, deposit insurance had proved effective. Although it had not prevented the run on Continental, it had prevented the kind of domino effect that could close down the entire banking structure—and the U.S. economy in the process. Fortunately, investors were able to separate the problems of one bank from the problems of the entire system. This type of discretion and restraint may allow regulators time to work with a troubled financial institution to solve its problems.

Savings and Loans Face Runs

In the spring of 1985, the theory of deposit insurance was tested again. Home State Savings, an Ohio S&L, failed. It had not been insured by the FSLIC but instead by a private fund that backed the deposits at seventy-one state-chartered Ohio S&Ls. The fund was too small to cover the losses, and Ohio Governor Richard Celeste closed all seventy-one S&L's for three days to prevent a run.[36] It was the first time that a wide-scale financial-institution closing had been ordered since President Franklin D. Roosevelt ordered a national bank holiday in 1933.

Even though the problem in Ohio had involved private and not government-backed insurance, the entire industry suffered. Many were reminded how complicated public confidence can be in banking. A more flexible environment may bring advantages to institutions and consumers, but the instability connected with a less stable environment can also cause difficulties that many had assumed ended with the Great Depression.

The problems in the banking and S&L industries have split Congress into two camps: One group believes that *reregulation* is necessary to increase confidence and stability in both traditional and innovative financial institutions. The other believes that there is no way to go back to the regulation of the previous decades, despite recent difficulties. Even with continuing institutional failures, no consensus has developed within Congress on the proper course of action.[37] As such, the situation remains ripe for the types of crises that have brought havoc to a once-predictable industry.

Congressional Inertia

Every year since 1982, when the Garn–St Germain Act was passed, hearings have been held by committees in both the House and Senate on various aspects of financial services deregulation. Substantial testimony notwithstanding, no conclusions have been reached. The easier steps in deregulation, such as removing interest-rate ceilings and ending fixed stock-brokerage commissions, have already been taken.[38] These actions were relatively simple because they did not fundamentally change the structure of the industry.

The remaining unresolved questions do not deal with specific issues (such as rates) in specific parts of the industry (such as stock brokerages). Instead, policy makers face major decisions about the way the *entire* industry will evolve. Deregulators assert that the increased competition from new powers will be better for consumers, while opponents of regulation argue that the market is ineffective or too unstable to provide the best and most reasonably safe mix of financial services.

Financial institutions themselves do not agree on the proper course for future deregulation. Bankers argue that they need a "level playing field" to compete with the unregulated businesses. They believe that all financial service providers should face the same kind of regulation, with no advantage allowed to any one kind of institution. Securities brokerages argue that the entrance of banks into the securities business would ruin the industry. And S&L's want to be freed from laws that require them to hold significant numbers of home mortgages; they are reluctant, however, to give up the favored status that the home-finance specialization has provided.

The issues of financial services deregulation do not divide neatly along party lines. Like airline deregulation, large urban states probably have more to gain than do lesser-populated rural areas. But unlike the airline example, the issues in financial services are extremely complicated and difficult to understand. Financial services reform is not the sort of issue that excites the voters, especially when they do not believe they are affected by any current crisis in banking.

In the House, banking legislation is controlled by banking committee chair Ferdinand St Germain, a Democrat (R.I.). He has generally opposed further deregulation, believing that banking today is risky enough without letting banks have new powers. He has complained of a "competition in laxity" among the various bank regulators and is a substantial voice against further bank deregulation.[39] In the Senate, Republican Jake Garn (Utah) chaired the banking committee from 1981 until the Democrats recaptured the upper house in the 1986 midterm elections. A proponent of some further deregulation, Garn would have liked to grant banks new powers to expand into securities, real estate, and insurance.[40] It remains to be seen whether his successor, Democrat William Proxmire (Wis.), will push for such legislation. Any future banking legislation, however, will almost certainly have to be a compromise acceptable to these two different points of view, a difficult task unless a significant crisis is at hand. President Reagan has been almost silent on issues of bank deregulation, leaving the development of new legislation to Congress.[41]

Many legitimate regulatory goals—fostering competition, ensuring safety, managing the money supply, allowing fairness among types of institutions—are in conflict.[42] Given these contending values and pressures, members of Congress are having a difficult time deciding how these goals should be ranked. Even if the priorities are clear, experts disagree on the kinds of laws that would best achieve any given set of goals. If banking law is hard to understand, it is even harder to write, and most in Congress would prefer to leave it alone.[43] Moreover, they seem equally unwilling to assign further responsibilities to federal regulatory agencies.

The prospects do not seem good for new, significant financial legislation in the short term. Minor adjustments in the regulatory structure are possible, but there are a number of important unresolved questions for which no easy solution can be found. The following section examines one major question.

The Unresolved Question

The financial services industry may have outgrown its old regulatory structure, but it is not obvious what the new regulatory regime should be. The basic question facing policy makers is, Which federal institutions, if any, should retain control over the industry? Relative to this question, the philosophical debate over regulation as a tool for the industry remains without clear resolution.

Banks are forbidden to offer many potentially profitable financial services. This strict separation between banking and other financial services was not always the case but has prevailed since the passage of the Glass–Steagall Act of 1933. A combination of regulations, economic conditions, and management decisions had kept the industry stable from the mid-1930s to the mid-1970s. It would be a terrible year if ten banks failed, a figure well below those of the depression.[44] For those with a clear memory of the depression, it is not surprising that safety was the dominant regulatory concern.

Not too many years ago, banks and S&L's saw themselves as the major competitors in the financial marketplace. Arguments were, by current standards, almost trivial, and centered on issues such as the interest-rate differential: S&L's were allowed to pay 5.5 percent interest on savings accounts, while banks could pay only 5 percent. Since the 1960s, differences between these two types of institutions have narrowed. Now, the more important debate is not between banks and S&L's but among depository institutions, other providers of financial services, and businesses engaged in general commerce. According to the *Congressional Quarterly,* "the fight over banking deregulation is at bottom a fight over one fundamental question: Does the role in the economy of 'banks'—in this case meaning depository institutions generally—justify treating them differently from other providers of financial services?"[45] This question grows more prominent as the influence of nontraditional institutions increases.

Bank Arguments for Increased Powers

Banks have much to gain by expanding their financial services. They want to establish, in any way possible, a financial relationship with a customer. Once the initial contact is made, banks believe that it will be easier to sell other financial services.[46] They also want the expanded powers in order to meet the threats they see from such competitors as Sears.

Modern-day financial service centers extend well beyond the limited banking opportunities of a generation ago. Sears, for example, wants to be the leading provider of financial services to consumers. It added to its Allstate Insurance Company by purchasing the Coldwell Banker real-estate brokerage, Dean Witter securities, and the Sears Savings Bank (formerly Allstate S&L), and is well-positioned to meet its goal.[47] In 1986, Sears introduced the Discover credit card, a competitor to Visa and Mastercard, to further expand its financial empire. The Sears approach seems to work in bringing in new customers: 60 percent of Sears's financial center customers have never done business with a brokerage before.[48] Banks want the right to compete for that sort of customer base.[49]

Over the past fifty years, a number of exceptions to the Glass–Steagall Act have been allowed. Banks, in some cases, have been allowed to deal in stocks and bonds. They can underwrite federal, state, and local government bonds, as well as state– and local-revenue bonds for housing or building universities. In 1982, banks underwrote about 40 percent of all municipal revenue bonds.[50] Taken together, these activities have not been held responsible for any significant number of bank failures since the depression.

Banks see clear advantages in offering a broad menu of financial services to customers. This fact alone, however, is not persuasive enough to bank regulators and others when setting policy. To win additional powers, banks will have to argue that not only their interests but also the interests of society as a whole will be served by such a plan.

Bank-industry representatives have been joined by would-be deregulators, who argue that Glass–Steagall and other limiting laws are outdated. Banks were denied the power to deal in securities when the securities industry was essentially unregulated; present laws, however, would protect the consumer in stock deals regardless of which institution served as the underwriter. The SEC and other regulatory agencies are what make the securities industry safe, not Glass–Steagall or other legal limits on banks.

Proponents of deregulation also contend that competition will help lower prices for financial services for consumers. In instances where banks have been able to exploit loopholes in state laws to sell insurance, results have been mixed. Selling insurance in several states, mutual savings banks have offered life insurance at rates approximately 20 percent lower than those offered by major life-insurance companies.[51] There is little evidence, however, that these savings are widespread.

This entire line of argument is underscored by the contention that any argument against expansion of bank powers is merely a smokescreen of self-interest. Some regulators agree. When Donald Regan was Secretary of Treasury, he said, "Instead of contriving arguments to keep banks and thrifts out of their business, the securities, insurance, and real estate industries could put their creative efforts to better use."[52]

Defense of the Status Quo

Opponents of expanded bank powers are concerned with a repetition of the bank closings of the 1930s. Because banks and other depository institutions allocate credit, society must ensure that this is done in an impartial manner—an impossible task if banks have a financial interest in other enterprises. A bank that owns another sort of business might effectively give itself loans at preferential rates while denying funds to a better-run competitor unconnected with the bank. Those who favor regulation argue that banks should provide loans for the best-run, most financially sound, and most promising business enterprises. If the bank owns or directly supports some of these businesses, then the conflict of interest hurts the economy as a whole. Bank-owned businesses, regardless of merit, will benefit; potential competitors, despite their value to society, will be hurt.

One of the strongest arguments against the expansion of banking powers stems from the federal insurance of bank deposits. The public grants banks a special trust that to a great extent stems from the federal guarantee their deposits carry. Traditional stockbrokers have no federal guarantees. Banks might win securities, insurance, or other accounts not by offering a better combination of service and price, but because people have faith in banks. This factor is especially important for securities regulation if, as at least one study suggests, clients with the least experience in the stock market are those most likely to be attracted to banks.[53]

Supporters of regulation are also concerned about the possible concentration of wealth if banks are able to offer a broad range of financial services. Even those who favor deregulation see this as a legitimate concern. Small banks worry that they will be taken over or driven out of business by huge money center banks such as Citicorp, which has already shown a desire for aggressive expansion.[54] Even without further deregulation, the concentration in financial services will increase. A study by the Arthur Anderson Co., a broad-based business consultancy, suggests that as many as 50 percent of today's banks will be gone by the end of the decade, most through merger or acquisition.[55]

Finally, the instability of the current situation leads many observers to fear significant change of any sort at the present time. With the "nationalization" of Continental and the run on S&L's in Ohio, opponents of deregulation have argued that banks are having difficulty with competition in the marketplace now, and new powers might lead to an increase in the already high rate of bank failures.[56] Few want to risk further change when the present is so unsettled.

The Future of Bank Powers

Given the plethora of characters and problem areas, it is unlikely that any quick fix will be found for the financial services issue. If anything, the multifaceted controversy has left it all but impossible to facilitate further change, even though current problems show no signs of going away. Meanwhile, banks have worked hard to skirt various regulatory limitations. Those that truly want to sell securities or insurance can almost always find a legal means to do so. Because a bank can choose its regulator by choosing its type of charter, it can usually find a regulator who allows the powers it seeks. For example, a state-chartered bank with federal insurance is regulated by the FDIC, even without being a member of the Fed. The FDIC, however, has stated that if a state law allows banks to offer full brokerage services and to underwrite securities, the FDIC will allow this arrangement.[57] The FDIC's position is unpopular with the other regulators, but they cannot change the situation.

For members of Congress, allowing others to set financial-services regulatory policy may not seem like such a bad idea. The risk of expanding bank powers by congressional mandate is likely to generate considerable enmity among those close to the nonbank banks. If deregulation succeeds, the most obvious winners would be the banks, who will find themselves better able to compete with their unregulated counterparts. The public, for the most part, is not especially concerned if Citicorp believes that Sears has an unfair advantage in attracting customers. On the other hand, if deregulation further destabilizes U.S. banking, society as a whole will suffer serious damage. All commerce depends on banking, and the economic repercussions of additional bank failures would quickly spread through the entire economy. Banks will almost certainly have to wait for the "level playing field" they seek.

In the absence of congressional action, state legislators, banks, and regulators are likely to move forward. Banks and nonbanks will develop new products, expand into new fields, and find ways around many restrictive laws. If Congress prefers not to deal with these issues, it may find that the debate is irrelevant; policy may be decided by others in a fashion that is anything but uniform.

Other Suggested Reforms

In addition to the question of powers for banks and other financial institutions, many other reforms have been suggested. Two possibilities focus on the restrictions on interstate banking and basing deposit-insurance premiums on the risk a bank takes.

Most possible reforms ask certain common questions: How should fairness between different sorts of institutions be balanced with fairness to the public? How can stability in banking be retained without ignoring the reality of the marketplace? How can we cope with a system where loopholes have come to dominate the laws and to change the laws is risky?

It is not surprising that Congress is reluctant to act. Members want to study and understand these complicated issues before acting. But economic conditions and financial markets shift so rapidly that by the time a detailed study is complete, the facts have often changed and Congress is faced with a new reality. After fifty years of substantial control, much policy is now set by institutions developing new products and services where no regulation exists.

Banking Regulation: Tying Theory to Practice

Much of the motivation for bank regulation meshes with the public-interest theory of regulation. As with much of the regulation from the depression years, there was a clear consensus that the federal government should act to repair serious problems for the public good. Unlike other sorts of regulation, however, few have argued that bank regulation was a "triumph of conservatism." Banking's critical role in the economy made it obvious to almost everyone that society as a whole needed more control over the industry.

The public interest and the needs of the industry were similar. Restored confidence in the financial system seemed to be the primary concern for everyone. Although the exact nature of the appropriate regulatory activity was debated, there is little doubt that legislators believed that banking regulation was reform in the public interest.

As events changed in the marketplace, so did the basis for regulatory reform. The turmoil of the 1970s and '80s might be explained by a combination of both capture and public-interest theories. The public interest continues to be a critical concern for all regulators, but each regulatory agency has become a champion of the type of institution it oversees. The FSLIC and FHLBB actively campaign for legislation favorable to S&L's; bank regulators such as the FDIC attempt to protect the interests of banks. Even though regulators may identify with their client industries, they are ultimately concerned with the safety and soundness of the financial system as a whole.

The "public interest" is likely to be defined quite differently by consumer groups and financial services companies. Because the issues are so complicated, disagreement is strong over the best way to provide financial safety and soundness while retaining the benefits of competition for consumers. Perhaps in no other area is the public-interest motivation of regulators so clear; but in no other area is the policy to achieve that interest so difficult to develop.

Conclusions

Both financial institutions and users of financial services are adjusting to the partial deregulation now in place. The total number of financial institutions has declined, and that trend is expected to continue.[58] The industry will never be as stable as it was under heavy regulation. More financial institutions will almost certainly fail. Despite these costs, however, some benefits have accrued from the new financial-services environment.

Consumers have found mixed blessings from deregulation. They may receive higher rates on savings and investments, but they also pay high rates for services. Under regulation, with artificially low interest rates paid to savers, banking-service prices did not always reflect the true costs to the banks of providing these services.[59] Although it is expensive to handle checking accounts, banks offered free or low-cost checking because regulations prevented the payment of interest on checking accounts. Banks could charge little for checking, because they made money by investing the deposits. Now, large checking accounts almost always receive interest, although the costs of maintaining an account and writing checks are higher for everyone. The new, higher bank charges have led to some calls for renewed regulation.

Is Banking an Essential Service?

When airlines were deregulated, the price subsidies to some protected groups under regulation were removed, leaving them to pay higher prices. These groups lobbied against deregulation, but the efficiencies of the market won. In banking, however, another question arises: What happens to those for whom the price of banking becomes too high? If deregulation forces a traveler to take a bus rather than fly, it is not considered of much harm to society. But it may be argued that if low-income consumers cannot afford basic financial services, all of society suffers from the inconveniences and discontinuities in the system associated with a lack of universal access to money sources and benefits.

When the first round of deregulation came, most financial institutions fought for the "upscale" customer—that is, the one most likely to use a wide range of financial services and to place a substantial amount of money in the bank. The low-income customer, with little savings, no interest in "cash management," and a checking account balance hovering around zero, offers little chance of profit for a bank. Service costs on these accounts are high, and banks can no longer use charges on large accounts to subsidize the low-income consumer. If one bank charges high fees on large accounts in order to provide inexpensive service to smaller ones, large customers will simply move elsewhere. Regulation formerly restricted exactly that type of competition, but now pressure is increasing for the government to assure that low-income people are not frozen out of the financial system.[60]

Consumer advocates argue that financial services are almost as essential in modern society as food and housing. They believe that banks should be forced to offer "lifeline" accounts with low fees for a minimum level of service—ten checks written per month, for example. If the poor, especially the elderly poor, are forced to use cash for all transactions because they cannot afford a checking account, the possibilities for crime increase. As a consequence, some congressional and state legislators would like to see the expansion of bank powers tied to bank willingness to provide such lifeline accounts.[61]

Industry response has been guarded. Selected banks already offer such service, especially to elderly customers. Proponents of lifeline service are somewhat reluctant to contend that all Americans have an absolute right to free or low-cost banking; after all, banking is a private business. By analogy, although clothes are essential, few would argue that department stores should be forced to carry inexpensive clothes. The more usual approach is to try to see that some minimum level of income is maintained for all people, not to force private businesses to give free service.

On the other hand, the industry readily concedes that basic access to banking is important, and while it does not support lifeline legislation, it does recognize that voluntary action is a reasonable solution. After a *Boston Globe* article described the case of a paperboy whose bank account was eaten up by monthly service charges, Massachusetts passed a lifeline law for those eighteen and younger or sixty-five and older.[62] Other states may follow suit. In fact, given the diversity of services and institutions throughout the country, many states will probably take the lead in setting such policies rather than leave them to the federal government.

The debate over lifeline banking underscores a strong fear connected with bank deregulation—that the ordinary citizen, the small bank, and the small town will all suffer. The public interest looms large in the financial-services deregulation debate, largely because so many millions of Americans will be directly affected by the outcome.

The Future of Deregulation

The banking industry will continue to push for deregulation. It is hard to write laws against new ideas in financial services, and institutions will certainly continue to innovate. According to one Bank of America senior vice-president, Irwin Guman, "[t]here's really no end to the kinds of things that imaginative bankers can come up with."[63] But the risk of change is great. Many in Congress fear that any further action might bring an unacceptable wave of deregulation. Moreover, an environment without rules could make it tough on providers and consumers alike. If powers are expanded to one set of institutions, the others are likely to want more as well. As for consumers, the shifting array of fast-paced changes could greatly increase the burden of making proper decisions.[64]

The economy in 1985 and 1986 gave Congress some breathing room. Lower interest rates and inflation took some of the pressure off banks and S&L's. At the same time, the threat to local banking from the giants became somewhat less compelling. Bankruptcies continued at an untolerably high rate, but public lawmakers accepted the industry's difficulties within the context of existing policies.

It is unlikely that financial services will be completely deregulated. A return to the days of bank panics and closings, uninsured deposits, and questions of confidence would destroy the economy. Congress must look beyond the needs of any one sort of institution—banks, S&L's, and others—and examine the larger questions posed by deregulation.

Financial institutions have a special role in the American economy. No other industry is so critical to all other sectors of the economy and yet so dependent upon public confidence to function effectively. The problem comes with the clash between the needs of a free market and the needs of society. For a free market to operate, banks must be allowed to make mistakes—and to fail. But the result to society from such failures may be unacceptable.[65]

The history of bank regulation has been one of reaction to crisis. In the absence of a critical reason for immediate change, little meaningful reform has occurred. This trend will probably continue. As long as the present mix of regulation and deregulation works reasonably well, calls for "fairness" among financial institutions are not likely to bring significant reform from Congress. The risk inherent in any truly meaningful reform will only be taken when it is clear that the alternative, no change, cannot work. Further financial services deregulation—or reregulation—awaits another crisis.

Notes

1. U.S. Department of Commerce, *Statistical Abstract of the United States, 1986*, 106th ed. (Washington, D.C.: U.S. Government Printing Office), p. 494.
2. *Ibid.*, p. 493.
3. Independent Bankers Association of America, *Independent Bankers Association of America*, (Washington, D.C., 1983) p. 17.
4. *Statistical Abstract, 1986*, p. 498.
5. *Ibid.*, p. 492.
6. Daniel J. Balz, "Regulatory Report 2: Bank Rules Inhibit Concentration and Competition," *National Journal*, 7, no. 10 (March 1975): 344.
7. Office of the Federal Register, National Archives and Records Service, General Services Administration, *The United States Government Manual, 1984/85* (Washington, D.C.: U.S. Government Printing Office, 1984): 440.
8. *Ibid.*, p. 497.
9. *Ibid.*, p. 504.
10. George G. Kaufman, *Money and the Financial System: Fundamentals* (Chicago: Rand McNally, 1975), pp. 69–71.
11. John Ranlett, *Money and Banking: An Introduction to Analysis and Policy,* 3d ed. (Santa Barbara: Wiley, 1977), pp. 34–36.
12. *Ibid.*, pp. 36–39.
13. Kenneth J. Meier, *Regulation: Politics, Bureaucracy, and Economics* (New York: St. Martin's Press, 1985), p. 50.
14 Kaufman, *Money*, p. 97.
15. See Milton Friedman and Anna Schwartz, *A Monetary History of the United States* (Princeton, N.J.: Princeton University Press, 1963), and Thomas Mayer, *Monetary Policy in the United States* (New York: Random House, 1968).
16. One example is the regulation of bank holding companies. See *Statistical Abstract, 1986*, p. 519.
17. Richard T. Pratt, "Deposit Insurance Needs an Overhaul," *San Jose Mercury News,* March 24, 1985, IV:5.
18. Balz, "Regulatory Report 2," p. 346.
19. R. B. Miller, "Conversations with the Reagan Regulators," *The Bankers Magazine,* 165 (March–April 1982): 41–42.
20. Robert Douglass, "The Outlook for Nationwide Expansion," *The Bankers Magazine,* 167 (November–December 1984): 8.

21. Expansion in these, and other areas, depended on regulation.
22. Miller, "Conversations," p. 47.
23. "Bank of America Rushes into the Information Age," *Business Week* (April, 1985): 110–111.
24. Andrew Gray, "In the Wake of Continental," *The Bankers Magazine*, 167, no. 6 (November–December 1984): 72.
25. Harvey Rosenblum, "Banks and Nonbanks: Who's in Control?" *The Bankers Magazine*, 167, no. 5 (September–October 1984): 13.
26. "The Revolution in Financial Services," *Business Week*, no. 2812 (November 28, 1983): 89.
27. Andrew S. Carron, *The Plight of the Thrift Institutions* (Washington, D.C.: The Brookings Institution, 1982), p. 10.
28. "Now Merger May Be the Thrifts' Only Hope," *Business Week*, no. 2861 (September 24, 1984): 124.
29. "The Revolution in Financial Services," *Business Week* (November 28, 1983), pp. 88–89.
30. "Bailing Out Banks: How Much Is Too Much?" *Congressional Quarterly Weekly Report*, September 15, 1984, p. 2244.
31. Gary Hector, "The Nationalization of Continental Illinois," *Fortune*, 110, no. 4 (August 20, 1984): 140.
32. G. Christian Hill, "Ohio S&L Crisis May Spur Industry Changes," *Wall Street Journal*, April 8, 1985, p. 6.
33. "Continental's Blow to a Safer Banking System," *Fortune*, 109, no. 12 (June 11, 1984): 93.
34. "Bailing Out Banks," *Congressional Quarterly Weekly Report*, September 15, 1984, p. 2246.
35. Hector, "Nationalization," p. 140.
36. "Ohio Governor Closes 71 S&Ls for Three Days," *San Francisco Examiner*, March 15, 1985, p. C6.
37. "Washington Wrangles as the Thrift Crisis Deepens," *Business Week*, no. 2896 (May 27, 1985): 128.
38. "Revolution in Financial Services," *Business Week*, November 28, 1983, p. 89.
39. "Bailing Out Banks," *Congressional Quarterly Weekly Report*, September 15, 1984, p. 2243.
40. "New Rules for Banks," *Fortune*, 112, no. 2 (July 22, 1985): 106.
41. "Bailing Out Banks," *Congressional Quarterly Weekly Report*, September 15, 1984, p. 2243.
42. Douglass, "The Outlook," p. 9.
43. "Populist Legacy Lives on in House Banking," *Congressional Quarterly*, 41, no. 36 (September 10, 1983): 1906.
44. Richard Whittle, "Financial Industry in Turmoil as Reluctant Congress Stalls on Bank Deregulation," *Congressional Quarterly*, 41, no. 36 (September 10, 1983): 1905.
45. *Ibid.*, p. 1094.
46. "The Peril in Financial Services," *Business Week*, no. 2856 (August 20, 1984): 75.
47. *Ibid.*, p. 54.
48. *Ibid.*, p. 55.
49. Debate on the Financial Services Competitive Equity Act, Sen. Slade Gorton, *Congressional Record*, September 13, 1984, p. S11139.
50. Sen. Jake Garn, *Congressional Record*, September 13, 1984, p. S11133.
51. "The Peril in Financial Services," *Business Week*, no. 2856 (August 20, 1984): 79.
52. Douglass, "The Outlook," p. 9.
53. Sam Scott Miller, "Banks Should Not Engage in Securities Activities," *The Bankers Magazine*, 167, no. 5 (September–October 1984): 86–87.

54. Whittle, "Financial Industry in Turmoil," p. 1908.
55. Burt Solomon, "Banks of Tomorrow," *National Journal,* 18, no. 37 (September 13, 1986): 2161.
56. "The Rush to Slow Bank Deregulation," *Fortune,* 110, no. 1 (July 9, 1984): 152.
57. "Bankers as Brokers," *Business Week,* no. 2785 (April 11, 1983): 71.
58. Donald Fraser, "Deregulation and Depository Institutions," *The Bankers Magazine,* 166, no. 1 (January–February 1983): 37.
59. Roger Skrentny, "Repackaging an Old Tradition: Bank Deregulation," *California Business,* 19, no. 4 (April 1984): 76.
60. Ann Cooper, "Low-Income Customers Discover Down Sides of Phone, Banking Deregulation," *National Journal,* (January 26, 1985): 204.
61. *Ibid.,* p. 205.
62. *Ibid.,* p. 204.
63. "The Rush to Slow," *Fortune,* July 9, 1984, p. 152.
64. D. R. Stephens, "Why Banks Fail," *The Bankers Magazine,* 169, no. 4 (July–August 1986): 61.
65. Bevis Longstreth, "In Search of a Safety Net for the Financial Services Industry," *The Bankers Magazine,* 166, no. 4 (July–August 1983): 32.

CHAPTER 7

The Auto Industry

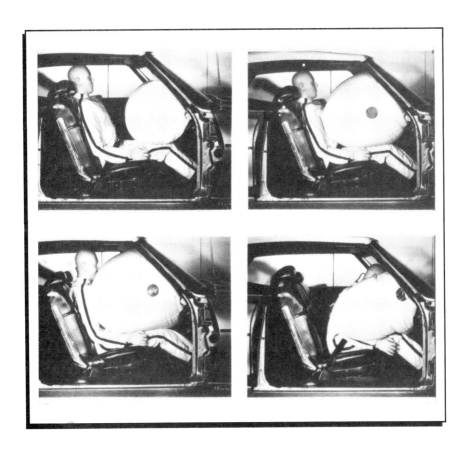

In 1953, company head Charles Wilson told the nation, "What's good for General Motors is good for the country." With this statement, Wilson bluntly asserted the importance of the U.S. auto industry to the economy. But his suggestion of a symbiotic relationship between corporate and public interests was unsubstantiated then and remains so today. Nothing is more demonstrative of the tension between business and society than the fight over the auto industry's behavior. In the past fifteen years, environmental and safety issues have caused significant disagreement between the industry and government over what constitutes "the common good."

The auto industry is critical to the nation's economy. It generates more employment opportunities than any other industry in the United States. According to the Motor Vehicle Manufacturers Association, "[o]ne in eight manufacturing dollars, one in six retail establishments and one in six privately employed Americans are part of the domestic motor vehicle manufacturing industry."[1] Perhaps more important, the health of the economy as a whole is tied to that of the auto industry because it generates demand for the products of so many other basic industries. Philip Caldwell, chairman of Ford Motor Co., notes that "(t)he production of cars, trucks, and parts in the United States has provided a market for 24% of the U.S. steel output, 17% of aluminum, 54% of iron, and 59% of synthetic rubber."[2] The carry-over effects for American business interests are enormous. When the auto industry is healthy, so usually is the economy.

The automobile industry has a profound impact on people's lives as well as on industry as a whole. The United States has more automobiles, in total and per capita, than any other nation in the world.[3] Unfortunately, the country also has high traffic mortality and injury levels to match. According to the National Safety Council, 47,800 people were killed in traffic accidents in 1986.[4] The resulting costs to society are staggering. The Insurance Institute for Highway Safety reports that "[o]f the leading causes of death to Americans, motor vehicle crash injuries are second only to cancer in their economic burden" (see Figure 7-1). In addition, these accidents are the leading cause of paraplegia and quadriplegia, severe facial lacerations and fractures, epilepsy, and brain damage.[5]

Aside from injuries and deaths, Americans pay heavily for other motor vehicle–related problems. The Department of Transportation estimates that the annual economic loss from auto accidents exceeds $57 billion.[6] These losses come in many forms: the costs of emergency medical services, hospital care, rehabilitation programs, lost wages, and the many social-welfare programs needed by families who find themselves devastated by death or injury. The noneconomic costs are even greater. A National Highway Traffic Safety Administration study on these other effects found that "in some families, financial costs paled in comparison to victims' continuing pain, disability, and pyschological stress. . . .

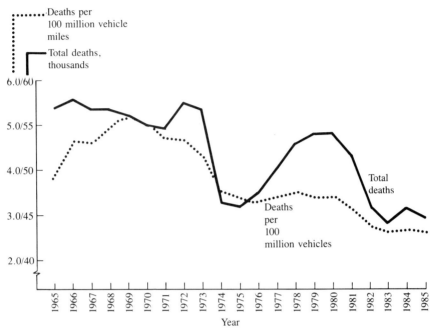

Figure 7-1. Traffic fatalities, 1965–1985
Source: *MVMA Facts and Figures 1983*, p. 89; *1985*, pp. 90–92

In others, economic hardship blighted the victims' convalescence and rehabilitation and deepened the entire family's misery."[7]

The costs of auto accidents, both in lives and dollars, are and will continue to be of significant concern to society. Because of these costs, auto-safety regulation has been and remains a critical problem for both the automobile industry and American society.

The Auto Industry: To Be or Not to Be Left Alone?

An impressive array of federal regulation governs the auto industry in the areas of emission control, fuel economy, and safety. Prior to the mid-1960s, federal regulations in these areas were virtually nonexistent and state regulations were minimal. In 1966, however, the industry was first subjected to national standards for vehicle safety. The area provides an excellent example of governmental efforts to balance competing demands of the private and public sectors, first by regulation and then by deregulation.

During the pre–federal intervention era, the auto industry's approach to safety was characterized by two beliefs. First, industry executives generally believed they produced safe cars; accidents were the fault of drivers, and therefore it was unfair to make manufacturers take extra care in designing cars just because they might be involved in accidents. Harry F. Barr, a vice-president for engineering at General Motors, summed up the industry's position: "We feel our cars are quite safe and quite reliable. . . . The driver is the most important [cause of accidents], we feel. If the drivers do everything they should, there wouldn't be accidents, would there?"[8] The solutions for traffic accidents, according to Detroit's executives, was simply to educate drivers to avoid them and to get the bad drivers out from behind their steering wheels.

A second objection to regulation stemmed from the industry's firm belief that the public did not want to pay for safety features. Executives viewed investment in safety as a nonrecoverable expenditure, one that could not be passed on to the public without a loss in sales.[9] Although the evidence on this point is equivocal, it does not appear that the public was making demands for safer vehicles.[10] Lester Lave, a senior fellow at the Brookings Institution has since reported that "(r)elatively few buyers have ordered optional equipment that would make their vehicles safer. . . . When given a choice, the vast majority of new car buyers choose an automobile with style, power, and comfort."[11]

Not surprisingly, auto manufacturers never gave safety considerations high priority until the federal government forced them to do so. Safety was such a peripheral concern that it was not until the 1950s that an auto executive was even given formal responsibility for safety; and where safety and style were in conflict, style almost always won out.[12] This does not indicate, as some consumer advocates might argue, that auto executives are immoral and uncaring; it appears instead to be a rationale of self-interest. Aside from the social desirability of safety features, auto executives saw little utility in trying to market them. In the mid-1960s, Lee Iacocca, then general manager of the Ford Division at Ford Motor Co., noted that the industry's belief was that "styling cars sells cars and safety does not."[13] Apparently, consumers felt the same.

Many commentators have argued that, despite a lack of demand, Detroit has a social obligation to engineer safety into its cars. The industry, however, has always viewed its business as selling cars, not the saving of lives. Still, both auto officials and antiregulation critics have admitted that federal intervention could have been forestalled if the industry had shown social responsibility when public concern was first expressed over rising traffic fatalities. Robert McNamara, onetime assistant general manager at Ford, for example, argued that the auto industry had a responsibility to deal with traffic safety issues or it risked governmental intervention.[14] But despite concern in some quarters, relatively few dollars were allocated to safety research. The nation was stunned in 1966 when auto executives admitted under questioning in Senate hearings chaired by Robert Kennedy (D.–N.Y.) that the industry had spent only $11 million on basic safety research in 1965, despite earning more than $2.5 billion in profits.[15]

Increasing the Pressure: Movement Toward Regulation

In 1965, the regulatory environment abruptly changed with the publication of Ralph Nader's *Unsafe At Any Speed*.[16] Nader argued that the automakers were largely indifferent to safety concerns. His harshest criticism focused on General Motors, whom Nader accused of marketing one automobile, the Chevrolet Corvair, despite executives' knowledge of major safety hazards resulting from design defects. Suddenly, the industry's *attitude* became an issue to the increasingly skeptical public.

With auto safety now a key item on the public's agenda, congressional critics considered new regulations for the industry. Concerned that the automaker's interests were not necessarily those shared by the public, congressional activists pursued a program to force manufacturers to assume responsibility for safety, and not to place blame solely on individual drivers. As Sen. Abraham Ribicoff (D.–Conn.) explained, "The automobile manufacturer has a part to play, taking into account that a human being is never going to be perfect. . . . (S)ince drivers make mistakes, and they are always going to make mistakes, . . . automobiles should be built in such a way as to minimize the damage done."[17]

The industry remained unconvinced. Rather than accept or seek a compromise on a series of mandated safety standards under the then-pending National Traffic and Motor Vehicle Safety Act (NTMVSA), the industry proposed a four-point program: First, the industry would formally commit to voluntarily adopting safety features; second, the federal and state roles in protecting the public interest would be strengthened by appropriate legislation that dealt with vehicle inspection, driver education, licensing, and highway programs; third, the industry would submit frequent reports to Congress and appropriate federal agencies on the progress of their voluntary efforts; and fourth, the industry would help carry out the voluntary program by creating a five-member, motor-vehicle safety board. The board would include the four presidents of the major auto companies; the fifth member would be appointed by the auto industry.[18] This would have allowed the industry to continue self-regulation, a practice of many major industries and one acceptable to government. Such self-regulation had not only been applied by the automobile industry, but also by tobacco, oil, and other private industries whose public accountability had traditionally been left to the private sector.

Passage of the National Traffic and Motor Vehicle Safety Act

Congressional hearings on auto safety began in 1965 with Senator Ribicoff's subcommittee on government operations taking the lead. Early in 1966, President Lyndon Johnson submitted a highway safety bill that would "arrest the destruction of life and property on our highways."[19] Following several months of heated debate, Congress passed the National Traffic and Motor Vehicle Safety Act. By enacting regulatory controls for a heretofore unregulated industry, Congress rejected the industry position emphasizing the driver-only approach to safety.

The 1966 act mandated the Department of Transportation (DOT) to "reduce traffic accidents and deaths and injuries to persons resulting from traffic accidents."[20] The Secretary of Transportation was authorized to issue motor-vehicle safety standards that "shall be practicable, shall meet the need for motor vehicle safety, and shall be stated in objective terms."[21] In issuing these standards, the secretary was required to consider "relevant available motor vehicle safety data, whether the proposed standard is reasonable, practicable, and appropriate for the particular type of motor vehicle . . . for which it is prescribed."[22] The act quickly became the cornerstone for governmental regulation of the industry.

As a result of the NTMVSA, automobile manufacturers have been required to install numerous safety devices including dual braking systems, padded instrument panels, lap and shoulder belt restraints, shatterproof windshields, head rests, and energy-absorbing steering columns. According to the DOT, federal safety standards have saved more than 80,000 lives since 1968 and are currently saving more than 10,000 lives each year.[23]

These regulations do more than save lives. As Joan Claybrook, former head of NHTSA, pointed out, vehicle standards have lowered insurance costs by more than $3 billion annually. In addition, a number of other negative effects from accidents have been reduced, including psychological trauma and family disruption; welfare, social security, unemployment, and disability payments; and long-term health care and rehabilitation costs.[24]

DOT further estimates that the efforts have been cost-effective: For each dollar consumers spend on safety features (a total of $370 per car, including industry profit), twenty-seven lives are saved.[25]

For the most part, auto industry leaders have continued to oppose federal safety regulations. Despite the benefits accruing from new safety features, the industry has viewed regulation as both costly and unnecessary. The opposition stems in part from the fear that government will not know when to stop. As Ralph Nader explains, "[e]very time (auto companies) oppose or . . . consider opposing a safety standard, their advisors tell them that if this standard gets accepted there is going to be another standard, and so on. So why not fight this one because you will stop the others or you will delay the others?"[26] Accordingly, the industry has felt compelled to fight each and every regulation effort.

Prior to 1980, the relationship between the federal government and the industry was almost always adversarial. Mistrust on both sides was so strong that federal officials believed that if the industry did not object to a proposed standard, the proposal must be too soft. The industry felt it was being persecuted by regulatory actions. Few words are as revealing as those of a former Ford executive in the early 1970s; according to him, "the bastards in Washington are pushing us around."[27] As the Consumers Union has argued, industry spokespersons respond negatively to any regulation proposal, regardless of its merits: "There is no proof that the proposed standard is needed or will serve any purpose. . . . Its terms and requirements are not clear. We cannot possibly put design and production changes in effect by the stipulated date. The matter needs much more research and study before a proper proposal can be written."[28] Ironically, the automobile industry fully approves governmental intervention in one area—import quotas—but it sees no role for government in its own affairs—the design and manufacture of automobiles.

The Air-Bag Standard: The Safety Debate Renewed

Of the many proposed Federal Motor Vehicle Safety Standards (FMVSS), Standard 208 has generated the most controversy and has epitomized the larger debate over the merits of regulation. Originally issued in 1967, FMVSS 208 required auto manufacturers to install seatbelts in all vehicles.[29]

The controversy began when NHTSA proposed an amendment to FMVSS 208 that would require manufacturers to install passive restraints. (The NHTSA is an agency within the DOT; its director is appointed with the approval of the secretary of transportation.) These do not require any actions by drivers or passengers, but will automatically protect an automobile's occupants in a collision. The two major restraints are air bags and passive seatbelts. Active restraints, on the other hand, require the user to take some action, such as fastening a seatbelt. FMVSS 208, like almost all other NHTSA standards, is a performance criterion, not a design-oriented regulation; that is, the standard specifies some level of performance that must be met. The debate over passive restraints has largely been a debate over the air bag. When NHTSA's predecessor, the National Highway Safety Board, first amended FMVSS 208 to include passive restraints, the standard was worded in such a way that only air bags could meet the requirements. Since then, auto-safety advocates have pushed this restraint as a vastly superior alternative to the passive seatbelt.

The auto industry has spent far more time, effort, and money in fighting the air bag than it has on any other proposed safety standard. The industry particularly dislikes the high cost of the standards, the most expensive ever proposed by NHTSA. As Yale economist William Nordhaus has explained, the air-bag proposal has come to symbolize all the negative effects of regulation to the automobile industry: "[T]hey feel that if they can beat this one, maybe the tide will have turned for them and they can beat back some other ones."[30] For the industry, the air-bag concept has come to represent the "last straw" of the regulation burden.

Industry opposition also stems from the potential regulatory impact of the air bag. The device requires major technological innovations, but if it were successful, saving thousands of lives and billions of dollars each year, the industry fears that the NHTSA's regulatory zeal would increase. Likewise, according to industry critic Ralph Nader, failure of the air bag would give the automakers hope for discrediting future government regulation. The air bag's success, then, has to be prevented, for if this regulation works, "[g]overnment might get the credit and such success might become contagious in other regulatory areas."[31]

In 1969, NHTSA first proposed that FMVSS 208 be amended to include passive restraints. Over the ensuing fifteen years, the standard has followed a tortuous path through the policy-making structure. The U.S. Court of Appeals for the District of Columbia stated that the standard has been "the subject of approximately [sixty] notices of proposed rulemaking, hearings, amendments, and the like between 1969 and 1981, (including) . . . successful as well as unsuccessful attempts in Congress to control the evolution of the regulation."[32]

From the time the passive-restraint standard was first issued, various organized interest groups have entered into both sides of the debate while others have commented from the sidelines. Those favoring passive restraints fall into two forces, the insurance industry and coalitions of consumer, health, and safety groups.

Led by the Allstate and State Farm insurance companies, 95 percent of the automobile-insurance industry has actively advocated the installation of passive restraints, particularly the air bag. The insurance industry stands to benefit when air bags are installed because companies will pay out fewer claims for deaths and injuries. Those insurance companies owned by auto manufacturers are the only exceptions to this position.[33]

The second group has forged a coalition of consumer, traffic-safety, and medical organizations, including the American Academy of Pediatrics, the American Epilepsy Foundation, the American Public Health Association, the Center for Auto Safety, the Consumer Federation of America, the International Association of Police Chiefs, the Insurance Institute for Highway Safety, the National Motor Vehicle Safety Advisory Council, and the National Traffic Safety Board. The American

Automobile Association first opposed air bags, but reversed itself and endorsed the standard in 1977.

The primary opposition to the air bag comes from an auto-industry coalition of the four major American auto manufacturers—General Motors, Ford Motor Co., Chrysler Corp., and American Motors—as well as the Motor Vehicle Manufacturers Association of the United States and the National Automobile Dealers Association. Some foreign manufacturers, especially Japanese companies, have also opposed the standard.

Chronology of the Struggle

During the fifteen-year conflict, every movement toward or away from the air-bag concept has been predicated on the acceptability of regulation as the means to induce industry cooperation. The struggle has seen three stages.

Stage One: April 1969 to June 1973

When they became convinced that government would not back down from its demands, auto industry leaders developed a multifaceted plan to fight the standard. Three major lines of attack dominated the first four years of the campaign against the air bag: First, the industry pressed NHTSA to delay the effective date of the standard; second, it advocated the increased use of seatbelts as a superior alternative; and third, it tried to have the regulatory standard overturned in federal courts. In June 1969, NHTSA issued an advance notice of rule making to require passive restraint installation in all passenger cars effective January 1, 1972. The industry asked for a postponement of the effective date and, after evaluating the situation, the NHTSA agreed in May 1970 to delay the proposed effective date for one year to January 1, 1973.[34] The extension, however, did not appease the industry and as soon as the extension was granted, it immediately began to press for another; this strategy would continue throughout the debate.[35]

Although "insufficient lead time" in tooling up production lines would remain a critical argument, the auto companies also attempted to neutralize the standard by offering the industry's traditional first defense to regulation: a proposal to voluntarily innovate. In August 1970, in an effort to buy time, Ford, Chrysler, and GM promised to install air bags in all 1975 vehicles. In return for these commitments, NHTSA delayed the effective date an additional six months.[36]

The industry further attacked the air-bag standard by promoting seatbelts as a superior alternative to passive protection. Seatbelts, when worn, have long been recognized to be effective in preventing death and injury in auto accidents. Although several analyses have shown that seatbelts and air bags save lives in *different* ways.[37] (air bags are superior in frontal collisions, seatbelts are superior in side collisions and rollover crashes), the automakers have argued that the two systems could substitute for one another. This position was based on figures that showed the *overall* death and injury reduction rates would be similar for passive and active restraints (given 100 percent air-bag installation and 70 percent seatbelt usage).

Encouraging public use of active restraints was appealing to some regulatory officials, who thought that seatbelts could save lives while the air bags were gradually installed in all new cars. The approach also appealed to auto manufacturers because they were already required to install seatbelts. Unfortunately, seatbelt use has never been very high. For example, a study by the Insurance Institute for Highway Safety (IIHS) in 1970 determined that the average seatbelt-use rate was 20 percent.[38] Since that time, the rate has declined: In 1984, NHTSA data showed a seatbelt usage rate of 12.5 percent for front-seat occupants.[39] Clearly, even though the auto industry has tried to increase the use of seatbelts through public education, their efforts have uniformly failed.*

The ignition interlock was the strongest attempt by the auto industry to increase seatbelt use. The device prevents a car's engine from starting unless the front-seat occupants fasten their seatbelts. Although the auto industry has called it another "harebrained" scheme of consumer advocate Ralph Nader, the interlock was actually one of Ford's "better ideas."[40] Henry Ford II and Lynn Townsend, board chairs of Ford and Chrysler respectively, met privately with President Richard Nixon in late 1970 to persuade him to ease the passive-restraint standard. The result of this meeting was White House pressure on the DOT to substitute the interlock for the air bag.[41]

More than ten years later, a transcript of the meeting confirmed its importance. At one point, the tape covered the conversation of Henry Ford II, Ford Co. president Lee Iacocca, and John Ehrlichman. The exchange revealed that while NHTSA is legally an independent agency, the White House could influence its policies.[42] While the official government agency responsible for auto safety took one public position, another, albeit higher, authority took a different and private position. Ultimately, DOT accepted the interlock proposal and a two-year delay in passive-restraint installation.

While the DOT considered the interlock, the auto industry began its third line of attack. In April 1971, Chrysler challenged the passive-restraint standard in the U.S. Court of Appeals. Joined by the other auto companies, Chrysler argued against the standard on two grounds. First, the company contended that NHTSA did not have the authority to promulgate standards that required automakers to develop new technology. The court disagreed, upholding NHTSA's legal authority by reaffirming

---

*Only after state governments passed mandatory seatbelt laws in 1984–1985 did seatbelt use increase.

"that the agency may issue standards requiring future levels of motor vehicle performance which manufacturers could not meet unless they diverted more of their resources to producing additional safety technology than they might otherwise do."[43]

But Chrysler succeeded in pressing its second argument. The safety act required that "objective" standards must be used to test the effectiveness of passive restraints; the court was persuaded by Chrysler that NHTSA's testing dummies did not adequately meet this criterion. The court thus ordered a delay in the passive-restraint standards until appropriate test criteria were reestablished.[44] The effects of the decision were ambiguous, and both sides claimed victory. The NHTSA was given a "green light" for requiring new safety technology, but Chrysler had won an indefinite delay in the requirement's implementation. At the end of this first stage, the battle lines were more clearly drawn. The auto industry had been unable to knock out the standard with one punch, but it had discovered that delaying the standard was not impossible.

Stage Two: July 1973 to May 1976

The second phase of the air-bag debate was marked by a significant retreat of GM's support for the air bag and congressional disavowal of the interlock substitution. The GM about-face followed a reassessment of commitments the company had made to NHTSA and to Congress to voluntarily install air bags in vehicles. The company went so far as to actually discourage the sale of the few air bag–equipped vehicles that were produced during this period. Furthermore, GM repeatedly cut back its planned air-bag production schedule; instead of the 1 million air bag–equipped cars it had pledged for a 1975 demonstration program, only 11,000 were to be produced.[45] As soon as the nation's largest automaker did this, the other manufacturers stiffened their opposition to the air-bag standard. After initial disagreement on the issue, the industry once again presented a united front.

As if to underscore this new resistance, GM informed NHTSA that the company would not offer air bags as optional equipment after the 1976 model year. The decision also had ramifications far beyond the immediate issue: The absence of air bag–equipped cars in operation significantly limited the amount of data regarding air-bag effectiveness in actual crashes. This lack of field testing (one of the stated purposes of the GM demonstration program) came to be used by the industry as a primary argument against the air bag over the next decade.

GM's active effort to discourage sales has been well-documented. One *Wall Street Journal* study found that GM dealers received little information about, and thus, did little promotion of the air bag. In fact, dealers, like most customers, knew "little about the air bag, did little to make buyers aware of it or whet their interest in it, and often sought to pour cold water on any interest that customers showed."[46] One would-be consumer gave a typical account of his efforts to learn about air bags from several GM dealers. Rather than encourage purchase, they told him falsely "that the air bag was too expensive; that it might suddenly pop out in his face, causing him to lose control of the car" and that it was not sold on the particular model in which he expressed interest.[47]

A 1983 study by the firm of Booz–Allen and Hamilton concluded that low sales of air bag–equipped cars could be explained to a significant degree by GM's lack of proper marketing: "With one exception, GM's major market research efforts on [air bags] occurred after the corporation had decided to cease marketing the option."[48] GM and other auto companies subsequently used the low sales figures from the demonstration program to argue that the public did not want the air bag, and that mandating air-bag installation would only lead to buyer hostility and depressed auto sales.

Although GM offered air bags on a small number of cars, the remaining vehicles were equipped with the ignition-interlock system. Almost immediately, the motoring public deluged NHTSA and Congress with complaints about the system's inconvenience: seatbelts had to be worn before the car would start. The interlock was criticized so severely that Congress nullified the requirement in October 1974, nearly banning the passive restraint standard in the process.

Sensing an opportunity to roll back reforms, auto manufacturers attempted to link the interlock and the passive-restraint standard. In a reinterpretation of past and present events, industry spokespersons called the interlock an example of excessive regulation originated by the DOT, implying that it was hardly the political favor they had earlier sought. Lee Iacocca, for example, blamed the government for wasting $500 million and urged that the passive-restraint standard be repealed as another example of regulatory excess.[49] The *Wall Street Journal* reported that the two issues had been carefully made inseparable elements of the automakers' antiregulation agenda: "Somehow, the two devices—each different from the other and based on totally contrasting approaches to auto safety—have become linked in the congressional mind. And lawmakers, deluged by a wave of public disgust for the starter–interlock, are on the verge of wiping out the air bag at the same time they kill the interlock."[50] Such confusion only heightened the demand for repeal of all regulations relative to auto safety.

The industry scored new gains in August 1974 when the House passed a bill that would, according to the Insurance Institute for Highway Safety, prohibit NHTSA "from requiring passive restraint systems (such as air bags), ignition interlock belt systems, or 'any warning device other than a warning light designed to indicate that safety belts are not fastened' on future cars."[51] The Senate did not agree, and passed an amendment that outlawed interlocks but retained the passive-restraint standard. The Senate amendment, however, did require public hearings before the DOT issued any restraint standard; furthermore, Congress had the power to veto any DOT restraint standard within sixty days of its issue.[52] When the conference committee met to resolve the two bills, the Senate version prevailed. The ability of the DOT to promulgate a passive-restraint standard had been retained, but the automakers benefited by the congressional oversight of DOT's rule-making process.

Meanwhile, air-bag proponents spent much of the second phase of the debate on the defensive. The auto industry raised doubts about the cost of air bags and the feasibility of air-bag technology in a variety of special circumstances, including cold weather, small cars, and out-of-position occupants. Some of these cases were questionable, but others presented legitimate concerns. The air bag did not receive much field testing, but lab studies helped to answer questions about the technology, and at the end of the period air-bag proponents had more effectively justified the device. Nevertheless, the air bag's merits failed to gain public support for the standard. The outcry that led to the 1966 NTMVSA was clearly absent from the new debate. Instead, consumers were annoyed with the ignition interlock and the subpar performance of new cars equipped with tougher pollution-control devices. They were more concerned about the cost of new auto-safety features than with the seemingly peripheral issue of increased accident probability. Several hundred dollars for an optional air conditioner or FM radio might offer the "good life," but that kind of money for a required but hidden safety device seemed silly. As its advocates came to realize, the case for air bags would have to be made without strong public support.

Stage Three: June 1976 to November 1980

The pro–air bag lobby continued to pressure the DOT to implement FMVSS 208. In June 1976, Secretary of Transportation James Coleman announced that he would hold public hearings in August on the future of the passive-restraint standard; he would make a final decision by January 1, 1977. At the public hearing, the auto industry restated previous testimony: Seatbelts were a superior option to passive restraints and air bags required additional testing before adoption. Secretary Coleman's decision, announced in December 1976, did not require passive-restraint installation, but it did urge the auto companies "to show 'social and corporate' responsibility by voluntarily entering into agreements with the Department of Transportation for a (passive restraint) demonstration program."[53] In return for the industry's agreement to voluntarily equip 500,000 cars with air bags, DOT would not mandate their installation. Coleman also forestalled voluntary air-bag installation on a "pilot" basis until the 1980 model year—three years later than the previous rule had required. Again, regulation had been forestalled.

With the election of Jimmy Carter that fall, Coleman's tenure ended. The next year, Carter's new Secretary of Transportation, Brock Adams, announced that he would review the Coleman decision. In March 1977, Adams voided Coleman's agreement with the auto manufacturers and scheduled another public hearing on the standard's status; he was clearly more receptive to safety concerns than his predecessor had been. In June, Adams announced that passive restraints would be required for front-seat occupants of future models. Installation would be phased in over three years, beginning September 1, 1981, for large cars.[54]

On the surface, the Adams decision appeared to be a victory for pro–air bag forces; in reality, however, the impact was less favorable than anticipated. While the DOT had finally issued a formal rule requiring passive restraints (as opposed to notices of proposed rule making), it had also given auto manufacturers their biggest delay—four years (from the 1978 to the 1982 model years).

Adams's decision was at least partly concerned with congressional reaction. While Adams was deciding what to do with FMVSS 208, the auto industry intensely lobbyied Congress for regulatory relief. Adams thus faced a dilemma: He could mandate air bags and risk having Congress overturn his decision, or he could appease the auto industry by opting for a weaker standard. In the end, he selected the second choice. Although the industry was satisfied, pro–air bag activists were dismayed. As the Center for Auto Safety, a consumer-oriented group, argued: "It is obvious from the Secretary's decision, which deviates so widely . . . from the recommendation of his staff experts . . . that political considerations and a fear of what Congress might do have produced a result that will cost thousands of lives."[55] What was "poor politics" to some was "practical" to others.

The cautious approach taken by Adams did not please everyone in Congress. On the same day that Adams announced his decision, two of Michigan's legislators, Rep. E. G. ("Bud") Shuster and Sen. Robert Griffin, introduced concurrent resolutions to overturn the DOT standard, considering even the watered-down solution too rigorous. Their efforts, however, failed in both houses. According to the 1974 legislation that had banned interlocks, a concurrent resolution of both houses of Congress was needed to block the standard, so when neither House nor Senate acted to disapprove it, Modified Standard 208 went into effect.[56]

Between the issuance of the final rule by Adams in December 1977 and the inauguration of Ronald Reagan in January 1981, many attempts were made to rescind or delay the effective date of the passive-restraint standard. Opponents of the air bag attached riders to appropriations bills that passed in 1978 and 1979; the riders prohibited the DOT from using any funds to enforce the passive-restraint standards.[57] These efforts had no real impact, since the effective phase-in date was still several years away;

they demonstrated, however, a continuing disapproval with the standard by certain members of Congress.

Emissions and Fuel Economy

Although the passive restraint standard was issued, delayed, and reissued, the federal government did regulate auto manufacturers in the areas of fuel economy and emissions control. Congress first attempted to control auto emissions with its 1965 amendments to the 1963 Clean Air Act. The old Department of Health, Education, and Welfare was given authority to set standards. Several were established, but their effective dates were set far into the future.

In January 1969, the Department of Justice charged the industry with conspiracy to delay pollution-control technology.[58] Consequently in 1970, according to the National Research Council, the Senate amended the Clean Air Act. The amendments ordered a 90 percent reduction of 1970 pollutant levels for hydrocarbons, carbon monoxide, and nitrous oxide by the 1975–76 model year. The Senate also required 5-year/50,000 mile warranties for the emission-control devices and gave enforcement responsibility to the new Environmental Protection Agency.[59]

The Energy Policy and Conservation Act of 1975 set fuel-economy standards for all cars sold in the United States, including foreign imports. The act established average mileage standards of 20 miles per gallon (mpg) for 1980 model cars and 27.5 mpg for 1985 model cars and light trucks.[60] The total cost to the consumer of these federal regulations is hard to calculate, although NHTSA estimates that safety and emission standards together have added about $500 to the price of a 1978 car, considerably less than 10 percent of the purchase price.[61]

Recently, the auto industry has been victorious in getting the fuel-economy requirements relaxed. GM and Ford did not meet the 1985 standard of a 27.5 mpg average and were successful in having the 1986 standard decreased to 26 mpg. In September 1986, GM and Ford again argued that they could not meet the 27.5 mpg level for 1987 and 1988 model-year cars without cutting thousands of jobs. GM estimated that meeting the standards would result in a loss of at least one million new car sales, forcing it to lay off 250,000 employees. Consequently, over NHTSA's objections, the DOT again eased the standard to 26 mpg for the industry. The decision met considerable criticism from energy-conservation groups and from Chrysler, which had spent billions of dollars in an effort to meet the original standards. The DOT decision allowed the lowest level of standards that did not require congressional approval, but was consistent with earlier Reagan administration actions to weaken the fuel-economy standards for particular model years.[62]

The Quest to Expand Deregulation

The auto industry has long resisted regulatory controls. In the late 1970s, its cries for regulatory relief intensified as the economy suffered from two shocks. First, in the spring of 1979, the Iranian oil embargo led to a doubling in the price of oil and an increase of about 50 percent in the price of gasoline.[63] Sales by U.S. auto companies dropped 15.5 percent as a result of increases in gasoline prices.[64] The second shock came when the economy was hit with a recession that began in February 1980.[65] Automobiles, like most other durable goods, are highly sensitive to economic downturns.[66] When times are tough, one of the first "big-ticket" items that a consumer postpones is the purchase of a new car. With the increase in gas prices, consumer preference shifted strongly toward smaller cars. Domestic manufacturers, tooled up to produce larger cars, could not meet demand for smaller cars. And many customers who did want the larger, domestically produced cars could not afford them. As a consequence, auto industry sales showed a precipitous decline, and imports took a greater share of the U.S. market (see Figure 7-2). By the end of 1980, U.S. auto firms had lost more than $4 billion.[67] More than 300,000 auto workers were indefinitely laid off, and twice that many were unemployed in supplier industries.[68]

The conventional explanation of these developments faults Detroit for its lower auto sales. Because the industry stressed large car production, it was unable to adapt to a changing market. This view is summed up by William Tucker, who argues that the automakers insisted on making large cars in search of equally large profit margins. Unaffected by unstable oil supplies, the auto companies "went on churning out the same old monstrosities as if all the gas pumps in the nation were plugged into a bottomless oil well. The motivation, of course, was obvious—profits. Detroit . . . made big profits on big cars and small profits on small cars."[69] Clearly, the industry believed that a minimum of regulation would allow the automakers maximum independence in choosing the production schemes most comfortable to them.

But an alternate explanation for the industry's decline faults the government. The Energy Policy and Conservation Act of 1975 was Congress's response to the energy crisis of 1973–1974. In addition to establishing fuel-efficiency standards, the act restored price controls for domestic oil. According to William Niskanen, this "prevented the U.S. price of gasoline from increasing to a level based on the world oil price. Thus Congress simultaneously reduced the market demand for fuel economy and mandated the production of more fuel efficient new vehicles."[70]

The net effect encouraged new car buyers to return to larger cars. The only compelling motive for buying smaller cars, it appears, was rising gasoline prices. With more stable prices, patriotic appeals to save energy fell on deaf ears. As former transportation secretary Neil Goldschmidt

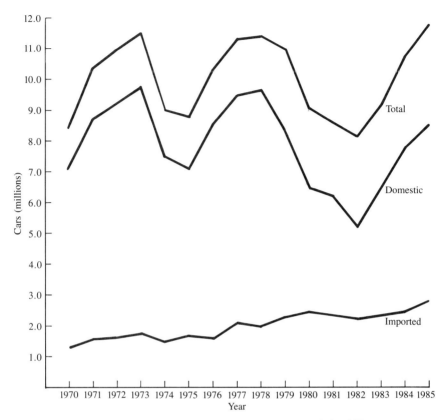

Figure 7-2.   U.S. retail passenger car sales, 1970–1985
Source: *MVMA Facts and Figures, 1983*, p. 18; *1985*, pp. 14–15

stated, "[b]ecause the political courage to deregulate the price of oil was not present in 1975, the U.S. government allowed the nation to go from importing one-third of its oil to nearly half, and the opportunity to make a gradual shift of the nation's automotive fleet from larger to smaller cars was lost."[71]

Although Detroit mostly produced large cars in the 1970s, in large part it was merely meeting public demand. It takes years to design and produce a new car line, and as consumer demand shifted to smaller cars in 1979 when gas prices increased, the auto industry was incapable of meeting the public need. If Congress had allowed gasoline prices to rise to true market levels, the industry might have better responded to changing circumstances.

Regulations save lives and dollars, but they are not without cost. When so many workers in the auto and related industries were out of work and the auto manufacturers were losing billions of dollars, the industry found its arguments to lessen regulation much better received. It was not so much any one rule but rather the combination of sometimes conflicting regulations that gave the industry its best argument in the fight for deregulation.

Many of the auto industry's problems were feverishly debated during the 1980 election campaign. Regulated in three areas (safety, fuel economy, and emissions) by two agencies (NHTSA and EPA), the industry justifiably argued that these regulations were often contradictory; moreover, they sometimes worked at cross-purposes and suffered from a lack of coordination. Thus, according to Lester Lave, "the law to control emissions also reduced the fuel efficiency by 7.5 percent, and a fuel efficiency law that has forced the building of smaller cars is estimated to reduce safety by resulting in an additional 1400 fatalities a year by 1984."[72] These results irritated people both in and out of the industry.

The conflicting nature of federal regulations and the high costs these standards imposed drove Detroit to seek regulatory relief. The industry's plea came at a time when it needed large amounts of capital to retool production lines in order to build the smaller, more fuel-efficient cars; but simultaneously, they faced their greatest financial losses since the depression. These conditions ensured that the industry had a sympathetic ear in the newly elected Ronald Reagan.

The Reagan Administration: Deregulation in High Gear

Ronald Reagan ran for the presidency on a pledge to deregulate society wherever possible in order to get government off the people's back. As a conservative Republican, Reagan strongly believed that the federal regulatory apparatus was choking American businesses, and at the time of his election, the U.S. economy was in the middle of a severe recession. The auto industry in particular was in dire straits.

Reagan's position on federal regulation and the auto industry was clearly stated during his campaign: "The U.S. auto industry is virtually being regulated to death. . . . It simply needs the freedom to compete, unhindered by whimsical bureaucratic changes in energy, environmental, and safety regulations."[73] Reagan told audiences in Detroit, "Federal regulations are the cause of all your problems."[74] He asked them to "vote for a presidential candidate who will close down the federal auto safety program."[75] Shortly after he assumed office, President Reagan set out to fulfill his campaign promise to reduce federal regulation. On January 29, 1981, eight days after his inauguration, the president directed all executive agencies to postpone any pending regulations (see chapter 3). The postponements were fixed in an executive order in February. The purpose of both moves was to allow for a reassessment and the possible rescission of federal regulations.[76]

The administration's views on regulation in general, and auto industry regulation in particular, were expressed by Reagan's Secretary of Transportation, Drew Lewis: "If I could do it, there would be a four-year moratorium (on new regulations). I know four years is unrealistic, but my point is that this administration opposes regulations."[77] But the new administration made good on its word. In April 1981, the administration announced a wide-ranging series of "relief measures" for the auto industry, claiming that the efforts would put 200,000 unemployed auto workers back to work within eighteen months. Key promises included "the relaxation of [thirty-four] environmental and safety regulations . . . intended to save consumers $9.3 billion during the next five years and the auto industry $1.4 billion while Detroit engages in a $70 billion retooling effort to make smaller cars and put itself in a better competitive situation with Japan."[78]

The auto industry greeted the administration's deregulatory efforts with great enthusiasm. According to Betsy Ancker–Johnson, GM vice-president for environmental affairs, comparing the Carter and Reagan administrations was "like the difference between night and day."[79] With Reagan, the auto industry felt it finally had a true friend in the White House.

Given Reagan's antiregulatory philosophy, industry officials thought that a golden opportunity existed to eliminate what they considered unnecessary and costly regulations.[80] Robert Simison of the *Wall Street Journal* reported that "some auto officials are determined to seek nothing less than a reversal of what W. Paul Tippett, Jr., the president of American Motors Corp., calls 'a disastrous period' of 'unrelenting warfare on the automobile.' "[81]

But not everyone shared this view. For example, the environmental group Friends of the Earth ridiculed Reagan's "regulatory reform" as little more than a shifting of power from the public to private sectors. Industry's increased influence in government decision meant "delayed action on many rules that are essential to protect the environment, health and safety, and increased emphasis on reducing costs to industry even where the result is increased risk for the public."[82]

In addition to a regulatory rollback, Detroit wanted the Reagan administration to provide the industry with favorable tax treatment and import quotas. One *Fortune* magazine account suggested that the industry needed a three-year freeze on Japanese imports in order to increase productivity, reduce costs, and adjust to the small-car market.[83]

It is important to understand that Detroit was not opposed to *all* governmental regulation; rather, it wanted the government to eliminate regulations that cost the industry money and to issue regulations that would protect it from foreign competition. But consistent with its philosophy of decreasing governmental intervention in the marketplace, the Reagan administration was reluctant to institute import quotas. The auto industry was helped, however, by a voluntary agreement to limit Japanese imports. The Japanese Ministry of International Trade (MITI), recognizing the U.S. automakers' plight and fearing the imposition of harsher protectionist measures, agreed to hold imports to 1.65 million cars a year or about 20 percent of the U.S. market. The voluntary restraint was extended in 1985, although increased to 1.85 million Japanese cars.[84] Since then, while exporting more vehicles, the Japanese have been careful not to overload the American market. Their concern has been largely because of the huge U.S. trade deficit and the danger that protectionist pressures would be renewed by displaced American auto workers.

According to the Department of Commerce, the auto industry spent $2.8 billion on safety and pollution controls in 1981, but the Reagan regulatory rollback saved the industry approximately $1.1 billion.[85] Although the auto industry gratefully accepted these savings, they were insufficient to significantly affect the industry's financial problems. Michael Wines of the *National Journal* reports that automakers "(do not) see much evidence that regulatory relief has given their industry a hoped-for economic boost. While deregulation has saved some money, the savings are minuscule compared with the $60 billion that [automakers] must raise for modernization and other capital needs in the next five years."[86]

Well into the Reagan administration, industry leaders concluded that deregulation is not a panacea for their problems. Former Secretary of Transportation Drew Lewis pointed out that "[w]hat we really need, is less inflation and lower interest rates. And until we reach those points, neither the automotive industry nor the economy in general will really be vibrant."[87]

As the economy improved in 1983 and 1984, so did the health of the auto industry. It remains to be seen if the industry has used the economic expansion to make needed changes both to better weather future economic downturns and to match the challenge from foreign competitors. In 1986, U.S. auto makers sold an estimated 8.4 million vehicles, up from 5.7 million in 1982. But despite Detroit's spending at least $40 billion to build state-of-the-art automated plants, the Japanese can still manufacture cars for much less. In 1979, the Japanese could build and ship a car to the United States for $1,500 less than it cost Detroit to build a similar car; in 1986, that gap had *increased* to $1,900.[88]

The Rescission of FMVSS 208

At the time Reagan took office, FMVSS 208 required passive restraints on all full-sized cars beginning September 1, 1981, all mid-sized cars beginning September 1, 1982, and all small cars beginning September 1, 1983.[89] But in February 1981, Secretary Lewis proposed to delay the standard's effective date for one year. Lewis pointed to the "difficulties of the automobile industry," citing a "very depressed level" of sales and losses "by even the largest of the domestic manufacturers."[90] Two months later, NHTSA delayed the passive-protection requirement for one year and proposed to eliminate it entirely. The White House announced both decisions in April, along with other proposed actions targeted to provide economic relief to the troubled industry.[91]

In October 1981, NHTSA amended FMVSS 208 by rescinding the passive-restraint requirement.[92] Although NHTSA cited concern over the cost of passive restraints and uncertainty over public acceptance, the requirement was principally voided because of agency concern about the ways that the automakers planned to meet the standard. The agency gave three justifications for its decision. First, it predicted that most car makers would meet the standard by installing detachable passive seatbelts rather than install air bags. Second, NHTSA argued that passive belts were functionally equivalent to the active belts already required. And third, it concluded that most people would simply disconnect the passive belts. Therefore, the benefits from implementation of the standard would fail to meet or exceed the costs.[93]

The decision to rescind the passive-restraint requirement provoked considerable controversy. Sen. John Danforth (R.–Mo.), chair of the surface transportation subcommittee, submitted a bill to force NHTSA to reinstate the standard.[94] In addition, the State Farm Mutual Automobile Insurance Co. sued the DOT and NHTSA in federal court under provisions of the 1946 Administrative Procedures Act to overturn the DOT's rescission. Even senior NHTSA staff members and aides to administrator Raymond Peck disagreed with the decision. Peck admitted that "there is great disappointment, great frustration, and great chagrin (among his aides). I don't think anyone on my staff agreed with all aspects of this decision."[95]

But the issue did not die there. In June 1982, in *State Farm Mutual* v. *DOT,* Judge Abner Mikva, writing for the U.S. Court of Appeals for the District of Columbia, held that NHTSA's decision was arbitrary and illogical for two reasons: First, the agency had offered no hard evidence in insisting that the standard was unjustified; second, it had failed to consider alternatives to the standard's elimination. Thus, concluded Judge Mikva, "[w]hen the agency so narrows its options that it fails to heed the goals that Congress has asked it to meet, the agency violates its basic legislative mandate. Simply put, NHTSA's discussion of ways in which Modified Standard 208 could have been amended was wholly inadequate, and rescission was therefore arbitrary and unlawful."[96]

In *State Farm,* the appellate court further delineated the flaws in NHTSA's decision. To begin with, NHTSA focused on the needs of "the economically depressed automobile industry—which is not the agency's mandate—at the expense of traffic safety, which is."[97] The agency's regulatory impact analysis had neglected or completely omitted the most logical amendments to Modified Standard 208. Two options—not allowing compliance with detachable belts or allowing compliance only with air bags—were never fully analyzed. "Absolutely no effort was made to compare the costs of airbags against their potential benefits," according to the court.[98] Although holding that NHTSA's decision was arbitrary and unlawful, the court did not require the imposition of either nondetachable passive seatbelts or airbags. Instead, it held that the final decision was up to the NHTSA; in fact, NHTSA could once again rescind the passive requirement, but it could only do so if it found nonarbitrary reasons to support its judgment.[99]

The Motor Vehicle Manufacturers Association of the United States appealed the *State Farm* decision to the U.S. Supreme Court. In June 1983, the higher court vacated the Court of Appeals' decision.[100] The Supreme Court agreed that NHTSA's decision had been arbitrary and capricious, but stated that the Court of Appeals had used an improper degree of review. In *State Farm*, the parties disagreed over the intensity with which the arbitrary and capricious test of the Administrative Procedures Act could be applied. The Court of Appeals had decided that regulatory agencies were under a heavier burden to justify the revocation of a standard than they were to impose a standard in the first place. The Supreme Court disagreed, holding that the justification in either case should meet the same standard of review. NHTSA was forced to reconsider its decision. After more than a year of additional delay, a new standard was issued.

The current passive-restraint standard was issued by NHTSA in July 1984. The agency decided to require "the installation of automatic restraints in all new cars beginning with model year 1990 (September 1, 1989) unless, prior to that time, state mandatory belt usage laws are enacted that cover at least two-thirds of the U.S. population."[101] In effect, NHTSA abandoned the air-bag approach as long as the country accepted seat belts on a widespread basis.

NHTSA's decision, announced by administrator Diane Steed, met with mixed reactions. The auto industry was disappointed. They had "strongly objected" to this alternative since they would be forced to plan and invest for a device that might not be required.[102] At the same time, however, the industry had received an additional three-year delay, and if enough states passed mandatory seatbelt laws, the specter of passive restraints would end.

Consumer advocates' reactions to the new regulation were mixed; some were happy that the standard was still alive, but others were upset that automakers had received yet another delay. Senator Danforth, who had accused a Reagan-appointed NHTSA administrator of seeking to cripple auto safety, expressed pleasant surprise at the decision to require future safety regulation. But Rep. John Dingell (D.–Mich.), chair of the energy and commerce committee, vowed to press on with the fight to permanently remove the air bag as a safety requirement. He called the device "overly costly and inadequately effective." Air-bag advocates, however, condemned the regulation. Joan Claybrook, head of NHTSA under Jimmy Carter, said the decision "assures another long delay before the public is able to buy air bags." Ralph Nader further characterized the rule as "a snare and a delusion" that would "gladden the evil hearts of the executives of General Motors."[103]

Air Bags: Deflated or Derailed?

Whether automatic restraints, air bags, or passive seatbelts will be mandated in the future is unclear. Some observers doubt that NHTSA's required two-thirds of the population can be covered by mandatory seatbelt-use laws by April 1, 1989, the deadline imposed by NHTSA. But as of this writing, twenty-seven states and the District of Columbia had passed mandatory seatbelt laws. The seatbelt laws for California and the District of Columbia, however, do not count in the total because their laws were intentionally written by their legislators to "self-destruct" if NHTSA were to use their populations in meeting the two-thirds goal. This leaves twenty-six states covering approximately 60 percent of the population, very close to the two-thirds target.[104]

Even though many states have passed mandatory-use laws, it is highly questionable whether any (other than New York's, which was grandfathered in by the NHTSA decision) can be counted since the laws often fail to meet all of NHTSA's qualifying criteria. Many states, for example, do not even levy a minimum $25 fine or allow for enforcement of their laws; other states exempt too many people from having to wear the belts. In yet another court case over the validity of NHTSA's decision to back down from mandatory airbags, the U.S. Court of Appeals for the District of Columbia in September 1986, declared that "none of these laws, however, apparently complies with the [DOT] Secretary's specific requirements."[105] Although it appears that airbags may finally be required, long-time auto-safety observers indicate that the decision may once again end up in the courts and that they will wait and see if all three U.S. auto manufacturers actually begin to manufacture autos with passive restraints.

Auto Safety and Theories of Regulation

The initiation of federal regulation of automobile safety quite clearly adheres to the public-interest theory of regulation. Under the prodding of outspoken private citizens and concerned legislators, government enacted the National Traffic and Motor Vehicle Safety Act of 1966 in an effort to lessen the tragic loss of human life from automobile accidents. The inability of the market to provide safer vehicles was demonstrated not only by the daily highway carnage but also by auto-industry actions and statements that placed the blame on drivers. The auto industry did not seek, as capture theory holds, safety regulation in an effort to stabilize its market, increase profits, or preempt state regulatory efforts, for the industry has been consistently and historically hostile to federal safety initiatives.

Over time, auto-safety regulation has begun to take on characteristics of the bureaucratic model. Following the mandate to issue standards meeting the need for motor-vehicle safety, NHTSA regulators and staff have almost always strongly favored auto regulation. Although the heads of DOT and NHTSA have sometimes tried to lessen automobile regulation, the agencies themselves have continued their efforts to increase auto safety. These agencies have exhibited at least some continuity from administration to administration; in part, this explains why the Reagan administration has not had more success in deregulating the auto industry.

Looking to the Future

In 1983, the automobile industry rebounded with multibillion-dollar profits. One account reported that Chrysler's profit of $701 million that year represented a four-fold increase over 1982. GM's profit of $3.7 billion was the company's best showing since 1978. Even Ford, which lost $658 million in 1982 despite protection from imports, earned $1.9 billion one year later.[106] Good times continued in 1984 with $7.7 billion in profits from the first three quarters of 1984—almost double the three-quarter total from 1983; and 1985 profits were at $7.6 billion.[107] Short-term profits, however, do not necessarily mean long-term health. In fact, analysts are concerned that the United States is entering a period of marginal sales growth. Increased operating costs and an ever-widening gap between new car prices and available incomes are likely to lead to a permanent change in buying habits, with consumers holding onto their used cars for longer periods of time.[108] Given these considerations, auto-industry pressures to roll back regulatory requirements will continue as shown by the 1986 fuel-standard rollback, which only required the automakers to maintain 1987 standards for 1988 models.

How much has the auto industry benefited under the Reagan administration? A quick review indicates that the flow of new regulations slowed to a trickle and other proposed rules were delayed. The regulation that remains, however, continues as a hodgepodge of inconsistent measures; safety, fuel-economy, and emission standards still lack coordination. Deregulation has only meant fewer new regulations, not fewer agencies issuing rules. The agencies' mandates have not changed; they are simply interpreting their goals differently. Even with the Reagan administration's commitment to relieve the regulatory burden on the auto industry, other players in the game—Congress, the courts, and career agency staffers—have often acted to counter the administration's efforts. If a less sympathetic administration is elected in 1988, in all likelihood the system to increase regulation will still be in place. But a "system in place" may not be enough. Given the unlikelihood of the April 1989 deadline being met, the Department of Transportation, prodded by the auto industry, has once again proposed an additional four-year delay, making 1993 the deadline year.[109]

Notes

1. Motor Vehicle Manufacturers Association, *MVMA Motor Vehicle Facts and Figures, 1983* (Detroit, Mich.: MVMA, 1983), p. 4.
2. Philip Caldwell, "The Automobile Crisis and Public Policy," *Harvard Business Review,* 59 (January/February 1981): 78.
3. Newspaper Enterprise Association, *The World Almanac and Book of Facts, 1983* (New York: NEA, 1982), pp. 497–581.
4. National Safety Council, *Accident Facts: 1987 Preliminary Condensed Edition,* 1987.
5. Insurance Institute for Highway Safety, *Policy Options for Reducing the Motor Vehicle Crash Injury Cost Burden* (Washington, D.C.: IIHS, May 1981), p. 1.
6. Joan Claybrook, *Retreat from Safety* (New York: Pantheon, 1984), p. 178.
7. Gladys Kaufman and Barbara Bilge, "Effects of Automobile Accidents upon American Families," prepared for NHTSA, Department of Transportation, Report no. DTNH 22-80-C-07695, August 1982, in Claybrook, *Retreat from Safety,* p. 179.
8. Jeffrey O'Connell and Arthur Myers, *Safety Last* (New York: Random House, 1966), p. 6.
9. Howard Bunch and Michael Kubacki, *An Analysis of Industry Responses to Federal Regulations in Safety Requirements for New Automobiles,* prepared for NHTSA, Department of Transportation, Report nos. DOT-TSC-NHTSA-78-26/HS 803 369, September 1978, pp. 6–7.
10. *Ibid.*
11. William Niskanen, "Interactive Effects: Toward an Automobile Industry Policy," in *Reforming Social Regulation,* eds. LeRoy Graymer and Frederick Thompson (Beverly Hills, Calif.: Sage Publications, 1982), p. 76.
12. Lester Lave, "Conflicting Objectives in Regulating the Automobile," *Science,* 212 (May 22, 1981): 894.
13. O'Connell and Myers, *Safety Last,* p. 5.
14. Bunch and Kubacki, *An Analysis,* p. 7.
15. Sen. Robert Kennedy, U.S. Senate Committee on Commerce, Science, and Transportation hearings, March 30, 1966, p. 208.
16. Ralph Nader, *Unsafe at Any Speed* (New York: Grossman, 1972).
17. As quoted in testimony by Clarence Ditlow, U.S. House of Representatives, Committee on Energy and Commerce, Subcommittee on Telecommunications, Consumer Protection, and Finance, *National Highway Traffic Safety Administration Oversight and Authorization,* 97th Congress, 2d Session, March 23, 1982, p. 187.
18. Automobile Manufacturers Association Safety Administrative Committee, U.S. Senate Committee on Commerce hearings, April 4, 1966, pp. 381–382.

19. *The Competitive Structure of the U.S. Auto Industry,* 1982, p. 80.
20. *49 Federal Register 28964,* July 17, 1984.
21. *15 U.S.C. Sec. 1392(a)* cited in *State Farm Mutual Automobile Insurance Co.* v. *Department of Transportation,* 680 F.2d 206, 209 (1982).
22. *15 U.S.C. Sec. 1392(f) (1), (3), (4),* cited in *State Farm,* 1982, p. 209.
23. Summary, "The Cost of Automobile Safety Regulations," NHTSA, Department of Transportation, March 1982, p. 1, cited in Claybrook, *Retreat,* pp. 167, 182.
24. Claybrook, *Retreat,* p. 182.
25. *Ibid.*
26. Ralph Nader, "Stenographic Transcript of NHTSA Hearings on Occupant Crash Protection," May 23, 1973, pp. S-144, S-145, quoted in "1977 National Debate Tournament Final Debate," *Journal of the American Forensic Association,* 14, no. 1 (Summer 1977): 22.
27. Jonathan Rauch, "Fasten Your Seatbelts—There Is Turbulence Ahead on the Safety Front," *National Journal,* June 27, 1981, p. 1159.
28. "The Reluctant Dragon," *Consumer Reports,* April 1969, quoted in U.S. Senate Committee on Commerce hearings, April 18, 1969, p. 252.
29. *32 Federal Register 2415,* February 3, 1967.
30. Rauch, "Fasten Your Seatbelts," p. 1159.
31. Ralph Nader, U.S. Senate Committee on Commerce hearings, *The Passive Restraint Decision by the U.S. Department of Transportation,* September 9, 1977, p. 294.
32. *State Farm* v. *DOT.*
33. A. R. Boe, letter, in U.S. Senate Committee on Commerce hearings, September 9, 1977, p. 304.
34. *Ibid.,* IIHS attachment 4, p. 153.
35. *Ibid.*
36. Benjamin Kelly, statement before NHTSA public meeting on FMVSS 208, May 19, 1975, reprinted in U.S. Senate Committee on Commerce hearings, September 9, 1977, p. 158.
37. William Haddon, U.S. Senate Committee on Commerce hearings, September 9, 1977, p. 139.
38. William Lawrence, "The Economic Impact of Air Bags," *American University Law Review,* Winter 1976, p. 374, fn. 18.
39. *Federal Register,* July 1984, p. 28983.
40. Helen Kahn, "Tape Tells of Ford Pitch to Nixon," *Automotive News,* December 6, 1982, p. 2.
41. Ralph Nader, "Washington Under the Influence: A Ten Year Review of Auto Safety Amidst Industrial Opposition," *Federal Consumer Product Safety Service Special Report #106,* April 1976, p. 2.
42. Kahn, "Tape Tells," p. 2.
43. John Bredell, "Seat Belts Anyone? Department of Transportation Attempts to 'Unbuckle' the Auto Industry from Passive Restraint Requirements: State Farm v. Department of Transportation," *University of Toledo Law Review,* 14 (Spring 1982): 1099–1101.
44. *Ibid.*
45. *32 Federal Register,* July 17, 1984, p. 28965.
46. Albert Karr, "Saga of the Air Bag, or the Slow Deflation of a Car-Safety Idea," *Wall Street Journal,* reprinted in U.S. Senate Committee on Commerce hearings, September 9, 1977, p. 160.
47. *Ibid.,* p. 161.
48. *Automotive News,* December 19, 1983, p. 7.
49. Nader, "Washington Under the Influence," pp. 24–25.
50. Karr, "Saga of the Air Bag," *Wall Street Journal,* September 17, 1974.

51. Insurance Institute for Highway Safety (IIHS), *Status Report,* August 16, 1974.
52. IIHS, *Status Report,* September 27, 1974.
53. IIHS, *Status Report,* February 3, 1977, p. 1.
54. IIHS, *Status Report,* July 26, 1977.
55. Center for Auto Safety, *House Hearings,* September 12, 1977, p. 270.
56. 680 F.2d 206, 223–224 (1982).
57. 680 F.2d 206, 212 (1982).
58. Automotive Panel, Committee on Technology and International Economic and Trade Issues of the Office of the Foreign Secretary, National Academy of Engineering and the Commission on Engineering and Technical Systems, National Research Council, *The Competitive Status of the U.S. Auto Industry: A Study of the Influences of Technology in Determining International Industrial Competitive Advantage,* 1982, p. 81.
59. *Ibid.*
60. Peter Behr, "Administration to Revise Auto Standards," *Washington Post,* April 5, 1981, p. A1.
61. Niskanen, "Interactive Effects," p. 74.
62. "Fuel Economy Standards Cut by U.S. to Save Auto Jobs," *San Francisco Chronicle,* Oct. 2, 1986, p. 22; "G.M. Asks U.S. to Ease Fuel Economy Standards," *New York Times,* Sept. 9, 1986, p. 13; "Car Fuel Economy Standard Said to Ease for Next Two Years," *New York Times,* Oct. 1, 1986, p. 18.
63. *Ibid.*
64. *Ibid.*
65. *Ibid.*
66. Jose A. Gomez–Ibanez and David Harrison, Jr., "Imports and the Future of the U.S. Auto Industry," *American Economic Review,* 72, no. 2 (May 1982): 319.
67. Niskanen, "Interactive Effects," p. 71.
68. Clyde Farnsworth, "Carter Acts to Speed Car-Import Study," *New York Times,* July 9, 1980, p. D4.
69. William Tucker, "The Wreck of the Auto Industry," *Harpers,* November 1980, p. 2.
70. Niskanen, "Interactive Effects," p. 78.
71. Tucker, "The Wreck," p. 3.
72. Lave, "Conflicting Objectives," p. 893.
73. Claybrook, *Retreat,* p. 173.
74. Bredell, "Seat Belts Anyone?" p. 1108.
75. *Ibid.*
76. *Ibid.*
77. Claybrook, *Retreat,* p. 180.
78. Jane Seaberry, "Auto Industry Relief Plan Outlined by White House," *New York Times,* April 7, 1981, p. A1.
79. Robert Simison, "Rollback Time? Auto Companies Press for More Deregulation in Safety and Pollution," *Wall Street Journal,* August 14, 1981, p. 1.
80. *Ibid.*
81. *Ibid.*
82. Bredell, "Seat Belts Anyone?" p. 1134.
83. Anne B. Fisher, "Can Detroit Live Without Quotas?" *Fortune,* 109, no. 13 (June 25, 1984): 20.
84. *Ibid.*
85. Michael Wines, "Reagan Plan to Relieve Auto Industry of Regulatory Burden Gets Mixed Grades," *National Journal,* 15, no. 30 (July 23, 1983): 1533.
86. *Ibid.,* p. 1532.
87. *Ibid.,* p. 1533.

88. "Detroit Stumbles on Its Way to the Future," *Business Week,* no. 2951 (June 16, 1986): 103.

89. IIHS, "Lewis Asks Delay in Automatic Restraints," *Status Report,* 16, no. 3 (February 25, 1981): 1.

90. *State Farm* v. *DOT,* p. 213.

91. *Ibid.*

92. *46 Federal Register 53,* 419 (October 29, 1981).

93. *State Farm* v. *DOT,* pp. 216–217.

94. IIHS, "NHTSA Abandons Automatic Restraint Standard," *Status Report,* 16, no. 17 (November 15, 1981): 1.

95. *Ibid.,* p. 2.

96. *State Farm* v. *DOT,* p. 230.

97. *Ibid.,* p. 240.

98. *Ibid.,* p. 233.

99. *Ibid.*

100. *Motor Vehicle Manufacturers Association of the United States* v. *State Farm Mutual Automobile Insurance Co.,* 103 S.Ct. 2856 (1983).

101. *49 Federal Register,* July 17, 1984, p. 28962.

102. *Ibid.,* p. 28978.

103. Stephen Gettinger, "DOT Rule May Shift Air-Bag Battle to States," *Congressional Quarterly Weekly Report,* 42, no. 128 (July 14, 1978): 1708.

104. Conversation with Michelle Field, IIHS, November 5, 1986.

105. *Ibid.*

106. Fisher, "Can Detroit Live?" p. 20.

107. *San Francisco Chronicle,* October 27, 1984, p. 50. MVMA, *Motor Vehicle Facts and Figures, 1985* (Detroit, Mich.: MVMA, 1985), p. 62.

108. *Wall Street Journal,* May 3, 1984, p. 18.

109. "Buckle or Bag?" *The Economist,* December 6, 1986, p. 28.

CHAPTER 8

Occupational
Safety and Health

The issue of health and safety in the workplace has been a long-standing item on the public agenda. Despite considerable attention, however, reformers have found it difficult to gain public support for governmental oversight. As a former AFL–CIO official described the issue at a congressional hearing, "[o]ccupational health and safety always has been the illegitimate child at the family reunion. No one gives a damn. If twenty-three people get swine flu, the whole government is turned upside down, but you can have carnage in the workplace and no one cares."[1] When it comes to worker safety, the implied assumption seems to be "let the worker beware."

The United States owes much of its high standard of living to the industrial expansion since the late 1800s. Hand in hand with the development of new industries, chemicals, and means of production have come increasing numbers of worker fatalities and injuries. The accident toll in the workplace is nothing less than staggering. For example, 292,000 servicemen died in battle during World War II, but more than 300,000 workers died in industrial accidents during the same period. And more than three times as many workers lost arms or legs as did soldiers.[2]

Today, workers are protected under the 1970 federal Occupational Safety and Health Act.[3] The act established the Occupational Safety and Health Administration (OSHA) within the Department of Labor to develop and enforce safety and health standards.

OSHA was created during a period of intense social-regulatory activity that witnessed the birth of many federal regulatory agencies. The organization, however, encountered criticism from its inception, despite the proregulatory atmosphere of the time and the clear need to do something about injury and death in the workplace.

Long mired in controversy, OSHA's story is that of an agency that has never been provided with the proper resources to accomplish its near impossible mandate: "[T]o assure so far as possible every working man and woman in the Nation safe and healthful working conditions."[4] Business and labor, adversaries in almost every other arena, agree that OSHA has been one of the federal government's most mismanaged and ineffectual agencies. OSHA provides an excellent study of how an agency reacts to deregulatory pressures, how deregulatory goals can be accomplished internally by an agency through administrative changes, and how society must make fundamental decisions about the value it places on the sometimes competing objectives of human safety and industrial–economic health.

Pre–OSHA Worker-Safety Legislation

Prior to the 1970s, protection of workers had largely been considered a state responsibility. Massachusetts was the first state to respond to occupational injuries. In 1867, the state established the Department of Factory

Inspection to deal with job safety; ten years later, the state enacted the first worker-safety law to require protective guards around spinning machinery in textile plants.[5] Other states soon followed with similar preventive-safety laws, but little attention was given workers once they had been injured. Although an employee could sue his or her employer for negligence, the chances of success were small because of the many common-law defenses. For example, one defense—assumption of risk—contended that by accepting a job, a worker also accepted the risks connected with it. This reasoning often prevailed in many suits.

In 1911, New Jersey became the first state to pass a worker's compensation law. The legislation offered employees money for certain injuries suffered on the job. This opened the floodgates, and by 1920, forty states had similar legislation.[6]

Although the states had recognized the issue of worker safety, their efforts to decrease worker injuries were largely unsuccessful. Although some of the major industrial states, including New York and California, had adequate job-safety laws, most were known for combinations of policies that included limited coverage, poor enforcement, and poor funding. As with other matters left to state jurisdiction, responses to these problems varied greatly. If a given industry felt hampered by a state's actions, its factories were simply relocated in a "friendlier" state.[7] The ramifications for employment patterns, taxes, and other policy areas were endless and unpredictable.

Competition was a cornerstone of American economic growth during the first half of the 20th century. Yet, market forces alone clearly would not provide safe workplaces. The demand for a comprehensive national law to establish and enforce worker safety and health standards followed partly from the inability (and in some cases, unwillingness) of industry to voluntarily adopt protective measures. Before OSHA was established, few workers were told about exposure to dangerous chemicals, the aftereffects associated with exposure, or how to protect themselves. Examples of such disregard for worker health are easily found. In the case of asbestos, "companies ignored studies made as early as 1933 that linked asbestos to chronic lung disease, and now the federal government estimates that 10 [percent] to 15 [percent] of all cancer deaths over the next [twenty-five] years will be related to asbestos."[8] The cumulative impact of unsafe working conditions has been almost impossible to estimate.

The issue of worker safety seems to be related to the age-old issue of costs versus benefits. Although some employers are generally willing to remove obvious hazards, they are not likely to go out of their way to voluntarily provide a healthy work environment if the costs are substantial. Paying for a safer work environment would necessitate higher-priced products; unless all companies uniformly adopted health and safety standards, those initiating such actions would be at a competitive disadvantage in the marketplace. Historically, too, it has been almost impossible to sue an employer for negligence; consequently, a firm has had little incentive to go beyond a minimum effort in providing a safe workplace. Ironically, worker-compensation laws, while providing relief to workers injured in job-related accidents, have limited employer liability to those few financial benefits that have been provided by law.

Prior to OSHA, business was not alone in its preference for the status quo. Labor was slow to press for health and safety initiatives. Even though they might desire a safe working environment for their members, unions have traditionally given higher priorities to wages and benefits when negotiating with management. During hearings on the Occupational Safety and Health Act, conservatives delighted in pressing labor leaders to explain why they had not demanded improvements when bargaining if workplace conditions were so deplorable.

Although the federal government had offered piecemeal legislation to cover coal-mine and railroad safety in the late 1800s, significant federal involvement was not seen until 1936 when Congress passed the Walsh–Healy Act. The impact of the act was limited, however, because it only included certain workplace hazards (e.g., noise, gas, chemicals), and coverage was restricted to those companies engaged in federal contract work. Yet even with these major limitations, the law was largely unenforced.[9] By the late 1960s, the Walsh–Healy Act, combined with several other narrowly drawn federal laws, provided minimal coverage for more than 25 million workers. Nevertheless, the workplace remained dangerous for many Americans. A 1967 U.S. Surgeon General's report concluded that although 65 percent of the workers in industrial plants were exposed to harmful chemicals, only 25 percent were adequately protected.[10] By this time, the stage was set for a comprehensive federal effort to decrease worker deaths and injuries.

The 1970 Occupational Safety and Health Act

Three factors led to pressure for passage of the 1970 Occupational Safety and Health Act. First, the number of worker injuries and fatalities had grown significantly during the 1960s. According to the National Safety Council, the number of injured workers increased 29 percent from 1961 to 1970. In 1970 alone, there were 2.2 million disabling injuries and more than 14,000 deaths from workplace accidents.[11] Additionally, government sources estimated there were as many as 100,000 deaths annually from occupational diseases, including workplace-induced heart disease and cancer.[12] Several major coal-mining disasters helped to accent the problems of worker safety, the most notorious occurring with the Farmington, West Virginia, explosion in November 1968, in which seventy-eight miners died. According to a subsequent study by the Ford Foundation, "the coal mine legislation and the congressional momentum thus generated helped pave the way for job health and safety legislation applicable to the rest of American industry."[13] Tragedies such as that at Farmington seemed to haunt the nation's conscience.

Increased activism by rank-and-file workers became the second factor that led to the enactment of OSHA. In his study of the act's origins, Patrick Donnelly argues that "the roots of the law can be traced to the rebellion of the rank-and-file workers across the United States. . . . Wildcat strikes, walkouts, rejected contracts, and violent confrontations expressed rank-and-file dissatisfaction with existing safety and health conditions."[14] This widespread protest was not limited to employers; it was also directed at union officials who paid little attention to health and safety issues when negotiating contracts.[15]

Political expediency was the third factor leading to passage of the 1970 act. On January 23, 1968, President Johnson told Congress of his intention to make the protection of American workers a national goal. The next day, an administration-sponsored occupational-safety-and-health proposal was introduced in Congress. Donnelly notes that "[t]he legislation was drafted and introduced at a time when the political support of rank-and-file workers was desperately needed by the incumbent president."[16] Unrelated political events, however, led to the bill's demise. With Johnson's withdrawal from the 1968 presidential election, the bill never reached the floor of either the House or Senate.

In 1969, Democrats reintroduced the worker-safety bill. The new Republican administration under Richard Nixon, however, introduced a bill of its own. A public-interest-group study under the direction of Ralph Nader suggested that the White House regarded a Republican occupational-safety-and-health law as necessary to demonstrate concern for "the silent majority" and "hard hats." In a period when many Republicans looked forward to a realignment of the two-party system, GOP strategists hoped such a law would help draw blue-collar workers away from the Democratic fold.[17]

The introduction of the White House-sponsored bill dramatically increased the chances of some kind of worker-protection bill becoming law. Business, which had vehemently opposed the Democrats' version, came out in support of the significantly more probusiness Republican bill. Major differences in the new bill included giving less power to the Labor Department, putting final enforcement powers in the hands of a presidentially appointed commission, and relying more on state governments for oversight; all of these changes had been suggested earlier by business representatives.[18]

Despite major fights between Democrats and Republicans in both the Senate and House committees, the final votes were extremely lopsided. The 1970 Occupational Safety and Health Act passed the Senate 83–3 and the House 384–5. The bill more closely reflected the Democratic rather than the Republican version; nevertheless, the administration was committed to some kind of federal legislation. Rather than appear to be against safety in the workplace, President Nixon signed the bill into law in late December 1970.[19]

Provisions of the 1970 act fell into two areas. First, the act created the Occupational Safety and Health Administration (OSHA) as an agency in the Department of Labor; it was to be headed by one of seven assistant secretaries of labor. The agency was charged with both promulgating and enforcing safety and health standards. Safety hazards are those that generally result in cuts, burns, broken bones, and loss of limbs or eyesight. Health hazards are those that often result in heart disease, cancer, respiratory disease, neurological disorder, as well as a shortening of life expectancy from general physiological deterioration.[20] Typically, these follow from exposure to toxic and carcinogenic chemicals and dusts. Enforcement of these standards is carried out by OSHA compliance officers inspecting workplaces. These inspectors are authorized to cite violators and propose penalties. Unless an employer contests a citation within fifteen days, it becomes final. If an employer does contest the action, the case is reviewed by the Occupational Safety and Health Review Commission, an independent three-member panel not associated with the Department of Labor.[21]

The second major provision of the OSH Act was the establishment of the National Institute of Occupational Safety and Health (NIOSH). Although independent of OSHA, the institute is, in effect, OSHA's research arm. The purpose of NIOSH is to perform and summarize research on occupational hazards and to recommend standards to OSHA.

OSHA: Regulation under Fire

Throughout its existence, OSHA has been in the unenviable position of being criticized by business, labor, Congress, and every president since Nixon. Even within the first year of its existence, approximately 100 bills to amend or repeal OSHA's enabling legislation were introduced in Congress.[22] The agency's ability to make so many enemies stemmed from its rather broad mandate—ironically, granted by Congress—to oversee the workplace. The more that OSHA made new rules, the more that it seemed to affect the public—and, indirectly, Congress—in a negative way.

By 1977, public-opinion polls showed that OSHA was the most hated of all federal agencies.[23] As one former administrator put it, OSHA perfected "getting off on the wrong foot to a near art form."[24] Complaints even developed among those congressional members most sympathetic to the agency. As one of OSHA's supporters told the agency's administrators, "I catch hell, you catch hell, and everybody catches hell about OSHA and the crazy standards you have."[25]

In addition to complaints from government, the private sector has criticized the agency for promulgating standards that are voluminous, overly technical, burdensome, and, in many cases, unrelated to safety and health. Industry spokespersons also argue that OSHA is nit-picking in enforcing standards at the expense of educational and consultation efforts. At the other end of the political spectrum, labor has criticized OSHA for failing to enforce the law *strictly enough,* focusing too much attention on trivial safety standards, and delaying the issuance of health standards.[26] Although OSHA's administrators have argued that criticism by both business and labor indicates they must be doing something right, other observers have quipped that perhaps it means OSHA is doing everything wrong. After reading a scathing 1973 General Accounting Office report on OSHA, Sen. Harrison Williams (D.–N.J.), coauthor of the original act, was forced to conclude that the act "has yet to be properly implemented . . . and has been shackled by administrative ineptness."[27] Almost overnight, OSHA became an agency without a constituency.

Although there are many explanations for OSHA's inability to properly regulate occupational safety and health, its failure can be explained in large measure by structural flaws within the agency. Concomitantly, the costs resulting from enforcement of the agency's standards have led to a political backlash that continues to this day.

Consensus Standards

The 1970 act required OSHA to adopt existing "national consensus" or established federal standards on safety and health "as soon as practicable," but no later than two years of the agency's start-up date.[28] The statute did give the Secretary of Labor the power to refuse to issue a consensus or federal standard if it was unrelated to fighting occupational disease or injury.[29] One month after the agency was created, however, OSHA Administrator George Guenther promulgated all existing consensus and federal standards as mandatory national standards—all this without the necessary staff, data, or funds to evaluate many of those standards, and with twenty-three months left to accomplish the task.[30] Although this provided immediate coverage to millions of workers, it also created numerous problems that still haunt the agency.

Many of the industry consensus standards were derived from optional measures, privately adopted by the American National Standards Institute and the National Fire Protection Association. According to Mark Rothstein, associate professor of law at West Virginia University, "Many of the [consensus] standards were poorly drafted, extremely general, vague, redundant, contradictory, or hopelessly outdated. . . . Other standards were advisory . . . and were never intended to be given binding effect."[31] Among the many trivial and outdated consensus standards adopted by OSHA were a prohibition on using ice in drinking water (originally directed at the nineteenth-century practice of using ice cut from polluted rivers and lakes) and a requirement that all toilets have a "hinged openfront seat."[32] The agency's new standards reached into virtually every corner of the private sector.

Adoption of the consensus standards need not have caused significant problems if OSHA inspectors had discreetly overlooked "trivial" violations. Instead, they adopted a tight enforcement policy for all violations uncovered. The problem was compounded by a poorly trained and understaffed inspection force. According to research by Rothstein, most inspectors had little formal safety and health education. Their training consisted of a bare-bones, four-week course before "being 'turned loose' on American business. Rather than viewing their mission as one of assisting in the elimination of workplace hazards, some inspectors were concerned only with citing employers for as many violations as possible."[33] In fact, prior to 1976, 95 percent of OSHA's citations were for nonserious infractions.[34] Both business and labor, adversaries on most issues, were angered by OSHA's policy of following up nuisance standards with nuisance citations and penalties.[35] Continued citations aroused the ire of industry in general and small businesses in particular, and the call for regulatory relief was soon loud and clear.

Safety versus Health Standards

Both labor and business were distressed at the way OSHA developed health standards. For its part, labor criticized the agency for its emphasis on safety standards to the exclusion of developing what it considered to be more-important health standards. But business was angry for different reasons. Industry leaders contended that those health standards that had been promulgated accrued too few benefits to justify their high costs.

Despite all their other complaints, OSHA's critics agree on one fact: The agency has a clear bias for safety. OSHA has always had many more safety than health inspectors and many more safety than health standards. In 1975, 99 percent of all citations were for violations of safety standards.[36] By the end of that year, OSHA had issued only three health standards; these covered exposures to vinyl chloride, a group of carcinogens, and asbestos.[37] To put this into perspective, it has been estimated that more than 25,000 toxic substances are generated or used by industry.[38]

Part of OSHA's problem has been the scarcity of trained industrial-health professionals. One estimate suggests that as recently as 1970 there were probably fewer than 2,000 industrial hygienists in the whole country, and only 600 of these were certified by their professional organization.[39] Even by 1976, OSHA had only 165 fully qualified industrial hygienists. Despite the need for a larger health force, OSHA could barely fill its existing openings.[40]

OSHA's poor performance in promulgating health standards can be partly explained by several problems associated with OSHA's de facto research arm, NIOSH. In NIOSH's first three and one-half years of operation, it issued just eighteen recommendations for health standards.[41] NIOSH's problems were twofold. First was a lack of funding. Dr. Marcus Key, the institute's director, declared in 1973, "NIOSH is not expanding, it's shrinking. It is getting the proverbial meat ax. . . . Our present laboratory space isn't even adequate for any kind of research."[42] Asked to update his statement in 1974, Key answered, "If anything, it's worse."[43] Without adequate funding, the research wing has found itself unable to carry out its mandate.

The second problem that NIOSH had was a lack of communication with OSHA; this was, in fact, the fault of both agencies. Essentially, they developed separate priorities and hardly ever coordinated research agendas. NIOSH's staff of health professionals originally came from the Department of Health, Education, and Welfare, and were widely regarded as having significantly greater scientific expertise than did OSHA's research staff. A notable rift developed between the two agencies as OSHA emphasized the development of safety standards while NIOSH focused on developing research documents to support health standards. OSHA administrator Morton Corn was forced to admit that by December 1975, effective communication between the two agencies had ceased.[44] The resulting waste of precious resources was astounding. NIOSH, for example, conducted extensive studies on heat stress only to discover later that the issue was well down on the list of OSHA's priorities and that no one at OSHA had even begun to work on a standard.[45] Given such poor coordination in addition to the other criticisms, it was clear that something had to be done to put OSHA's house in order.

The Initial Reassessment: The Ford Administration

In December 1975, Morton Corn, a former professor of occupational health and chemical engineering at the University of Pittsburgh, was sworn in as OSHA's new administrator.[46] Recognizing that the agency was in deep trouble, Corn began to reorganize and shift its priorities. Under Corn's direction, the agency instituted better training programs for its inspectors, created a departmental task force to determine the problems of small business in complying with OSHA regulations, and changed the agency's emphasis from safety to health standards.[47] Although OSHA had begun to set more specific goals and became more cohesive, the reforms alone were insufficient for the agency to change its notorious image as an enforcer of nuisance standards.

Among the many people displeased with OSHA during this period was President Gerald Ford. During 1975 and 1976, Ford made a number of statements criticizing governmental regulation in general and OSHA in particular. Taking the cue, administration economists on both the Council on Wage and Price Stability and the Council of Economic Advisors tried to intervene in a variety of OSHA rule-making procedures in order to minimize OSHA's effects on business.[48] During his 1976 campaign, Ford made opposition to "overregulation" a key theme, and OSHA, despised by businesses large and small, became a favorite Ford target. In May that year, at a bicentennial salute to small business, Ford proclaimed "a declaration of independence from the needless regulations of government."[49] To help meet this goal, Ford announced the creation of a presidential task force that would "simplify and streamline government regulations."[50] The task force would start by reviewing the regulations of OSHA and the Federal Energy Administration. These agencies, Ford continued, could do their jobs "without needlessly harassing the American businessman."[51] Ford chose Paul MacAvoy of the Council of Economic Advisors, an outspoken OSHA critic, to head the task force.

The president's announcement alarmed both OSHA and labor officials, who saw the task force as a Republican attempt to solidify business support by weakening OSHA and rescinding the regulations that business did not like. Labor's suspicions were spelled out by Anthony Mazzocchi, citizenship–legislative director of the Oil, Chemical, and Atomic Workers International Union of the AFL–CIO: "The appointment of the task force is another code word to industry that the Administration wants to emasculate OSHA. Ford is saying OSHA is a thing of the past if he's returned to the White House."[52]

Although OSHA defenders feared the task force as a major force for deregulation, in the end it was given little power to revise OSHA's regulatory agenda. MacAvoy originally wanted a broad investigatory role for the task force but he was to be disappointed. According to a close observer at the time, the Labor Department successfully convinced MacAvoy that "he would be out of his mind to have a proposal to zap OSHA—the political opposition from labor would be too great."[53] Consequently, the task force's final work plan provided no authority to examine, much less alter, existing OSHA regulations. The task force could only assist OSHA with an internal review process already underway and aimed at increasing the relevance of the original consensus standards.[54]

Although the Ford administration saw the stirrings of the deregulatory movement, OSHA managed to survive the early pressure to lessen regulation. Nevertheless, the message was clear, and critics and defenders alike knew that the efforts to reform OSHA would arise again.

Keeping Deregulation on the Public Agenda: The Carter Administration

In 1977, the victorious Jimmy Carter installed a new team of players at the Department of Labor. Both Ray Marshall, Carter's Secretary of Labor, and Eula Bingham, OSHA's new administrator, recognized the need to clean up OSHA's tarnished image. Marshall declared: "We need to bring common sense into the occupational safety and health programs. . . . We've been chasing minnows and letting whales get away. I think that's a bad way to fish."[55] In effect, the Republican stirrings of the Ford administration were now echoed by Democratic voices. OSHA reform proposals had taken on a bipartisan character.

Business, while welcoming a "common sense" approach to occupational safety, was not overjoyed by Carter's selection of Bingham, an eminent toxicologist, to head OSHA. Not only had she been proposed by the AFL–CIO for the job, but also she had headed the OSHA committee that set controversial coke-oven emissions standards. "All told," *Business Week* reported, "numerous businessmen view her background as decidedly antibusiness."[56] Her connections with organized labor immediately made Bingham suspect.

When she assumed office, Bingham understood her agency's tenuous position. Believing that OSHA's future would remain in jeopardy unless the agency improved its public image, she immediately sought to put OSHA's house in order.[57] OSHA began to concentrate on health rather than safety standards, ignored technical violations, simplified existing regulations, and beefed up its scientific staff. Labor still criticized OSHA for being too slow, but under Bingham the agency doubled the number of health standards on the books. New regulations limited worker exposure to cotton dust, arsenic, benzene, lead, and certain pesticides.[58] Bingham's attempt to refocus OSHA's priorities, however, soon brought her into sharp conflict with deregulatory pressures from business, Congress, and the White House on the one hand and proregulatory pressures from labor on the other.

Eliminating the Consensus Standards

During the Carter administration, pressure on OSHA to remove existing standards sharply increased. In 1977, Congress attached an amendment to an appropriations bill requiring OSHA to eliminate "nuisance standards."[59] At the same time, the legislative branch expressed its displeasure with OSHA by approving legislation that eliminated the agency's authority to regulate farms with ten or fewer employees.[60] Carter noted the extent of business displeasure with OSHA and strongly supported the efforts to reduce its regulations. Declared Carter, "If I can clean up the mess in OSHA, I can be [reelected]."[61] As with Ford, Carter misjudged both the agency and his chances for reelection.

OSHA administrators clearly understood the demands for change. For several years there had been a movement within the agency to revise existing safety standards. In December 1977, OSHA officials formally proposed the revocation of more than 1,100 safety regulations, most being the original ill-advised "consensus" standards adopted at the agency's birth.[62] Organized labor, however, fought any change and expressed anger over its sudden distance from OSHA's management. Union officials interpreted OSHA's move as a reversal of the agency's commitment to job safety, and further demanded public hearings over any proposed changes. Recognizing the threat of court challenges by labor, OSHA officials responded by meeting with union officials.[63] This consultative position, according to one student of OSHA politics, "helped reduce the intensity and pervasiveness of union opposition to standards revisions. Union leaders saw the proposed alterations far less as capitulations to business in an ongoing war than changes that should be debated on their specific safety merits."[64] For the time being, OSHA officials mended fences with labor leaders, but the links were weak.

After extensive comments by both business and labor representatives, OSHA deleted more than 900 safety standards in October 1978.[65] Although most groups except labor were pleased with the remaining safety standards, business was still upset about OSHA's new drive to promulgate health regulations.

The Cotton-Dust Standard

OSHA's attempt to establish a standard that limited textile workers' exposure to cotton dust became another critical juncture in the agency's existence. For the first time, a president would intervene on behalf of a specific occupational-safety regulation. It also became the first time that an OSHA regulation would cause open warfare between different government agencies. The controversy over cotton dust, described below, exemplifies the difficult decisions that society must make between the human and financial costs caused by worker injuries. Even under an administration committed to worker safety and supported by organized labor, OSHA was forced to pay heed to the effects of its standards on the financial health of the industries it regulated.

In December 1976, OSHA formally proposed a health standard to protect workers from exposure to cotton dust; the standard proposal was continued by the Carter administration. The standard called for decreasing worker exposure through engineering controls (air-cleaning equipment) from 1.0 to 0.2 milligrams per cubic meter (mg/m^3) of air.[66] The standard sought to protect workers from byssinosis, a progressive respiratory disease caused by the long-term inhalation of cotton dust. In its more severe forms, it is a disabling and irreversibly chronic pulmonary disease known popularly as "brown lung."[67]

White House economists on the Council of Economic Advisors and the Council on Wage and Price Stability tried to convince OSHA to relax the cotton-dust standard, arguing that the costs of the mandated engineering controls were excessive compared to the expected benefits; furthermore, they said, the lower costs of alternatives such as personal protective devices (respirators) made them more desirable.[68] The debate between the two groups raged on amid threats of resignation and court-imposed deadlines; the issue received extensive coverage in the newspapers, which featured photographs of White House economists working at their desks wearing respirators.[69] Recognizing the need to tread carefully between labor unions and a president who was dependent on political support from the cotton-growing South, OSHA modified its original proposal and allowed exposure levels to vary from 0.75 to 2.0 mg/m^3 for different cotton-processing stages. Although OSHA had never before adopted a variable exposure level, and the compromise standard decreased the estimated compliance costs from $700 to $500 million, all but one of the White House economists were satisfied.[70]

Faced with OSHA's refusal to further revise its proposed standard, Charles Schultze, then-chair of the Council of Economic Advisors, appealed directly to Carter to overrule OSHA. Inasmuch as the agency was housed within the Department of Labor, the president clearly had the authority to do so. Labor, however, was not about to capitulate on the issue. Faced with opposition from George Meany of the AFL–CIO and members of Congress, Carter called Schultze, Marshall, and Bingham to a top-level conference. But as a result of the conference, Carter changed sides and supported OSHA.[71] Neither business nor labor, however, was pleased with the compromise. Labor sued, claiming that the standard was not stringent enough. Business interests also challenged the standard in court as being unnecessary to protect workers and neither economically nor technologically feasible.[72] Carter and his administration suddenly found themselves surrounded by hostile forces.

Ultimately, the issue was settled in the U.S. Supreme Court, which upheld the compromise cotton-dust standard. In the meantime, two effects became clear. First, Carter had alienated himself from all sides in the cotton-dust issue, and he was thus in a "no-win" situation. Second, the courts emerged as the only institution capable of breaking the logjam on proposed OSHA regulations.

Deregulation and the Courts

Filing suit in federal courts was nothing new to either business or labor. Because the first party to file a suit determines which court hears the case, and because different federal courts are known to be sympathetic to different arguments, major OSHA decisions have actually produced races to the courthouse door. Thus, both business and labor groups not only sued for different issues but chose different court sites for their battles in their efforts to gain the upper hand on their opponents.

In their early suits, business hoped to win issues dealing with the *way* OSHA enforced the law. Business lawyers argued that inspectors, by citing and proposing penalties, violated a company's constitutional right to trial by jury. These issues languished in federal district courts for five years. When the issue finally reached the U.S. Supreme Court, the justices upheld the OSHA regulation, ruling that "Congress, when public rights are involved, indeed does have the authority to grant OSHA-type enforcement and penalty powers to an agency created to regulate the problem."[73] Business was more successful when it argued that OSHA inspectors must produce search warrants before beginning an inspection. Although the Supreme Court agreed with business on this issue, Steven Kelman has noted that "the court decision established liberal criteria for granting such warrants, and . . . does not appear to be having much effect on OSHA inspection activities."[74] In the early rounds, OSHA's arguments prevailed over those given by business. The fight, however, continued on other fronts.

As OSHA focused its attention on health standards, business changed its strategy from contesting OSHA's methods to fighting the *actual standards* in court. Because health standards require industry to spend millions of dollars in compliance, virtually every OSHA health standard has met with a lawsuit.[75] Business interests finally won a major victory in a Supreme Court decision that involved OSHA's benzene standard. In *Industrial Union Department, v. American Petroleum Institute,*[76] the Supreme Court declared that before OSHA may regulate a toxic substance, it must first prove that a significant risk of health impairment exists and that the risk can be eliminated or lessened.[77] The decision had the dual effect of invigorating industry and demoralizing OSHA, and the pressures to deregulate escalated as industry persisted in its attacks on OSHA in the courts and through Congress.

Deregulation and Congress

Since the passage of the Occupational Safety and Health Act in 1970, every session of Congress has witnessed the introduction of bills to revise, limit, or revoke OSHA's regulatory power. Although most efforts have failed, some have altered the agency's role. In 1976, small farms were declared exempt from OSHA's inspections. In 1979, the Senate and House passed an amendment offered by Sen. Richard Schweiker (R.– Penn.) to exempt firms in selected industries with ten or fewer employees from regularly scheduled OSHA inspections and from penalties for first infractions. OSHA estimated that 37 percent of the nation's workplaces would be thus exempt from inspections under the bill.[78] But because the amendment was part of the 1980 appropriations bill, it was in effect for just one year.

In December 1979, buoyed by the passage of his legislation, Schweiker introduced a far more sweeping bill to limit OSHA's power to regulate occupational protection. In the words of the AFL–CIO, Schweiker's new bill "posed the most serious threat to OSHA in the act's decade-long history."[79] Labor was particularly alarmed because Schweiker had been a long-time OSHA advocate and friend of labor.

Schweiker's new bill called for the exemption of approximately 90 percent of all workplaces and 70 percent of all workers from OSHA inspections. Sensing disaster, labor unions across the country banded together to give the measure's defeat top priority. Richard Warden, the AFL–CIO's legislative director for the industrial-union department, remarked, "I've seldom seen the industrial unions and the labor movement as a whole so unified on any issue."[80] Although, in the end, labor won the battle over the Schweiker bill, many analysts believe that it lost the war for worker safety with the 1980 election of Ronald Reagan.

Making the Final Push: The Reagan Administration

Deregulation of occupational health and safety has been a major priority of the Reagan administration. This posture was quickly signaled by Raymond Donovan, Reagan's first Secretary of Labor, in January 1981. Donovan announced the withdrawal for "re-evaluation" of seven health and safety standards issued at the end of the Carter administration. When taking this action, Donovan did not consult with OSHA's outgoing director, Eula Bingham, or any of the agency's existing staff; he did not even wait until OSHA's new director, Thorne Auchter, was installed.[81]

Unlike Ford and Carter, who appointed experienced occupational-health-and-safety scientists to head OSHA, Reagan appointed a 35-year-old business executive, Thorne Auchter. Since graduating from college, Auchter had worked at his family's construction company, first as a supervisor and later as executive vice-president. Some critics have speculated that Auchter's appointment had more to do with his position as Reagan's 1980 campaign director for special events in Florida than with any particular expertise he had in the job-safety area.[82] In fact, his only previous experiences with OSHA were highly unflattering. Although he had served on a Florida task force to set up a state OSHA program in the early 1970s, his company had been cited for forty-eight safety violations, six of which were serious.[83]

Once in office, Auchter wasted no time in implementing a variety of policy changes to make OSHA more palatable to business. Auchter's top priority was to eliminate OSHA's adversarial relationship with business by transforming the agency into a "cooperative regulator."[84] The result, according to the *National Journal,* was that after six months in office, Auchter "relaxed enough inspection guidelines and industry rules to mollify, if not totally delight, the agency's sharpest business critics."[85] Others, however, were not happy. Consumer advocate Ralph Nader declared, "The Reagan administration, using code words such as 'voluntary compliance' and 'nonadversarial' has shackled OSHA and changed it from an enforcement agency against industrial hazards to an industry-indentured, demoralized bureaucracy."[86] Although there was considerable disagreement over the propriety of Auchter's new policies, they clearly evidenced a strong deregulatory agenda.

With Reagan in office, both the Heritage Foundation, a conservative "think-tank", and the probusiness U.S. Chamber of Commerce proposed numerous changes in OSHA policy, including the abolishment of OSHA's "policeman's orientation," use of cost–benefit considerations to set safety standards, and the transfer of significant enforcement powers to the states.[87] For the most part, these suggestions have been implemented. The AFL–CIO has complained that at the end of Auchter's first year, he had "put into effect or has proposed effecting two of the Chamber's three 'first priority' goals, all but one of its second priority goals and two of its four third priority goals. The Heritage Foundation had four programs for immediate revamping of OSHA. All have been put in place to some degree."[88] Most of these changes have been in direct conflict with the objectives of organized labor.

Changes in OSHA's policies have been instituted through administrative directives issued by Auchter rather than through congressional mandates. Some critics have argued that the effect of these administrative changes has been to dismantle and carry away OSHA's regulatory structure, bolt by bolt, through the back door, far away from congressional scrutiny.[89]

What little congressional oversight that did take place did not help OSHA achieve or even maintain its regulatory goals. Under prodding from Reagan, Congress cut OSHA's 1982 budget by 25 percent and NIOSH's by almost 40 percent. The cuts sharply curtailed OSHA's ability to promulgate new standards or to enforce those already on the books. The number of inspectors, for example, decreased from 1,700 in 1981 to 1,200 in 1982. Even Secretary of Labor Donovan, a strong supporter of Reagan's efforts to trim the budget, admitted, "We're no longer cutting into fat; we're cutting into muscle."[90] Nevertheless, the cuts continued under the joint rationales of deregulation and the philosophy that "less government is the best government." Under Auchter, deregulation of OSHA proceeded by weakening the enforcement of safety standards and by rescinding and revising health standards through administrative directives.

The Deregulation of Safety Standards

Auchter's voluntary compliance and targeting programs highlighted his deregulatory program. Under the voluntary compliance program, OSHA was to retreat from its role as policeman of the workplace and become a "cooperative regulator." According to Auchter, "consultation and education will be . . . improved. The states will play a larger role. We will begin encouraging employers to do self-inspection of their workplaces. And OSHA will become the catalyst to encourage various employer/ employee approaches to workplace safety and health."[91] This change in philosophy fit in well with the Reagan administration's general goal of shifting a number of federal responsibilities to the states.

To encourage voluntary compliance with federal standards, Auchter has created several programs. At the same time, the agency has embraced a "cooperative regulator" attitude, rather than assuming an adversarial position. OSHA's training institute, which now gives health-and-safety training to private businesses and state officials, has had its staff and budget increased. Finally, great strides have been made in relinquishing enforcement duties to the states. Seven states and territories have been added to the list of jurisdictions certified to run their own health-and-safety programs. Auchter also removed all federal inspectors from twenty-one states that had their own state-run OSHA programs.[92]

Although many analysts have approved of these steps, there has been sharp division over OSHA's decreased enforcement role. The decrease in OSHA inspectors has been matched by a sharp decline in violations cited and penalties given and a significant decline in the number of inspections from the highs of the Carter administration (see Figures 8-1, 8-2, and 8-3). In the first year of Reagan's administration, workplace inspections decreased 18 percent, follow-up inspections decreased 73 percent, serious citations were down by 37 percent, and fines by 65 percent.[93]

Enforcement of penalties for violations of the Occupational Safety and Health Act has not been a major priority of the administration. As Auchter explained, "Our job is health and safety. We're not interested in crime and punishment."[94] Patrick Tyson, Auchter's top deputy concurred. "We're not out there pushing for penalties, because we don't think they're that important."[95]

As part of OSHA's new image, Auchter ordered several changes in the way OSHA inspectors actually performed their jobs. Informal complaints (those made by word of mouth or by anonymous sources) of extremely hazardous conditions were to be no longer investigated unless imminent danger was alleged.[96] Citations for separate violations were now allowed to be grouped into a single violation category, thus resulting in fewer citations issued and lower fines.[97] The number of citations also decreased because Auchter ordered his enforcement staff to keep OSHA out of court by decreasing the number of citations that businesses might contest.[98]

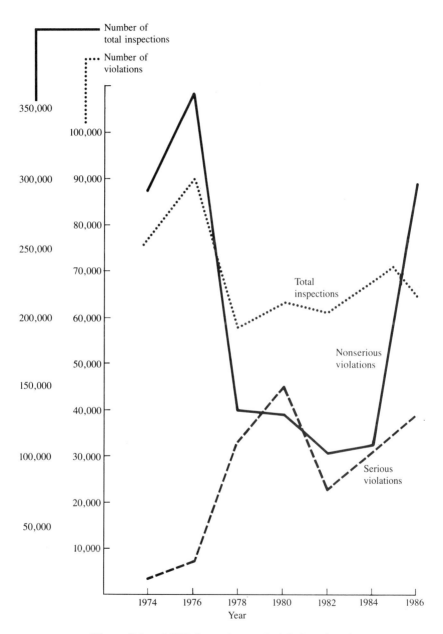

Figure 8-1.   OSHA inspections and violations found
Source: Mark A. Rothstein, *Vanderbilt Law Review,* 34 (January 1981), and telephone conversations with OSHA/Management Data Systems and Information Office

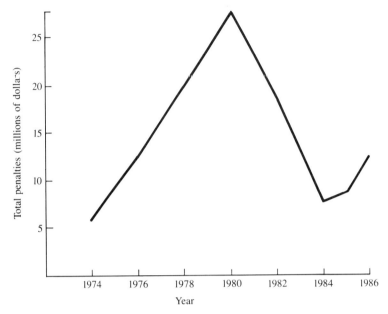

Figure 8-2. OSHA penalties proposed
Sources: Mark Rothstein, *Vanderbilt Law Review,* 34 (January 1981),
and telephone conversations with OSHA/Management Data Systems and
Information Office

Finally, for those citations that remained, Auchter set up a system of
"informal conferences." That is, to avoid legal battles, OSHA area
directors were empowered to confer with companies to lessen the severity
of citations, reduce penalties, and extend the deadlines for hazard
abatement.[99] These conferences have reduced penalties from 50 to 90
percent.[100]

While industry has been delighted with the informal conferences, labor
has fumed. According to Philip Simon and Kathleen Hughes of the
Center for Study of Responsive Law, the problem has been that "no
formal guidelines govern the process. Settlements are arbitrary and undermine an inspector's field work. Worse, they signal industry that
OSHA no longer takes its enforcement efforts seriously."[101] More than
ever, organized labor senses the current OSHA administration to be an
enemy, not an ally.

Auchter's targeting program was designed to allow OSHA inspectors
to focus on high-risk, hazardous industries. Although Senator Schweiker's amendment had exempted certain firms from OSHA inspections for
only one year, Auchter kept the amendment in effect by administrative
fiat. In October 1981, he exempted from routine safety inspections those
manufacturing firms with ten or fewer workers and manufacturing industries and individual firms that had fewer workdays lost from injuries

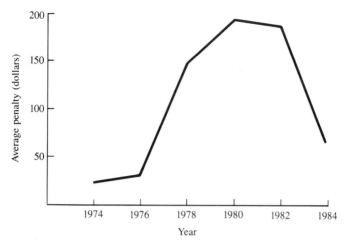

Figure 8-3. Average OSHA penalties assessed
Sources: Mark Rothstein, *Vanderbilt Law Review,* 34 (January 1981),
and telephone conversations with OSHA/Management Data Systems and
Information Office

than the national average. The effect, according to an AFL–CIO analysis, has been to remove approximately 13 million workers from the federal protection afforded by inspections.[102] Furthermore, when an inspection does occur, it is far less comprehensive than they had been under previous administrations. The AFL–CIO has reported that "nearly 50 percent of the general scheduled visits to manufacturing firms in fiscal year 1982 were merely reviews of paper records, not workplace inspections."[103] In other words, if a company's paper work seems in order, an inspector will never set foot into the workplace to check actual compliance. Many analysts have argued that the deterrent effect of inspections under this system is more than somewhat questionable.[104]

Although business and labor argue over the desirability of OSHA's new enforcement policies, they agree that the Reagan administration has orchestrated a significant shift in enforcement from previous administrations. Not all laws are enforced with equal zeal under any administration, but some critics have noted a startling contradiction in the Reagan administration between an easygoing attitude toward worker-safety conditions and a hard-nosed approach to "law and order" issues. As Joan Claybrook of Public Citizen laments, "No one in the Reagan administration has ever proposed a 'voluntary' approach when it comes to food stamp fraud or illegal immigration. . . . Mention safety and health in the workplace, however, and Reagan's enforcers are decidedly more casual. . . . Needless to say, American business has been pleased that its transgressions against people's health are treated more sympathetically by the government."[105] Such criticism points out more than a difference over approach; it points to changing priorities.

The Deregulation of Health Standards

Under Auchter, approximately thirty suggested health standards were scheduled to be completed. Almost every one of these, however, was not a proposal to develop a new regulation, but an attempt to weaken an existing one.[106] Among the standards the Reagan administration has moved to weaken or delay are exposure limits to lead, benzene, noise, ethylene dibromide (EDB), asbestos, and cotton dust. Auchter's standards-review policy effectively tied up OSHA's staff, preventing it from completing work on new standards. In Auchter's first year, for example, two-thirds of OSHA's standard-setting staff was reassigned to review and reassess existing standards.[107] Although neither a failure to regulate nor a decrease in the rate of increased regulation are the same as deregulation, the effect in this case has been clear: The government's commitment to improve occupational health through OSHA has been halted.

The aforementioned cotton-dust standard was one of the more notable attempts by the Reagan administration to weaken existing regulation. Originally proposed in 1978 (see pages 181–182), the standard had been in the courts for three years on the issue of economic feasibility before reaching the U.S. Supreme Court. Fearing that the Court might prohibit any consideration of economic feasibility, Auchter requested that the Court drop the case and send it back to OSHA for reevaluation. The Court refused, and in March 1981, it ruled that the threat posed to a worker's health was the overriding criterion that determined the appropriateness of a standard. A standard could only be declared economically infeasible if it caused general financial ruin of the industry. Specifically, the court ruled that OSHA was neither required nor permitted to use cost–benefit analysis in determining whether a standard was feasible.[108]

Yet, one month after clearly winning the case, OSHA indefinitely withdrew the cotton-dust standard to perform an "economic feasibility analysis."[109] When the standard reappeared more than two years later, it had been significantly weakened. Among the changes were that more than 340,000 employees in nontextile and knitting industries would be exempted, employers in covered industries would be allowed to seek exemptions from important provisions, and the installation of engineering controls could be delayed for some parts of the industry for up to two years.[110]

Auchter's policy to weaken existing standards also placed less emphasis on and need for OSHA's scientific staff. As a consequence, many professional staff members, demoralized and disgusted, simply quit, tired of having both their advice on health matters and their concern with the direction of the agency's regulatory policies ignored. Others were not so lucky, and were fired, demoted, or reassigned. One major case of scientific "muzzling" occurred shortly after Auchter assumed office. Dr. Peter Infante, one of OSHA's top scientists, publicly stated that the agency's official policy was that formaldehyde was a likely carcinogen. The formaldehyde trade association, however, did not wish to have its industry cited as a possible regulatory target and complained to Auchter, who, in turn, tried to fire Infante. It took a congressional hearing into the issues of scientific independence and free speech and its attendant publicity to persuade Auchter to reconsider. Although Infante stayed on, reports of staff intimidation continued.[111]

Under Auchter, there were notable exceptions to the deregulatory trend. The most significant involved the asbestos standard. Apparently at odds with Reagan's deregulation agenda, the asbestos standard actually has been the exception that proves the rule. At the end of the Carter administration, OSHA officials had been preparing an asbestos standard, and in August 1981, NIOSH scientists concluded that unless a tough asbestos standard were adopted, an additional 500,000 workers would develop lung cancer.[112] Five months later, however, in January 1982, Auchter revoked the standard's development schedule. The following year, under fire from Congress for failing to issue new standards, Auchter reversed himself and announced that OSHA would soon propose an asbestos standard.

To some observers, Auchter's reversal did not indicate a change in heart so much as a fear of what Congress might do in the wake of the toxic Superfund mismanagement scandals at the EPA. Joan Claybrook reports that "[i]n the highly charged political climate surrounding the scandals at the EPA, Auchter was undergoing heavy fire and knew his number might be next if he did not take action against *some* health hazard."[113] Still, whatever the motive, workers in the asbestos industry are now afforded better protection from lung cancer.

OSHA After Auchter

After three years of controversy, Auchter resigned as head of OSHA in March 1984. While President Reagan was searching for a permanent replacement, deputy administrator Patrick Tyson took over as acting director. In July 1984, President Reagan nominated Robert A. Rowland as Assistant Secretary of Labor for Occupational Health and Safety.[114] For the previous three years, Rowland had chaired the Occupational Safety and Health Review Commission, a federal agency that considered employer appeals of OSHA citations. Rowland, a wealthy Texas attorney, had played a key part in the 1980 Reagan–Bush campaign, as had many of Reagan's appointees.[115]

Rowland's tenure as OSHA director, while lasting less than a year, was in many ways just as controversial as Auchter's had been. From the beginning, Rowland came under fire from union officials. Labor argued that Rowland's record of siding with business while he was a member of the review commission demonstrated his antilabor bias. A more appropriate head of OSHA, according to labor, would be an expert on worker safety, not another Reagan campaign worker.

During Rowland's time in office, very few new health and safety standards escaped unchanged. In fact, several congressional studies became highly critical of OSHA's job performance. The Office of Technology Assessment, for one, argued that OSHA "may have further reduced an already weak regulatory effort" in an attempt to minimize confrontation between the agency and industry.[116] In a report prepared by the House Government Operations Committee's subcommittee on manpower, OSHA was heavily criticized for a "grossly inadequate" effort to inspect toxic-waste sites. According to the report, the result of OSHA's "great neglect" was to expose "a great number of working people to real danger."[117]

With renewed charges that OSHA failed to adequately regulate against and police workplace hazards, Rowland became the target of criticism. In hearings before Congress, he and his administrators were accused of using scare tactics and violating federal regulations to "root out" staff "troublemakers" and "communists" in an "almost McCarthy-like crusade for political conformity within OSHA."[118]

Adding to Rowland's troubles were several conflict-of-interest charges. These became apparent when Rowland was accused of not issuing standards on the use of certain chemicals and when OSHA was charged with a lack of attention to sanitation and clean drinking water facilities for farmworkers. In both instances, critics charged, Rowland held stock in the very companies that would have been negatively affected if the standards were issued. Rowland countered that his stocks were held in a qualified blind trust and, thus, were beyond his personal management. To this end, a probe by White House Office of Government Ethics cleared him of any wrongdoing; still, there was considerable controversy over the appropriateness of his actions.[119]

In May 1985, after less than eleven months on the job, Rowland, who had yet to be officially confirmed by the Senate, resigned. Once again, Patrick Tyson took over as acting director while another search was conducted for a replacement. Given the agency's poor reputation, Labor Secretary William Brock had a hard time finding someone who was willing to take the job as director. Finally, one year after Rowland had resigned, John Pendergrass was confirmed by the Senate as the new OSHA head.[120]

Pendergrass had been an executive at 3M of St. Paul for twenty-two years; his last position had been as manager of hazards-awareness products. Although labor raised some questions about the appropriateness of his corporate background, Pendergrass faced little opposition in the Senate. But on assuming office, Pendergrass was faced with numerous problems. The agency had been without an official director for more than two years and had suffered from the lack of leadership. Attacked from virtually every quarter, it was under fire by those in labor, business, and government. Moreover, staff morale was extremely low due to the resignations and terminations of many long-term employees.

It is much too soon to determine the extent to which Pendergrass will be able to deal with the challenges facing his office. There are signs, however, that the administrative deregulation of the Auchter era has been slowed, if not reversed. In early 1986, OSHA revised its job-inspection policy to allow spot checks of companies that were normally excluded from full-scale OSHA inspections as well as comprehensive inspections of companies in high-hazard industries.[121] And in June 1986, after years of study and controversy, OSHA significantly tightened the rules governing exposure to asbestos fibers despite the opposition of the OMB.[122] Although these policy commitments are a mere fraction of the agency's activities, they do suggest a change in direction.

OSHA and Regulation Theory

In a sense, OSHA's life can be divided into two periods: 1970 to 1980 and 1981 to the present. These periods have shown remarkably different attitudes among those in positions of authority. Concomitantly, they have reflected two different models of regulation.

In the early years, OSHA regulation seemed to follow the public-interest theory. Concern about a lack of safety precautions and high death and injury rates prompted presidents and Congress to act to protect the interests of all workers. The market, through voluntary actions by business and labor, had been ineffective in preventing workplace injuries or in compensating those who were adversely affected by workplace hazards.

OSHA may have originally seemed to follow the public-interest theory of regulation, but in the last several years it has more closely resembled the capture theory; in effect, it seems to have been co-opted over time so that its policies benefit those it regulates. There is, however, an important distinction to be made. In this case, it was not the regulated group that co-opted the agency—it was the White House.

Under a deregulatory mandate from President Reagan, successive OSHA administrators and government officials within the OMB rewrote OSHA's regulatory and enforcement agenda to directly benefit those who were regulated. Admittedly, business pressured the White House for regulatory relief, but in large measure OSHA actions were guided by a White House philosophy of lessening the "regulatory burden." Thus, from a regulatory perspective, the case of OSHA seems to reflect a variation on capture theory. The regulated group, business, benefits from regulation but it does so because of intervention by another branch of government. Absent White House intervention, it is unclear what direction OSHA would have taken if it had been subjected to normal political tensions—i.e., being caught between labor and business.

Regulation of the Workplace: Who Wins, Who Loses?

Throughout its history, OSHA has had few friends and many enemies. Given an enormous task, but limited resources, the agency's problems have been compounded by poor management, ad hoc decision making, and vanishing support in critical political quarters. Confronted with criticism from both business and labor, OSHA has faced persistent pressures for deregulation from Congress and the White House. Significant deregulation did not occur, however, until the Reagan administration.

There is much disagreement over how to assess the Reagan administration's deregulation. Business representatives have been pleased with the relaxed inspections and decreased penalties. But more important, the rescission, revision, and delay of health standards has saved their industries billions of dollars, which in some cases was desperately needed. Already weakened by a serious recession in the early '80s, many faced other pressures as well. Textile manufacturers, for example, have increasingly faced stiff competition from imported goods produced in countries with low wages and almost nonexistent worker protection. Other industries have desperately needed to modernize aging, outmoded plants.

Labor unions, on the other hand, have felt betrayed at what they see as the dismantling of an agency that was designed to protect their members' health. Occupational-health problems have always been far more serious than injuries, and effective deregulation began precisely at the time when OSHA had existed long enough to research and develop effective health standards. Labor leaders were especially dismayed that the agency had been significantly weakened just when it might have become a truly effective protector of worker health.

The debate over OSHA has been complicated by the actual effects of the agency's standards. Analysts point out that in the last decade, work-related fatalities have generally decreased, but workdays lost to illness and injury have generally risen.[123] Studies of the issue have not been greatly illuminating: Several focusing on OSHA's inspections have found little (3 to 5 percent) or no reductions in injuries.[124] Other studies came to significantly different conclusions. For example, the Center for Policy Alternatives at MIT concluded that "because of OSHA more than 350 deaths and between 40,000 and 60,000 accidents that resulted in lost workdays were prevented in 1974 and 1975 alone."[125] The cost to society, however, has been high. The U.S. Chamber of Commerce estimates that between 1970 and 1981, business spent approximately $48 billion in capital expenditures on safety and health measures.[126]

A key question for policy makers is whether the benefits justify the costs of regulation. Unfortunately, there are no simple answers. In the field of occupational safety, there are both large costs and large potential benefits. Balancing these trade-offs is difficult. Analyses of OSHA standards, however, should account for the fact that with or without regulation, someone must pay for unsafe workplaces. Dr. Sidney Wolfe, director of the Public Citizen Health Research Group, points out the differences between the costs of regulatory and deregulatory action: Until OSHA was created, the cost of dangerous workplaces had been largely avoided by industry. It had been borne by taxpayers through Social Security disability payments, and to a lesser extent through worker-compensation payments; the largest costs, however, had been borne through the death, disease, and disablement of workers themselves—a toll that can never be reversed, compensated, or expressed in dollars.[127] The costs of safety come from somewhere, be it the private or public sector. The perennial questions are, Who should pay, and is it worth it?

If nothing else, OSHA has raised the safety consciousness of business, labor, government, and the public. Lloyd McBride of the United Steel Workers Association, insists that "[e]ven under the most adverse conditions, OSHA has uncorked a bottle of knowledge on workplace hazards and unleashed an educational process which has awakened workers to the dangers they confront on the job. It has put all employers on notice of the regulatory intent of the government."[128] Some businesses have instituted voluntary programs to decrease workplace hazards, and many unions have pressed for worker health and safety programs in their collective-bargaining negotiations.

To the extent that government deregulates occupational safety, however, there is more than a fair probability that business will read such actions as evidence of decreased concern for worker protection. If pre–OSHA history is any guide, it is doubtful that a return to voluntary action will lead to better on-the-job protection. On the other hand, relations between business and the agency have improved significantly and its reputation for silly standards is fading. Under these circumstances, if OSHA chooses to focus on the important issues of worker safety and health, it might finally realize its mandate to protect the workplace.

Notes

1. Quoted in Joan Claybrook, *Retreat From Safety* (New York: Pantheon, 1984), p. 75.
2. "Why Nobody Wants to Listen to OSHA," *Business Week,* no. 2436 (June 14, 1976): 65.
3. Occupational Safety and Health Act, Sec. 2(b), *29 U.S.C. 651(b),* 1970.

4. *Ibid.*
5. Nicholas Askounes Ashford, "Crisis in the Workplace: Occupational Disease and Injury: A Report to the Ford Foundation" (Cambridge, Mass.: MIT Press, 1976), p. 47.
6. *Ibid.*, pp. 47–49.
7. John Stender, "Enforcing the Occupational Safety and Health Act of 1970: The Federal Government as Catalyst," *Law and Contemporary Problems*, 38, no. 4 (Summer–Autumn 1974): 641–642.
8. Vicky Cohan, "The Overhaul That Could Give OSHA Life Under Reagan," *Business Week*, no. 2671 (January 19, 1981): 88.
9. Ashford, "Crisis," p. 51.
10. Paul M. Bangser, "An Inherent Role for Cost–Benefit Analysis in Judicial Review of Agency Decisions: A New Perspective on OSHA Rulemaking," *Boston College Environmental Affairs Law Review*, 10 (1982): 370–371.
11. Ashford, "Crisis," p. 3.
12. *Ibid.*, p. 47.
13. *Ibid.*, p. 46.
14. Patrick G. Donnelly, "The Origins of the Occupational Safety and Health Act of 1970," *Social Problems*, 30, no. 1 (October 1982): 22.
15. *Ibid.*, p. 13.
16. *Ibid.*, p. 20.
17. Steven Kelman, "Occupational Safety and Health Administration," in *The Politics of Regulation*, ed. James Q. Wilson (New York: Basic Books, 1980), p. 241.
18. Donnelly, "The Origins," p. 13.
19. Kelman, "Occupational Safety," p. 242.
20. Ashford, "Crisis," pp. 8–9.
21. Stender, "Enforcing," p. 646.
22. Frank J. Thompson, "Deregulation by the Bureaucracy: OSHA and the Augean Quest for Error Correction," *Public Administration Review*, 42, no. 3 (May–June 1982): 204.
23. "OSHA Befriends Industry, but Draws Fire," *Washington Post*, July 5, 1983, p. A12.
24. "Why Nobody," *Business Week*, June 14, 1976, p. 68.
25. Thompson, "Deregulation," p. 204.
26. James W. Singer, "A New OSHA Tries to Put Its Pieces Back Together Again," *National Journal*, 9, no. 27 (July 2, 1977): 1046.
27. "Senate Report Slaps OSHA's Record," *Industry Week*, 182, no. 13 (September 23, 1984): 7.
28. Timothy B. Clark, "What's All the Uproar Over OSHA's 'Nit-Picking' Rules?", *National Journal*, 10, no. 40 (October 7, 1978): 1595.
29. Thompson, "Deregulation," pp. 203–204.
30. Thomas R. Bartman, "Deciding What to Regulate: Priority-Setting at OSHA," *Virginia Journal of Natural Resources Law*, 2, no. 1 (Spring 1982): 95–96.
31. Mark A. Rothstein, "OSHA After Ten Years: A Review and Some Proposals," *Vanderbilt Law Review*, 34, no. 1 (January 1981): 73–74.
32. Thompson, "Deregulation," pp. 203–204.
33. Rothstein, "OSHA After Ten Years," pp. 94–95.
34. Thompson, "Deregulation," p. 204.
35. *Ibid.*
36. Bartman, "Deciding What to Regulate," p. 96.
37. James W. Singer, "New OSHA Head May Signal Change in Agency's Approach," *National Journal*, 7, no. 51–52 (December 27, 1975): 1730.
38. Rothstein, "OSHA After Ten Years," p. 78.
39. Bartman, "Deciding What to Regulate," p. 91.

40. "Why Nobody," *Business Week,* June 14, 1976, p. 67.
41. Rothstein, "OSHA After Ten Years," p. 78.
42. Joseph A. Page and Peter N. Munsing, "Occupational Health and the Federal Government: The Wages are Still Bitter," *Law and Contemporary Problems,* 38, no. 4 (Summer–Autumn 1974): 654.
43. *Ibid.,* p. 655.
44. Bartman, "Deciding What to Regulate," p. 111.
45. "Why Nobody," *Business Week,* June 14, 1976, p. 67.
46. Singer, "New OSHA Head," p. 1725.
47. "OSHA: Hardest to Live With," *Business Week,* no. 2477 (April 4, 1977): 79. See also Singer, "New OSHA Head," p. 1728.
48. Kelman, "Occupational Safety," p. 261.
49. Steven Kelman, *Regulating America, Regulating Sweden: A Comparative Study of Occupational Safety and Health Policy* (Cambridge, Mass.: MIT Press, 1981), p. 101.
50. James W. Singer, "New OSHA Task Force—Political Payoff or Fake Alarm?", *National Journal,* 8, no. 28 (July 10, 1976): 973.
51. *Ibid.*
52. Singer, "New OSHA Task Force," p. 975.
53. Henry Perritt, Department of Labor, quoted in Kelman, *Regulating America,* p. 102.
54. Kelman, *Regulating America,* p. 102.
55. Quoted in Clark, "What's All the Uproar," p. 1596.
56. "OSHA: Hardest to Live With," *Business Week,* April 4, 1977, p. 79.
57. Singer, "A New OSHA," p. 1046.
58. *Ibid.* Also see Claybrook, *Retreat,* p. 77.
59. Thompson, "Deregulation," p. 208.
60. *Ibid.*
61. Clark, "What's All the Uproar," p. 1594.
62. Thompson, "Deregulation," p. 205.
63. *Ibid.,* p. 210.
64. *Ibid.*
65. *Ibid.*
66. "The Cotton Dust Case," *Regulation,* 5, no. 1 (January–February 1981): 5.
67. Bangser, "An Inherent Role," p. 384.
68. "The Cotton Dust Case," *Regulation,* January–February 1981, p. 5.
69. *Ibid.,* p. 6.
70. *Ibid.,* p. 5.
71. Kelman, "Occupational Safety," p. 262.
72. Bangser, "An Inherent Role," p. 387.
73. Quoted in Michael A. Verespej, "OSHA's Power Reaffirmed," *Industry Week,* 193, no. 2 (April 25, 1977): 54
74. Kelman, "Occupational Safety," p. 261.
75. Rothstein, "OSHA After Ten Years," p. 79.
76. *448 U.S. 607 (1980).*
77. Bangser, "An Inherent Role," p. 382.
78. James W. Singer, "Labor Lobbyists Go on the Defensive As Political Environment Turns Hostile," *National Journal,* 12, no. 11 (March 15, 1980): 442.
79. Margaret Semivario, "OSHA's Future: Fighting Perennial Battles," *AFL–CIO American Federalist,* 87, no. 7 (July 1980): 20.
80. Singer, "Labor Lobbyists," p. 444.
81. Kitty Calavita, "The Demise of the Occupational Safety and Health Administration: A Case Study in Symbolic Action," *Social Problems,* 30, no. 4 (April 1983): 441.
82. Claybrook, *Retreat,* pp. 72–74.

83. *Ibid.*, pp. 72–73.
84. Michael Wines, "They're Telling OSHA Horror Stories, But the Victims Are New," *National Journal*, 13, no. 45 (November 7, 1981): 1985.
85. *Ibid.*
86. Martin Tolchin, "Nader Says OSHA Is Shackled Now," *New York Times*, September 5, 1983, p. 9.
87. "The Crippling of OSHA," *AFL–CIO American Federalist*, 89, no. 4 (April–June 1982): 17.
88. *Ibid.*, p. 19.
89. Wines, "Horror Stories," pp. 1987–1988.
90. Calvita, "The Demise," p. 443.
91. Claybrook, *Retreat*, p. 73.
92. Michael Wines, "Auchter's Record at OSHA Leaves Labor Outraged, Business Satisfied," *National Journal*, 15, no. 40 (October 1, 1983): 2009.
93. Calvita, "The Demise," p. 443.
94. Claybrook, *Retreat*, p. 99.
95. *Ibid.*
96. "The Crippling of OSHA," *AFL–CIO American Federalist*, April–June 1982, p. 19.
97. Wines, "Auchter's Record," p. 2010.
98. Claybrook, *Retreat*, p. 104.
99. "OSHA, The Industry's New Friend," *New York Times*, September 5, 1983, p. 19.
100. Claybrook, *Retreat*, p. 104.
101. *New York Times*, September 5, 1983, p. 19.
102. "The Crippling of OSHA," *AFL–CIO American Federalist*, April–June 1982, p. 18.
103. Claybrook, *Retreat*, p. 101.
104. Rothstein, "OSHA After Ten Years," p. 108.
105. Claybrook, *Retreat*, p. 99.
106. Wines, "Auchter's Record," p. 2011.
107. "The Crippling of OSHA," *AFL–CIO American Federalist*, April–June 1982, p. 18.
108. Bangser, "An Inherent Role," pp. 396–397, and Claybrook, *Retreat*, pp. 83–84.
109. Calvita, "The Demise," p. 442.
110. Claybrook, *Retreat*, pp. 83–84.
111. *Ibid.*, pp. 74, 111–112.
112. *Washington Post*, July 7, 1983, p. A-12.
113. Claybrook, *Retreat*, p. 96.
114. Cathy Trust, "OSHA Chief Resigns After 11 Months As He's Cleared of 'Conflict' Over Stocks," *Wall Street Journal*, May 28, 1985, p. 7.
115. "Can Bill Brock Strike a Balance," *Business Week*, no. 2891 (April 22, 1985): 105.
116. "Job Safety Effort Said to Languish," *Facts on File*, 45, no. 2319 (May 3, 1985): 325.
117. "OSHA Site Inspection 'Inadequate,'" *Facts on File*, 45, no. 2325 (June 14, 1985): 441.
118. " 'Fear tactics' cripple OSHA, House panel is told," *San Jose Mercury News*, May 10, 1985, p. 26A.
119. *Wall Street Journal*, May 28, 1985, p. 7.
120. "OSHA head clears hurdle," *Engineering News Record*, 216, no. 22 (May 29, 1986): 100.
121. "Job-Safety Inspection Policy Set," *Facts On File*, 46, no. 2356 (January 17, 1986): 16.
122. "Asbestos Job Rules Tightened," *Facts on File*, 46, no. 2379 (June 27, 1986): 469.
123. Wines, "Auchter Record," p. 2013.
124. John Mendeloff, *Regulating Safety* (Cambridge, Mass.: MIT Press, 1979), p. 117. Also see Robert Stewart Smith, "The Estimated Impact on Injuries of OSHA's

Target Industry Program." Paper presented to Department of Labor Conference on Evaluating OSHA, Annapolis, Md., 1975.

125. Michael Verespej, "Has OSHA Improved?", *Industry Week,* 206, no. 3 (August 4, 1980): 54.

126. Wines, "Horror Stories," p. 1989.

127. Quoted in Claybrook, *Retreat,* pp. 112–113.

128. Verespej, "Has OSHA Improved?" p. 54.

PART THREE

Deregulation in Perspective

CHAPTER 9

Alternatives to Regulation

Over the years, regulation policies and the deregulation movement have coexisted uneasily, an indication of the contradictory beliefs held by the public and political leaders alike. Most citizens, for example, tend to believe that government is too involved in the daily activities of the private sector as well as in the affairs of the public at large. Yet, when pressed on specifics, the public strongly supports governmental protections in the environmental, consumer, and occupational spheres. Moreover, the public's endorsement of the involved federal regulatory agencies and their activities remains, even when people are made aware of the costs of these protections.[1]

Although governmental regulation has satisfied some sectors of society, it has seen considerable resistance from others. Dissatisfaction with economic regulation has a long history, and several presidential commissions have all recommended substantial change. The Landis study under John F. Kennedy, the council headed by Roy Ash under Richard Nixon, and the Domestic Council Review Group on Regulatory Reform under Gerald Ford all recommended major revisions in economic regulation.[2] Under the Carter administration, significant reform and deregulation took place. But even though deregulation has received the lion's share of publicity, other options have remained available to policy makers.

Ronald Reagan has also repeatedly stressed the problems of regulation. Two days after his inauguration, he created the Presidential Task Force on Regulatory Relief, headed by Vice-President George Bush (see chapter 3).[3] The Bush Committee differed from its predecessors in two respects. First, it billed itself as a committee on "relief," not on "reform"; that is, its goal was to decrease regulation. Second, it dealt not only with economic but also with social regulation.

The current enthusiasm for regulatory relief as expressed among those in government may not be shared by the general population, at least not beyond the "gut level" desire for less red tape and more common sense. Most political leaders have come to view economic regulation as unnecessary; accordingly, the fight for economic deregulation has been strongly bipartisan. The reconsideration of social regulation, however, has been more controversial. Social regulation still finds considerable, if not overwhelming, support.[4] After a decade of experience with what has been called "command and control" regulation, policy makers have begun to consider a variety of alternatives. The use of traditional checks on business excess or omission, supply-and-demand based incentives, and enhancement of information are all potential means to achieve regulatory goals in place of the federal agency setting regulatory standards.

Alternatives to regulation can and should be evaluated for their potential effectiveness, efficiency, equity, and feasibility.[5] The desire for less regulation without less governmental protection can be met only through the consideration of different approaches. Such choices must also be judged in accordance with the regulatory agency in question. Thus, the

CAB may have been anachronistic for air travel, but the ICC may still be necessary, albeit in a restructured role, for other forms of travel by land. One fact is certain in light of the public controversy over regulation: the most obvious alternative is deregulation. Yet even this is not without its own confusion.

Not all reformers mean the same thing when they advocate deregulation. Some call for a complete dismantling of any government structure that experts control over a particular industry; others want a relaxation of rules while the basic regulatory structure is maintained. In either case, the lack of a regulatory agency or rules does not mean that a business is free to do whatever it wants. Almost all advocates of deregulation stress that the traditional protections offered to citizens are adequate.

The remainder of this chapter examines alternatives to both economic and social regulation. The possibilities described are not rigid; some strategies could be used in reforming both economic and social regulation. Inasmuch as economic and social regulation respond to different goals, their alternatives differ as well.

Alternatives to Economic Regulation

Alternatives to economic regulation usually stress economic incentives in the absence of regulatory agencies. In most cases, these incentive strategies are already available, and would not require new agencies or significant changes in rules. In fact, outright deregulation is most commonly mentioned. Those who favor deregulation usually assume that other checks, either private or public, will provide adequate protection.

Laissez-Faire

Since the time of Adam Smith, the power of a free market to provide necessary checks and balances has been extensively analyzed and debated. The idea that each person, acting only in self-interest, can provide for the public good is still at issue today: No individual "intends to promote the public interest. . . . [H]e intends only his own gain, and he is in this, as in many other cases, led by an invisible hand to promote an end which was not part of his intention," Smith once wrote.[6]

Most economists agree that under certain conditions, a free market will produce the best mix of products through the most efficient means of production. Among other conditions, these include that there are many buyers and sellers, each too small to influence price; perfect information; the mobility of resources; and the absence of externalities. Are such conditions likely to exist in a modern industrialized society? Few observers agree that all are now present in the American economy. Even so, many subscribe to the basic premise that the inefficiencies resulting from imperfect markets are outweighed by the disadvantages from governmental intervention.

Yet even among political conservatives, this view has little credibility. Most accept the necessity of some role for government in certain circumstances, and the conditions necessary for a free market to be efficient are simply not met. Both buyers and sellers influence price, and resources are fixed, at least in the short run. More relevant to regulation, the social costs of many actions are radically different from the private costs. And the information needed to make rational choices tends to be insufficient, if not completely inadequate.[7] Workers often have no idea about the hazards in their workplaces, and consumers cannot judge in advance the purity of the food or drugs they might purchase. In short, the theoretical justifications for governmental intervention in the economy are satisfied.

Those who advocate an abandonment of governmental intervention in some form often downplay the fact that regulation usually resulted from the discovery of serious problems—appalling conditions in meat-packing companies, dangerous safety defects in automobiles, or rivers that caught fire. In such cases, various social regulations were enacted where a free market had failed to satisfactorily achieve certain goals.[8] Regulation originally passed to protect an industry, however, is usually harder to defend than regulation passed to help the general population; it is not accidental that most deregulation is economic rather than social.

Antitrust Laws

Many observers believe that antitrust laws are yet another form of regulation. Most, however, see it as an alternative, because these laws attempt to create the conditions for a competitive market rather than to regulate the market itself.[9] In addition to breaking up monopolies, antitrust laws seek to prevent predatory pricing, price-fixing, anticompetitive mergers, price discrimination, and tying contracts (agreements where companies must buy packages of products or services, rather than only the items they want).[10] If the particular problem that a regulator seeks to solve involves the lack of a potentially competitive market, then enforcement of antitrust laws may be a relevant alternative to regulation.

There are two problems with the use of antitrust laws instead of regulation. First, antitrust charges can be difficult to prove and whatever changes result can take an incredible length of time to bear fruit. The antitrust cases against such industry giants as IBM and AT & T seemed to go on forever, and even when they ended, some critics wondered who the *real* winners and losers were. The requirements for evidence and the difficulty of proving a case make antitrust a slow remedy at best. Second, in most cases, an antitrust action usually does not remedy the problems that a regulator is seeking to solve. Few believe that monopoly is the major cause of pollution or unsafe products. And although market power may make some problems worse, the presence of market power is not a violation of antitrust laws.

Still, antitrust laws can provide an important check in a deregulated market. Many members of congressional banking committees would insist upon stronger bank antitrust laws before deregulation of the financial-services industry proceeds any further. Because regulation and antitrust often seek different, although complementary, goals, antitrust action alone is seldom an adequate substitute for regulation.

Nationalization

Typically, regulation combines government control with private ownership. As such, intervention is not intended to replace corporate enterprise as much as it is designed to modify the efforts of private entities. Whereas most arguments against regulation focus on attempts to limit government involvement, another legitimate—if radical—proposal would be outright governmental ownership. In the United States, this has happened on a limited basis. Two examples include the Tennessee Valley Authority (TVA) and the Postal Service, although even the latter has been deregulated in part.

Some industrialized nations in the non–Communist world have nationalized major industries to varying degrees. The most active examples are found in Western Europe, where virtually every country has some government-owned industries or services. Perhaps the best example is Great Britain, where the leaders of the nation's two major political parties, the Conservative and Labour, have nationalized and denationalized several industries since the 1920s. Such actions have caused considerable anguish and confusion among corporate stockholders, the public, and government leaders.

Although nationalization remains a possibility in the United States, its likelihood is extremely remote. For the past ten years, the consensus among those in virtually all positions along the political spectrum has been to advocate less, not more, government intervention in the economy.

Conclusions

Traditional economic regulation sets prices, restricts the number of companies in an industry, and makes other economic decisions. Few alternatives exist to this sort of activity. The primary justification for deregulation assumes that the market works best for these issues, although government ownership is a remote possibility. Social regulation has broader goals and many more alternatives. With this in mind, we turn to the second aspect of regulatory behavior.

Alternatives to Social Regulation

Alternatives to social regulation usually fall into one of three categories: traditional, economic-incentive, and information strategies. Although some strategies, such as self-regulation, would significantly decrease the role of government, others, such as taxes, would simply change the type of government intervention. Each strategy tries to identify and correct some of the difficulties with regulation.

Traditional Strategies

Self-Regulation

Although the market may not be perfect, some observers believe that businesses can work together as well as with consumers toward desirable results without governmental intrusion. After all, voluntary cooperation is critical to every regulatory program presently in place. It is impossible for the federal government to enforce the millions of regulations on the books today; thus, regulators must assume that most of the regulations are followed reasonably well most of the time.[11]

The regulatory process is often adversarial, and perhaps with more cooperation, business could work more toward the public interest in addition to its pursuit of private profits. Under regulation, the purpose of rules can be distorted—just the case with the passive-restraint standard, which became a symbol of the problems of regulation to the auto industry. Regulation can be opposed for reasons exclusive of the rule itself. Were the relevant parties able to meet and discuss rules, more reasonable standards might be set in some cases.

Several information-sharing organizations have already been established.[12] With increasing concern about competition from Japan, the model of a business–government–labor–consumer partnership, seen as the Japanese approach, has been receiving new attention. Self-regulation is most likely to work when the goals of these groups are similar; the chances for success increase when the costs to businesses from a lack of standards are high. In most cases, such companies have strong motives to provide quality products, and the new emphasis on quality in American businesses is encouraging to those who advocate fewer rules.[13]

Self-regulation and cooperative efforts do not necessarily imply the absence of government. In most cases, it is assumed that if voluntary standards do not suffice, government intervention will follow.[14] Voluntary action, however, can often work well in combination with regulation. If rules are developed in a cooperative spirit and then made law, compliance is likely to be substantially higher. Adherents of this approach point to the widespread discussion of safety standards for DNA research among scientists, the government, and the public *before* rules were set—a classic example of the creation of good regulations cooperatively. Perhaps fewer and better rules would be written if the interested parties dropped the traditional assumptions that business cares little for safety and quality, that governmental intervention in business is always counterproductive, and that consumers and workers want perfection from businesses without paying for it. Such a belief, a mainstay of the Reagan administration, is based upon the notion of voluntary relationships in place of hostile governmental interference.

Liability Law

Liability law is one of the oldest alternatives to regulation, and long before social regulatory agencies existed, victims of pollution, faulty products, or dangerous workplaces could seek relief in court.

The courts offer several advantages as arbitrators of appropriate regulatory activities. The first is flexibility. Each court-ordered relief is on an individual basis. Penalties fit the severity of the harm caused and the needs of the injured party. Only those whose actions cause harm are punished; businesses with safe workplaces and clean production methods are not required to deal with the government. That is, in those cases brought to court, the arguments of those parties who are directly affected, rather than the priorities of a bureaucrat, will hold sway. Finally, courts are not likely to be "captured" by businesses, unlike regulatory agencies.[15]

As an alternative to regulation, liability has drawbacks. The burden of proof is always on the party who has been hurt. In some cases, proving the exact cause of damage is almost impossible, especially in the areas of pollution and occupational health problems; in these, it is extremely hard to meet the legal standards of proof. Moreover, the courts are slow and lawsuits are expensive. Many people with reasonable cases might be understandably reluctant to press a case against a large corporation. Even if the potential award is substantial, by the time that all appeals have been exhausted and the case is finally settled, the money may come too late to aid an injured party. In such cases, lawyers' fees will almost certainly take a large portion of the award.[16]

Defendants can also be poorly served by liability law. The damages that a company might pay for an accident can vary considerably depending on the judge or the jury involved. Many people with legitimate suits have been overwhelmed by the legal system; some corporations have also suffered when a judge or jury awards an enormous settlement to an individual simply because a company is large and has the money.[17] In addition, uncertain outcomes are a problem for both sides in a liability case.

Some conditions have very long latency periods. Workers who inhaled asbestos forty years ago are just now discovering they face shortened life spans and greatly increased risks of lung disease. A worker may be exposed to a substance that causes lung disease, but may not see signs of the trouble for twenty years or more. In the meantime, he or she may smoke cigarettes or live in an area with air pollution. It is rarely possible to determine the extent to which such problems, especially cancers, have been caused by conditions remote in time. Evidence regarding the exposure is gone, and sometimes the companies that might be responsible are gone as well. Similar conditions might prevail with a person's exposure to food that has been processed with unsafe additives.

Finally, liability works well only when businesses can be expected to react to the incentives created by the law. Businesses might not have adequate information to take precautions to prevent liability suits. They may be unaware of the potential harms from chemicals or the dangers posed by a machine or product. In the absence of regulation, each business will have to guess at such risks.[18] Liability law can only react; it has to rely on indirect incentives to prevent harm, and experience has shown that these incentives are often ineffective.

Some advocates of liability law as an alternative to regulation concede these problems and support changes in the laws to make the system more effective. In many cases, injured victims can claim damages only if the company involved has been proved negligent. Yet even "negligence" is open to redefinition in the wake of scientific advances. Saccharin was initially considered a safe alternative to the banned sweeteners, cyclamates. Now, many consumer advocates believe that saccharin, too, is carcinogenic. Manufacturers who substituted saccharin for cyclamates are unlikely to be considered negligent; this will require that those who suffered in the interim must find other forms of compensation or redress.

A shift from a negligence standard to a strict liability standard would force businesses to be more cautious. Under strict liability, a consumer need not show that a manufacturer was negligent in making a product that caused injury, but only that the cause of the injury was the product.[19] Some states are now moving toward such strict liability standards in these cases.

Reforming liability is difficult. There is no single standard, so laws differ from state to state and case to case. Case judgments vary accordingly. Moreover, it is difficult to tell in advance how a proposed reform might, in fact, work.[20] Businesses are not anxious to replace regulation with enhanced liability rules. Many fear a rash of unfounded lawsuits from plaintiffs lured by large awards. Thus, regulation has come to provide businesses with a defense in lawsuits. If a business has complied with all appropriate regulations, it can argue that it has taken all reasonable precautions. Regulations can provide some degree of certainty, while lawsuits cannot. But the current crisis in liability insurance will significantly limit the use of this alternative. Although, in theory, liability law can provide appropriate checks on business, the reality of the present insurance system leaves both businesses and consumers with significant doubts.

A week seldom passes without some news story about the crisis in liability. Ski areas, skating rinks, and swimming pools are closing down because they cannot get insurance; cities and businesses are going uninsured rather than pay the enormous costs that new policies entail. In 1985, 40 percent of the members of the U.S. Chamber of Commerce found that their liability-insurance premiums had more than doubled; for 25 percent of that group, fees increased by 500 percent or more. As a result, seven out of every twenty businesses now operate without insurance.[21]

Insurance companies contend that the problem lies with both liability laws and the jury system. Between 1974 and 1984, the number of product-liability suits in federal courts increased by 680 percent. In 1985, the *average* liability award was greater than $1 million.[22] Juries have awarded multimillion-dollar settlements to injured parties, even when the companies involved have done all they can to manufacture safe products. Companies have also been held liable for gross misuse of their products. Since there have been many awards of such large proportions, the insurance companies claim that they must either charge extremely high premiums or choose not to offer many types of insurance at all. Businesses, in turn, pass along insurance costs to consumers or abandon production of good products because the potential costs are too high.

Consumer groups respond that the "insurance crisis" is one of the insurance industry's own making. In the early 1980s, companies were willing to write policies on anything, and the current high premiums are a way to cover up past management mistakes. Present fees are much too high, given the level of risk. Still, property and casualty insurance companies reported a pretax loss of $5.5 billion in 1985.[23]

The crisis has caught the attention of legislatures in every state. Legislation that would increase the regulation of the insurance industry, limit awards to plaintiffs in liability cases, or both have been considered in each of the fifty states; more than half the states have already adopted some reform measures. Many business and consumer groups are now pushing for federal reform in areas that have traditionally been the responsibility of the states. The proposed federal reforms are given little chance of passage, but their consideration alone is proof that the crisis is a serious concern for all involved.[24]

Even if the liability-insurance crisis is resolved, liability as an alternative will have serious limits. The experience of the past several years has shown that some problems are almost impossible to solve after the damage is done. Two companies—asbestos producer Manville, and A. H. Robins, maker of the Dalkon Shield, an intrauterine contraceptive device found to have caused significant damage to many women—filed for bankruptcy when consumers were awarded large amounts in product-liability suits. As a result, if a company goes under, those injured by its products are left without compensation.

Insurance

Insurance is another alternative to regulation. In theory, it works much like liability. Insurance is a way to pool risk and to see that funds are available to pay injured parties. Companies can purchase liability insurance, professional athletes can obtain injury insurance, and doctors can buy malpractice insurance; that is, almost any activity can be insured. If the premiums a company or individual pays accurately reflect the risks involved, insurance can add another incentive for businesses to incorporate the social costs of their goods and production methods.

One of the best examples of insurance is workers' compensation. Employers are required to pay into the fund, and when a worker is injured on the job, he or she receives compensation from the fund. The viability of such a system depends on the degree to which a firm's payments reflect the number of injuries it might cause its workers. If a company finds that it has to pay exceptional premiums because its workers are more likely to draw compensation, the company clearly has an incentive to make the workplace safer.[25]

Insurance can offer several advantages. It is often cheaper and easier for a worker to prove a case to a compensation board than it is to prove a liability case in court. Workers receive less spectacular but more certain awards than they might receive from injury suits. Businesses benefit because one case will not radically change the fortunes of the business, and patterns of safety are rewarded with lower premiums.

It is difficult, however, to imagine a large number of cases where insurance can completely replace regulation. Similar risks must be pooled for insurance to work. Insurance companies must be able to set premiums based on adequate information. Few insurance companies would want to write policies to protect firms against unknowns. Like liability, the potential for effective insurance has always existed, but it has not prevented the problems that regulation attempts to solve.

Bargaining

Those who favor bargaining as an alternative to regulation believe that by getting together the interested parties—workers, consumers, and businesses—more efficient and equitable strategies can be developed. Like liability, bargaining has the advantage of flexibility. A rule can be designed to meet the needs of the specific parties involved, which may differ from location to location; it will reflect the priorities of a regulator. Finally, it may be easier to enforce because interested parties have agreed on its terms, rather than being subjected to a rule imposed from outside.[26]

Occupational-health-and-safety matters often present difficulties that beg for alternatives to regulation. Each workplace is different, and occupational rules have been singled out among current regulations as being ineffective and lacking in common sense. Labor unions exist to help ensure the health and safety of their members, and they are the logical representatives to bargain with companies. Because OSHA rules are often disrespected by managers and workers alike, bargaining may offer a superior alternative.

Bargaining does have limits, however, as chapter 7 explained. To win concessions on health and safety, workers might have to give up benefits or wage increases. Thus, they might prefer that a government agency determines health and safety so that the costs of such rules are more widely dispersed.[27] Also, a significant majority of workers are not unionized, so there is no obvious mechanism for their protection.

The present regulatory laws exist, in part, because of the inability of bargaining to achieve resolution within the private sector. This does not mean, however, that there is no future for bargaining. Experiments are spreading beyond the labor–management arena to other areas. In some cases, bargaining has even been used to help resolve environmental disputes. Consumer groups and environmental organizations have thus represented the interests of the general public in such proceedings.[28]

It is difficult, however, to know which groups legitimately speak for the public. Not everyone agrees with the positions taken by environmental groups, for example. Some people might prefer lower taxes, but more pollution. "The public" is not a uniform group with one set of preferences, and "the public interest" is not always represented by one group. There is no clear way to decide who should speak for the public or what this spokesperson should say. The same is true for business, environmental, and labor interests. This question of legitimacy must be solved if bargaining is to work on a widespread scale.

Conclusions

Each of these alternatives—self-regulation, liability, insurance, and bargaining—was used prior to the creation of the social regulation agencies that took over their functions. For this reason, it might seem that each is now an unlikely alternative to regulation. Yet there are several reasons why these alternatives still have merit. In some cases, regulation has not lived up to its promise. Either the problems requiring governmental intervention have not been solved or the new regulatory agencies have created new difficulties in the process of attempting to correct the old ones.

The roles of the various actors have also changed. When many social regulatory agencies were formed, business interests generally opposed them as a matter of principle. But some of the reformers of the 1960s and early 1970s are now managers in the corporations they once sought to reform. Some goals once considered controversial are now thought to be desirable by a broad spectrum of business leaders and reformers alike. Under these conditions, nonregulatory solutions may be more effective than they were twenty years ago. Equally important, some of them deserve to be looked at anew in light of the political and economic environment of the 1980s.

Economic Incentives

Economic incentives compose a second class of alternatives to social regulation. Some critics have claimed that the major problem with regulation is that it ignores rather than imitates the incentives of the market. In fact, most regulation is modeled on a legal system of rules and remedies.[29] Systems based on economic incentives are often overlooked. Economists, however, make a strong case for regulation based on market incentives; that is, by incorporating the efficiencies of market decisions into regulation, they contend that regulatory goals can be achieved in the most efficient manner.

Taxes and Subsidies

The most popular economic alternative to regulation replaces standards with taxes or subsidies. Regulatory standards do not necessarily create effective incentives to achieve a given goal at a minimal cost. First, standards are almost always uniform, and do not account for differences between companies. With pollution, for example, different companies may dump different amounts of effluent into a given area; moreover, they may have different costs to clean up the same pollutant.

To implement a fee, government must be able to measure each unit of pollution. It must have some idea about the marginal costs of cleanup for each company to be able to set a tax at a level that will prevent the undesired level of pollution. If the tax is too low, pollution will not be significantly decreased. If the tax is too high, production will be stopped when the benefits exceed the costs. In theory, one can easily adjust the fee to achieve the desired level of pollution control, but in reality, most companies cannot easily adjust their pollution technology, and a series of fee revisions could be very expensive for business and society alike. Moreover, the monitoring costs and bureaucratic problems associated with such a program could make regulation seem like a relatively simple alternative.

Marketable Permits

To overcome some of the fee-related problems, some agencies have developed an incentive system that uses marketable permits. In instances of water quality, the government body sets a pollution maximum, and permits are auctioned off in small units up to that maximum. Because the firms with the highest cleanup costs will bid the most for permits, the market incentives to clean up pollution at the lowest cost remain, the primary advantage of taxes or fees.[30]

Pollution is not the only problem where marketable permits might provide a solution. In the airline industry, deregulation has created a situation where airport landing gates and times have become scarce commodities. The Reagan administration has proposed a permit system to auction off landing rights. In effect, airlines that most highly value a particular landing time and gate would pay the most for the permit to land.

Marketable permits have several obvious advantages, but such a policy can run into difficulty. The potential for strategic behavior by competitors is especially troublesome. A large, strong company could buy up all the pollution permits in a given region not because its cleanup costs are high, but because it might block production by its competitors.[31] The stockpiling of permits might also undermine the efficiency of the scheme, thus conflicting with the best interests of society. Currently operating airlines might buy all the landing gates at a given airport, thus denying new companies a chance to compete. But if some permits are held back for each company, independent of their willingness to pay, some market efficiency is lost as well.

Conclusions

Economists have long argued that market-incentive systems are superior to the present systems of regulation in many cases. But market-based alternatives are seldom used. By concentrating on the theoretical advantages of market schemes, economists often overlook the realities of such policies in practice.[32] How, exactly, should pollution be measured? What limits should be placed on the purchase of marketable permits? Practical problems arise when we attempt to answer these sorts of questions.

Most companies do not always behave like the theoretical competitive firm of economic models. These models assume, for example, that a small change in an effluent fee would be matched by small changes in pollution control, so that adjustment to the optimal level of pollution is easy. In reality, once fees are set, a firm might respond with a particular type of technology. If fees change, the firm cannot easily change its technology. No easy trade-off exists between fees and pollution. Instead, companies will choose from among several costly technologies; once a decision is made, the cost of converting to a new technology will be quite high.[33]

Market systems do not seem to gather much enthusiasm outside of the economic profession. The public simply does not think in terms of economic incentives for all behavior.[34] The congressional preference for standards, or "command and control" regulations, is clear. Nevertheless, a tax system of sorts has been adopted with regard to hazardous waste, the "feedstock tax," which charges firms that produce hazardous chemicals by the level of such production. The heated debate over the implementation of this tax has provided Congress with some experience with regard to the advantages and disadvantages of market-based approaches.[35]

A final problem with a change to market-based incentives was explained by former EPA administrator Russell Train, who complained that substitution of emission charges for regulations would slow down the ability to implement effective policy: "It would be quite disruptive to make such a change until the initial objectives of the new environmental legislation of this decade are achieved."[36] Considerable time and money have been spent to develop a consensus from which progress in environmental quality and other improvements can be achieved. To suddenly change this system without clear evidence of benefits might be foolish.

At least in the short run, it is unlikely that entire regulatory systems will be scrapped in favor of market-based systems. Perhaps the best policy is to implement incentive systems to deal with newly discovered problems, as Congress did with the feedstock tax. Such an approach might provide evidence of the benefits to market approaches in practice, and provide experience in solving some of these practical questions without incurring the large costs of change from the regulatory system now in place. The potential benefits from taxes, subsidies, and other market incentive systems are too great to ignore. With more information, they might provide a superior alternative to traditional regulation in many cases.

Information Strategies

Lack of information constitutes one of the primary justifications for regulation. Because a worker cannot reasonably judge the safety of a workplace, or a consumer cannot judge the purity of a medicine or the risks in a food additive, adherents of the "public good" philosophy assert that the government should intervene to correct these informational inadequacies.

The usual method of intervention is standard-setting. Workplace safety rules are established, drug purity standards are enforced, and dangerous food additives are banned. But information or education could serve as an alternative to this form of government intervention. Such alternatives seek to disclose information on facts and the risks associated with jobs, products, or behaviors. Educational alternatives try to convince the public to change its behavior. In either case, the government does not force action on either business or consumers. Decisions are made with the existing costs and benefits unchanged. Public agencies or commissions seek only to make these choices more informed.[37]

Disclosure

Disclosure works best when a specific commodity or item exhibits a wide range of quality and price. For many consumer products, the difference between the highest and the lowest quality can be substantial. For example, one can spend between $15 and $300 or more for a baby stroller. If a single standard is imposed for such goods, substantial choice is lost. Some consumers would prefer a reduced price, with somewhat less safety and lower quality. Others prefer the safest possible item irrespective of cost. These preferences are not irrational. If the government can provide information so that consumers are aware of the differences between products, then information disclosure may be the best policy.[38]

Information strategies are currently pursued in several areas. Drug labelling informs consumers of the risks and side effects of nonprescription medicines. Banks and other financial institutions must disclose the true rate of interest on credit cards. Securities laws force companies to disclose substantial amounts of information before offering stock.[39] In each case, the goal is to aid in better decision making without restricting information.

Disclosure has several advantages over regulation. The cost to society of such policies is usually quite low. Adjustments to specific cases are managed with relative ease. Moreover, disclosure does not mandate behavior, an important consideration in a free society.[40] To the contrary, disclosure attempts to correct informational market failures in the least intrusive manner.

Although those firms developing mandated information statements might disagree, there are few significant disadvantages to information. At worst, it is ignored. The effectiveness of disclosure, however, is unclear. The idea has strong intuitive appeal, but available evidence indicates that its effect is minimal.

At the most basic level, it is a surprisingly difficult task to compose information that can be easily understood by most people.[41] The model of the consumer who actively compares products before each decision is not accurate. In fact, most people do not search and compare extensively, even with expensive items. Even though information on many products is available, studies have shown that very few people actively look for it.[42]

Consumers have tolerance levels with respect to the information they are willing to consider. Most people are unlikely to pay attention to detailed, numerical comparisons; even if they do, there are strong doubts that they retain such information. Unless the information appears in a useful format, it is ignored.[43] Finally, few people are able to understand or evaluate the information they receive, and so most consumers cannot use the information they are given. When the risk of getting cancer from a product is quantified as 1 in 100,000, most people do not understand what that means. A message delivered is not always a message received.[44]

Education

Information alone does not cause significant changes in behavior. When either Congress or a regulatory agency attempts to promote a particular choice, education may be the preferred alternative to the random distribution of information. Some private choices have social costs. People who smoke, drive without seatbelts, or eat unhealthy foods foster higher insurance and medical costs for everyone. In these cases, government can only attempt to persuade people to avoid smoking, to wear seatbelts, and to eat nutritious foods.

Education can enhance information as an alternative to regulation. People exposed to an informational message may not use its content, but with education, the information becomes more effective than the information by itself. Disclosure regarding the nutritional value of food is more effective when the public understands the components of a nutritious diet.

Many critics have argued that our society already suffers from "information overload." We receive so much information from so many different sources, it is hard for yet another fact to gain our attention. Life moves much too quickly to read the labels on each product we buy, or to completely analyze each decision we make.[45]

Consumer polls almost always indicate strong preference for disclosure independent of regulation. When these same consumers make major purchases, however, they ignore the available information. It could be that other information sources—previous experience, recommendations of friends, and advertising, for example—are the critical determinants of a purchase. The discrepancy between the stated desire for disclosure and the minimal use of such information raises questions over the utility of disclosure as an alternative.

Consumers may also assume that any product on the market already meets some government standard. Such an unstated expectation may invite regulatory activities at higher levels than might otherwise be expected. We may assume, for example, that if saccharin were really harmful, the government would ban it rather than require a statement about its ability to cause cancer in laboratory animals. People rely upon the government to analyze the available information and make decisions. If information takes the place of standards, people may take more risks than appropriate because they implicitly trust the government to provide minimum levels of product and other types of safety.

Some studies show promise for disclosure as an alternative to regulation in selected areas. An investigation into the effectiveness of energy-efficiency labelling for major appliances concluded that people both understood and used the provided information.[46] Another research effort concluded that even if people hear and understand the message, they may continue to behave exactly as they did before.[47] The difficulties with seatbelt education as mentioned in the auto case study are indicative of the trouble that governmental educators face. Studies of such situations have shown that the probability of an actual change in behavior is low.[48]

The government's educational messages must compete for consumer attention with ads that are usually far more effective and entertaining, if not more accurate or informative.[49] Of special concern for policy makers is that the least educated and less well-off members of society seem to be the least likely to be influenced by education.[50] A policy that abandons standards in favor of education and information may impose the largest costs on those least able to bear them.

Conclusion

Education and disclosure have strong appeal because they recognize individual choice while offering some protection from unhealthy or unsafe decisions. Unfortunately, there is little chance that either will be as effective as standards are in leading to safer products or more responsible behavior. Further research is needed on the extent to which people assume and prefer that minimum standards for products are being met. Perhaps the combination of minimum standards and information or education would best provide protection and choice.

Evaluating the Alternatives

When it intervenes in the market, government is not limited to standard setting. The range of traditional alternatives (liability, insurance, and self regulation), market-based incentives (taxes, subsidies, and marketable permits), and information provision (disclosure and education) offers a wide variety of potential policies.

Each alternative is more promising as a specific application than as a broad-based remedy. Deregulation combined with traditional protection can be promising as an alternative to economic regulation. The economic regulatory agencies are relatively old, and experience shows that the costs of their activities are usually high while the benefits are uneven.

Economic incentives work best in cases where social costs from private actions are a significant problem, such as with pollution. In these cases, schemes can be designed so that social costs are incorporated into private decisions while efficiency is retained in decision making. Information and education can work best when public policies refrain from interfering with private choice but remain unwilling to accept the market result. Information and education can thus influence private, individual decisions.

One remaining alternative to regulation deserves brief reconsideration. In theory, nationalization or public ownership of an industry can replace the need for standards. A nationalized industry does not experience the difficulties caused by the differences between public and private goals.[51] This alternative is most likely in cases of economic regulation. But American history and the values of most citizens strongly argue against this alternative. Thus, the likelihood of nationalized industries in addition to the TVA and Postal Service is slim, particularly given the public mood of the past decade.

There is no one alternative that can substitute for all of the present regulatory schemes. But used carefully and creatively, regulation and its alternatives can be combined to provide potentially effective policies. One proposed "mixed strategy" would be to mandate that insurance companies offer lower payments to those who wear seatbelts than to those who do not. If an auto injury suffered when a seatbelt is not worn is compensated at only 50 percent of treatment costs, then people might clearly see the benefits of seatbelt use.[52] This incentive scheme could be combined with education to ensure that people are aware of the costs of auto accidents when seatbelts are not worn. Such an approach has been successful already: information and standards, for example, have been combined to improve gasoline mileage in automobiles. Fleet standards required auto manufacturers to produce more fuel-efficient cars; information rules that required EPA mileage ratings gave consumers the data needed to make informed choices about the gas-saving features of particular models.

If the assessment above suggests any conclusion, it is that different problems require different solutions. Increased flexibility and openness to alternatives would probably allow the government to better design interventions to meet specific needs.

Reforming Regulation

Some policy makers reject the alternatives to regulation as outlined above. Instead, they argue, we should accept the present system, but reform it to make it more effective. Better management of the existing regulatory agencies through better oversight, coordination, and other reforms might improve the "command and control" system now in place.

Cost–Benefit Analysis

One common argument suggests that governing agencies should subject each regulation to some form of cost–benefit analysis before it is issued. Indeed, as we have seen, reforms under both Carter and Reagan have worked to increase the use of cost–benefit analysis by many regulatory agencies. Presently, however, many agency mandates do not account for the costs of regulation. Instead, these agencies are instructed by Congress to ensure that specific goals are met—provide a clean environment, safe workplaces, pure food and drugs, or safe automobiles.[53]

A cost–benefit requirement would restore some balance to many agencies' decisions. But if strictly implemented, it could lead to serious problems. As discussed in chapter 4, some benefits are hard to measure. The value of a clean lake or a life saved cannot be easily analyzed in dollars and cents.

Such concern does not mean that cost–benefit analysis is of no use in policy making; rather, it means that it is only one tool to use in forming policy. All decisions are based on an informal and unquantified cost–benefit analysis. We decide on any policy because we believe its benefits outweigh its costs, however those are defined. Thus, the quantification of costs and benefits, in the proper framework, can be a useful policy tool.

Coordination

Many studies of regulation have concluded that most agencies suffer from poor coordination.[54] The auto case study, for example, examined the problems of an industry that has been working to meet goals designed by different agencies, sometimes at cross-purposes.

Although everyone agrees that better coordination is needed, few can agree on a practical application. The power of a "superagency" to review all rules would be immense, and present agency supporters are not likely to willingly surrender these areas of power. Fears are also common that the coordinator or coordinating agency would be open to political manipulation. In fact, attempts under the Carter and Reagan administrations to coordinate regulation ran into difficulty over these issues.

Sunset Laws

Sunset laws stipulate that a particular regulation or regulatory activity will expire after a given period of time unless they are renewed by the appropriate legislature. Because thousands of rules are obscure and seem to serve little purpose, sunset laws prevent these rules from becoming institutionalized. As conditions change, the need for regulation changes, so sunset laws force a periodic examination of laws in light of current conditions.[55]

But there are costs to such laws. Time, staff, and money are limited. The energy spent on examining old laws and rules might be better focused on new problems and solutions. In fact, if old issues are continually reexamined, new issues may be ignored.[56] Although sunset laws are useful where goals are likely to change, they are less useful when there is agreement on need for action and where conditions are relatively constant.

Regulatory Budgets

Periodically, the suggestion has been made that regulation be limited by "regulatory budget." In effect, each agency would have to consider the costs that its rules impose on society, and each agency would have a limit on the total cost of the rules it could implement in any one year.[57] For example, NHTSA might be limited to imposing rules that cost a maximum of $500 million in any year, even if the benefits of further regulation outweighed the costs.

The proposal has never been adopted for several reasons. First, the cost estimates would be inexact at best. Second, a consideration of costs without a discussion of benefits might not be the most appropriate policy.[58] Large, comprehensive systems of public-expenditure analysis add significant costs of their own, often without adding useful information. This sort of reform is unlikely to have a significant impact on the real structure of regulation in the United States.

Summary

The country has had substantial experience with regulation, usually by agency standard setting. Although the problems that each agency faces are different, the approaches tend to be the same. One task for the future is to look at the alternatives to regulation, and to match the solutions more closely with the problems.

Perhaps this is the message from public-opinion polls that show support for the goals of regulation but dissatisfaction with regulation itself. The public does not want less government, but better and more innovative government. In this light, alternatives to regulation deserve strong consideration.

Notes

1. Roger Thompson, "Regulatory Reform," *Editorial Research Reports,* 1, no. 18 (May 11, 1984): 363.
2. Congressional Quarterly (CQ), *Regulation: Process and Politics* (Washington, D.C.: Congressional Quarterly, 1982), p. 62.
3. *Ibid.,* p. 66.
4. Michael D. Reagan, "The Politics of Regulatory Reform," *Western Political Quarterly,* 36, no. 1 (March 1983): 154.
5. Energy and Environmental Analysis (EEA), Inc., *Alternatives to Regulation; Possibilities; Experience; Prospects.* Prepared for the U.S. Department of Commerce. August, 1978, p. C-3.
6. Adam Smith, *Wealth of Nations,* quoted in Paul Samuelson, *Economics,* 11th ed. (New York: McGraw-Hill, 1980), p. 784.
7. Lester B. Lave, "The Strategy of Social Regulation," *Studies in the Regulation of Economic Activity* (Washington, D.C.: The Brookings Institution, 1981), p. 10.
8. Alan Stone, "Economic Regulation, the Free Market, and Public Ownership," *Economic Regulatory Policies,* ed. James E. Anderson (1976), p. 196.
9. Stephen Breyer, *Regulation and Its Reform* (Cambridge, Mass.: Harvard University Press, 1982), pp. 156–157.
10. See, for example, F. M. Scherer, *Industrial Market Structure and Economic Performance,* 2d ed. (Chicago: Rand-McNally, 1980), chs. 18–21.
11. Thomas P. Grumbly, "Self-Regulation: Private Vice and Public Virtue Revisited," in *Social Regulation: Strategies for Reform,* eds. Eugene Bardach and Robert Kagan (San Francisco: Institute for Contemporary Studies, 1983), p. 102.
12. J. Ronald Fox, "Breaking the Regulatory Deadlock," *Harvard Business Review,* 59, no. 5 (September–October 1981): 100.
13. George Eads, "Increased Corporate Product Safety Efforts: A Substitute for Regulation," in Bardach and Kagan, *Social Regulation,* pp. 302–303.
14. EEA, *Alternatives to Regulation,* p. C-21.

15. Eugene Bardach and Robert Kagan, "Liability Law and Social Regulation," in Bardach and Kagan, *Social Regulation,* p. 265.
16. Breyer, *Regulation,* p. 176.
17. Susan Tolchin and Martin Tolchin, *Dismantling America: The Rush to Deregulate* (New York: Oxford University Press, 1983), p. 240.
18. Bardach and Kagan, "Liability Law," p. 251.
19. *Ibid.,* p. 252.
20. Breyer, *Regulation,* pp. 175–176.
21. "The Insurance Crisis: Now Everyone Is in a Risky Business," *Business Week,* no. 2938 (March 10, 1986): 88.
22. "America, Your Insurance Has Been Cancelled," *Time,* 127, no. 12 (March 24, 1986): 20.
23. "The Insurance Crisis," *Business Week* (March 10, 1986): 88.
24. Michael Brady, "When Products Turn into Liabilities," *Fortune,* 113, no. 5 (March 3, 1986): 24.
25. EEA, *Alternatives to Regulation,* p. C-20.
26. Lawrence S. Bacon, "Private Bargaining and Public Regulation," in Bardach and Kagan, *Social Regulation,* pp. 217–220.
27. *Ibid.,* pp. 208–209.
28. Douglas Amy, *Ecology Law Quarterly,* 11 (1983): pp. 15–17.
29. Stone, "Economic Regulation," p. 189.
30. Bryer, *Regulation,* pp. 171–172.
31. Donald R. Ryan, "Transferrable Discharge Permits and the Control of Stationary Source Air Pollution: A Survey and Synthesis, Comment," *Land Economics,* 57, no. 4 (November 1981): 640.
32. Edwin T. Clark, *Regulatory Reform Seminar, Papers and Proceedings,* U.S. Department of Commerce, October 17, 1978, p. 58.
33. EEA, *Alternatives to Regulation,* p. C-4.
34. Alice Rivlin, *Regulatory Reform Seminar, Papers and Proceedings,* U.S. Department of Commerce, October 17, 1978, p. 60.
35. See, for example, the debate over the relative merits of a feedstock tax, a waste-end tax, or other policies to prevent the production of or aid in the cleanup of hazardous waste. The feedstock tax charges those companies that produce toxic chemicals a fee based on the amount produced. The revenues go to clean up the waste. This increases the price of such chemicals, and thus includes some of the cost of cleanup. A waste-end tax, on the other hand, charges for each unit of hazardous waste produced. Other critics would like to have standards only. U.S. Congress, Senate Committee on Environment and Public Works. *Hearings, Superfund Improvement Act of 1985,* February 15, 1985.
36. EEA, *Alternatives to Regulation,* p. C-15.
37. *Ibid.,* p. C-20.
38. Michael O'Hare, "Information Strategies as Regulatory Surrogates," Bardach and Kagan, *Social Regulation,* p. 225.
39. Breyer, *Regulation,* p. 162.
40. O'Hare, "Information Strategies," p. 222.
41. Robert S. Adler and R. David Pittle, "Cajolery or Command: Are Education Campaigns an Adequate Substitute for Regulation?" *Yale Journal on Regulation,* 1, no. 1 (1984): 165.
42. Howard Beales, *et. al.,* "Consumer Search and Public Policy," *Journal of Consumer Research,* 8, no. 1 (June 1981): 12.
43. Debra L. Scammon, "Information Load and Consumers," *Journal of Consumer Research,* 4, no. 3 (December 1977): 148.
44. Allen R. Ferguson, *Regulatory Reform Seminar,* October 17, 1978, p. 64.
45. Adler and Pittle, "Cajolery or Command," p. 166.

46. Dennis L. McNeill and William L. Wilkie, "Public Policy and Consumer Information: Impact of the New Energy Labels," *Journal of Consumer Research,* 6, no. 1 (June 1979): 9.
47. Adler and Pittle, "Cajolery or Command," p. 162.
48. Richard Staelin, "The Effects of Consumer Education on Consumer Product Safety Behavior," *Journal of Consumer Research,* 5, no. 1 (June 1978): 35–36
49. Beales, "Consumer Search," p. 21.
50. Adler and Pittle, "Cajolery or Command," p. 167.
51. Stone, "Economic Regulation," p. 199.
52. EEA, *Alternatives to Regulation,* p. C-7.
53. Lave, *The Strategy,* p. 21.
54. Richard Lesher, *Regulatory Reform Seminar,* October 17, 1978, p. 71.
55. Clark, *Regulatory Reform Seminar,* October 17, 1978, p. 73.
56. Christopher C. DeMuth, "The Regulatory Budget," *Regulation,* 4, no. 2 (March–April 1980): 30.
57. Lawrence J. White, "Truth in Regulatory Budgeting," *Regulation,* 4, no. 2 (March–April 1980): 44.
58. Rivlin, *op. cit.,* p. 70.

CHAPTER 10

Deregulation in Perspective

When Ronald Reagan campaigned for the presidency in 1980, he vowed repeatedly to "get government off the backs of the people." Although such promises are regular features of electoral contests, in this instance, Reagan's words echoed an increasingly popular refrain. His immediate predecessors—Nixon, Ford, and Carter—had actually moved, albeit tentatively, in the direction of regulatory reform as a means of cutting unnecessary red tape. But Reagan did not advocate "reform"; rather, he argued for the wholesale elimination of unnecessary regulation.

Shortly after he assumed office, the new president attempted to make good on his promise. With the signing of Executive Order 12,291 in February 1981, he consolidated jurisdiction of executive branch regulatory responsibilities by requiring that all proposed changes be subject to stringent cost–benefit reviews by the Office of Management and Budget. Only legal restrictions prevented extension of the executive order to the twenty-two independent agencies whose powers and functions were determined by Congress. Nevertheless, the message was clear: This administration intended to take an active role in reversing regulatory growth.

Deregulation has become a critical issue on the public agenda. Once the darling of a few conservative politicians and economists, the topic now occupies center stage in the American political debate. No single presidential administration has stressed this theme as vigorously as the team under the leadership of Ronald Reagan. As we near the 1990s, we look back now at the 100-year record of economic regulation and the 50-year record of social regulation and see how these efforts have withstood the challenges of the 1980s.

Economic Regulation:
Government Oversight at a Crossroads

On the eve of Ronald Reagan's presidential inauguration, Milton and Rose Friedman wrote of regulation as the tragic outgrowth of big government: "[T]hese days the government is the major source of interference with a free market system—through tariffs and other restraints on international trade, domestic action fixing or affecting individual prices, including wages, government regulation of specific industries, monetary and fiscal policies producing erratic inflation, and numerous other channels."[1] As with many philosophical opponents of regulation, the Friedmans were rather one-sided in their criticism of governmental involvement in private lives. According to them, save for matters of defense, police protection, roads, and other commonly used resources unaffordable to individuals, as well as providing for a few souls who are totally unable to take care of themselves, the best government is one that permits individuals to direct their own lives on their own terms. Regulation is therefore perceived as an unacceptable intrusion of government into private affairs.

Some of these objections also became concerns for elected officials. By the late 1970s, even before the Reagan revolution, President Jimmy Carter had issued his own executive order to eliminate unnecessary regulation. In addition, Congress had passed legislation that selectively deregulated specific areas of the economy. But even if these events were the first signs of deregulation, they paled in comparison to the efforts of the 1980s. Efforts alone, however, do not lead to change, and many of the Reagan attempts fell short of the mark, all rhetoric aside. In other instances, the administration seemed downright inconsistent.

Independent Economic Regulatory Agency Management

From the Interstate Commerce Commission to the Nuclear Regulatory Commission, Congress intended that independent commissions be kept free from immediate pressures. Independent agencies have long been known for having their own mandates of responsibility. The elements of required bipartisan membership, overlapping appointments, and lengthy terms of office have all been part of an effort to isolate these agencies from congressional or executive control. But, in fact, they have never been completely free from pressure. Congress flexed its muscle in 1980 when it responded to unfavorable regulation by reducing the powers of the ICC.

At the presidential level, Ronald Reagan has used conventional means—board-member appointments—to force his will on independent agencies. Indeed, by 1987, the bounty of two successive terms allowed Reagan to appoint all sixty-three members of fifteen key independent agencies. All of this suggests that "independent" agencies exist only in a relative sense. But aside from these facts, independent agencies have been slow to direct their policies in a less regulated direction.[2] Most available information suggests a slowdown rather than a reversal of independent agency activity during the 1980s. For example, during the first three years of the Reagan administration, the budget for the ICC was reduced by 25 percent. At the same time, the FCC and SEC budgets were increased by 3 and 15 percent, respectively.[3] All of these figures decline somewhat when accounting for inflation.

Perhaps dismantlement of the CAB represents the single greatest example of deregulatory success. In 1984, the fifty-year-old independent agency closed its doors for good. A few responsibilities were transferred to the FAA, but otherwise the CAB's functions were eliminated. Even this instance was not as it seemed, however, since the initial legislation to eliminate the CAB occurred during the Carter administration. Yet it is the Reagan regime that has gained prominence for the "less is best" approach.

Ironically, in some areas of economic regulation, the Reagan administration has actually promoted government intervention. Perhaps the best example can be seen in the banking industry. Although approximately eighty savings institutions in a less regulated environment failed in 1984, the Reagan administration and Congress did not hesitate to guarantee loans in excess of $4 billion when Continental Bank of Illinois, the nation's eighth largest bank, appeared on the verge of collapse (see chapter 6). Although Reagan seems to be sincere about "getting government off the backs of the people," his administration's methods will be tempered if they are likely to result in economic chaos.

Executive Branch Economic Agencies

As noted earlier in this book, regulatory agencies within the executive branch do not have the autonomy enjoyed by independent agencies and commissions. As such, the executive agencies' policies are more susceptible to direct control by the president and, in recent years, the Office of Management and Budget. Data for the executive branch–dominated agencies indicate a mixed record of budget increases and decreases in recent years. Between 1981 and 1983, for example, allocations for the FDA actually grew by 7 percent, while the NHTSA's budgetary commitments declined by 17 percent.[4]

Clearly, the impact of Executive Order 12,291 is the most visible indication of executive branch regulatory activity in the 1980s. Although one study revealed that between 1978 and 1983 the number of regulations published in the *Federal Register* declined by about one-third,[5] the numbers of changes may not be as important as the shifts in policy direction. In 1985, for instance, the NHTSA backed away from a long-term commitment to passive restraints (air bags) in favor of less costly active restraints (seatbelts). In the same year, the FDA moved away from its once-strident "no risk" carcinogen principle to the principle that "some risk is acceptable provided that it is minimal."[6] Such subtleties are the stuff of policy shifts, although their impact may be difficult to quantify in loss of life or financial cost.

Judged in perspective, however, economic regulatory policies and functions have not changed dramatically over the past decade. It is now axiomatic that the national mood favors less economic regulatory activity, and, in fact, such changes have taken place only in selective areas. Yet in some instances, governmental regulatory activity has actually increased.

Social Regulation: Battered but Surviving

With roots in Franklin Roosevelt's New Deal and Lyndon Johnson's Great Society, social regulatory agencies have had a higher collective profile than have their economic counterparts. As we have seen, social and economic agencies were designed to meet different goals. Economic regulatory bodies originated in large part as a means of government protection for troubled industries; social regulatory agencies were designed to address various public problems, conditions that were sometimes created by those industries already under economic regulation.

Yet another fact separates these two types of governmental oversight: Economic regulation was organized to accommodate narrow needs, but social regulation was created to satisfy broad public concerns. Thus, pollution is an example of the latter with its numerous causes and its harm to broad segments of society. So too are working conditions, which can be troublesome in a variety of environments ranging from small convenience stores to huge industrial plants.

Most agencies responsible for social regulation are under the jurisdiction of the executive branch. As such, their powers are monitored by the president or the cabinet-level department in which they are housed. Because of their close proximity to executive oversight, these agencies also may find their responsibilities subject to redefinition. Given their vulnerability to immediate political pressures, it is easy to understand why these agencies have changed so dramatically in recent years. Deregulation has been more observable in this area than in those independent agencies responsible for economic issues.

Independent Social Regulatory Agencies

Virtually all social regulation occurs at the hands of executive-branch agencies. Responsible to either the president or cabinet department heads, these agencies' directors have tended to adopt the policies of those above them; significant examples are cited in the following section.

One prominent independent commission is the FTC. That the agency was initially designed to protect business is important only for historical purposes.[7] By the late 1960s, the agency was invested with new responsibilities. A landmark decision by the U.S. Supreme Court in 1972 (*FTC* v. *Sperry and Hutchinson*) combined with the Magnuson–Moss Act of 1975 to give the agency expanded powers. By the mid-1970s, the FTC had thus become a public-interest advocate to the extent that it "began to pay consumer groups so that they could come to Washington and testify on pending rules."[8] But this new direction was short-lived.

Sensing an agency "out of control," Congress attempted to harness the FTC. Powerful interest groups ranging from the American Medical Association to the U.S. Chamber of Commerce had complained of the agency's new zeal, and so, under the guise of the Federal Trade Commission Improvements Act of 1980, Congress barred the FTC from pursuing investigations in a number of controversial areas. The congressional efforts show the possibilities for potential checks on regulatory agencies. After the 1980 election, President Reagan aligned himself with Congress, although for philosophical reasons other than opposition to the FTC.

Consequently, during the first three years of the Reagan administration, the agency's funding was reduced by 5 percent, while its employee staff shrunk by 9 percent.

Executive Branch Regulatory Agencies

In their critique of deregulation, Tolchin and Tolchin write that of all the resulting changes, "the social regulatory agencies have become the government's orphans, attacked by both management and labor."[9] Such a result has not been accidental or come without careful thought. Through such devices as Jimmy Carter's Regulatory Analysis Review Group (RARG) and Ronald Reagan's Executive Order 12,291, presidents have demonstrated increased abilities to control the actions of regulatory agencies within their purview.

Perhaps no two agencies illustrate the current contempt for regulation more than do the EPA and OSHA. Both agencies historically have had the ability to enact widespread, costly changes. Following a decade of controversy, OSHA became the first obvious example of the Reagan administration's movement toward deregulation. According to one account, shortly after the Reagan team took office, OSHA citations for willful violators decreased by 90 percent as the administration embarked on a conscious policy of seeking voluntary compliance from industry.[10]

Similar problems confronted the EPA when Anne Gorsuch Burford, Reagan's appointee to head the agency, declared that the EPA had become a thorn in the side of private enterprise; she followed that declaration by announcing a program of intentional opposition to unnecessary environmental regulation. Burford's actions were consistent with her rhetoric. By 1983, EPA enforcement actions had plummeted by 84 percent, and the agency had also reduced its initiation of court suits by 78 percent.[11] Only after Congress had discovered questionable management of the EPA's Superfund for toxic waste cleanup was Burford forced to resign. In this instance, appointment of an individual to an executive-branch agency worked to the president's disadvantage. Had Burford been ensconced in an independent commission or agency, she probably would have been insulated from a thorough congressional investigation.

Presidents have decidedly more control over some policy areas than over others. Within his own branch, the president can move with relatively little resistance. For example, by placing like-minded personnel in positions of authority, President Reagan has successfully reduced the government's commitment to social regulation in a number of areas. Whereas such efforts may be reversed by future presidents, Reagan's current efforts here are perhaps the most graphic examples of his deregulation intentions.

To Regulate, Deregulate, or Reregulate?

Over the past fifteen years, and four presidential administrations, the nation has reassessed the utility and wisdom of regulation. Hardly a knee-jerk reaction of one branch of government or one political party, the deregulation movement has come to represent a well-conceived, broad-based, and purposeful effort. The tensions from a century of economic restraints and a half century of social management have gotten the attention of many political leaders. In one recent study, Martha Derthick and Paul J. Quirk wrote that "[t]he steady and seemingly inexorable expansion of government activities has caused adversely affected interests, policy analysts, elected officeholders, and an increasingly disillusioned public to ask whether outmoded and excessively burdensome government policies can ever be revised."[12] Although Derthick and Quirk chronicle three cases of successful deregulation—the airline, trucking, and telephone industries—in only one instance (airlines) was the responsible agency actually dismantled. Moreover, they point to a series of other industries and issue areas where deregulation efforts failed.[13] Deregulation may be a movement of the 1980s, but it is not advancing equally on all fronts.

Approaching Deregulation on a Case-by-Case Basis

During ideological movements, individual changes quickly become part of the "big picture." Such periods of activism swept the nation into fundamental change during the Progressive Era, Franklin Roosevelt's New Deal, and Lyndon Johnson's Great Society. Each of these periods witnessed increased regulatory activity simultaneously across a wide range of issues.

In the 1980s, much the same sort of activism has been attempted with the *undoing* of regulation. Thus, in describing the philosophical tone of the Reagan efforts, Eugene Bardach adopts the administration's assumption "that all regulation is contaminated by unreasonableness and that large chunks of it can simply be lopped off or systematically shrunk with only minor, if any, detriment."[14] Perhaps the key idea here is "simple." For the advocates of deregulation, to make government simple is to make government best. But even though this has been the battle cry of the deregulation movement, meaningful change has occurred in only a few instances.

Other than the dismantling of the CAB, virtually all deregulation efforts have yielded partial changes on an *ad hoc* basis. Particularly since 1981, most regulatory agencies have witnessed incremental budget reductions, personnel reductions, and redefined responsibilities. Thus, rather than undergoing wholesale change, they have experienced modification.

Why have regulatory agencies withstood the demand for elimination? One common argument is that their close association with powerful interest groups leaves them well-defended against intrusion.[15] But deregulation has occurred to varying degrees in the economic arena, the one environment supposedly most invulnerable to interference. And supposedly, areas of social concern have no obvious protection from vested interests; yet their creations—notably the EPA, OSHA, and the U.S. Civil Rights Commission—remain intact despite protests from all points along the political spectrum.

An alternate explanation for the inability of political actors to effect wholesale deregulation holds that a lack of public intensity has accompanied the anti–regulatory agency sentiment. The work of regulatory agencies is neither exciting nor observable. In fact, they were designed to be low-key, methodical forces of policy making. Behind their long names and in their mysterious buildings, these agencies affect our lives to a much greater extent than is commonly acknowledged. It is their invisibility that works in favor of the status quo. Other than those few people who have constant association with regulatory agencies, they are commonly viewed as just another part of the maze known as "government."

Public-opinion polls suggest that the majority of citizens opposes regulation in principle, but has no desire to give up clean air, safe water, noncarcinogenic food, and a variety of other necessities that have been subject to regulatory activity.[16] This inconsistency is enough to diffuse and deflect a good deal of the energy associated with the deregulation movement. In short, the cross currents of politics have neutralized one another to the extent that most regulatory agencies have remained reasonably intact.

In some instances, the limited deregulatory activities that have taken place have met with considerable negative reaction. Critics have not only questioned the elimination of governmental authority but also demanded the resumption of that authority. Known as the *reregulation* movement, this school of thought suggests that government must regain its lost oversight functions. Similar concerns have been voiced by industry and government officials alike. Thus, with respect to the deregulation of the financial-services industry, Henry Kaufman, executive director of Salomon Brothers, a major brokerage house, has warned that in the postderegulation period "the performance and conduct of financial institutions should not be determined by the market alone. They must not only be the instruments of policy, but they, themselves, must experience the force of policy."[17] In the case of the deregulated airline industry, similar criticism has been aired by government officials who feel that the abandonment of governmental responsibilities may have gone too far. Commenting on the rash of crashes in 1985, former NHTSB director Charles Miller bluntly stated, "I've felt all along that deregulation has had an adverse effect on safety." He called one disaster involving the rapidly expanding Air Florida a "deregulation accident."[18]

If there is any truth to the axiom that every action has a reaction, so it can be said for deregulation, which has brought a cry for reregulation. The more that particular areas have been removed from governmental intervention the more that pressure has developed to reverse the direction of change.

Institutional Changes

The deregulatory movement shows signs of long-term change, much of which is due to its increased visibility on the public agenda. Whereas its concerns were once limited to academic seminars and business retreats, they now attract public attention on the front pages of daily newspapers. Moreover, the deregulatory debate has led to the reordering of priorities within both the executive branch and many key independent agencies. This is not to suggest, however, that activity has been limited to these areas; it has only been most pronounced in these areas. Although it is difficult to project whether today's concerns will outlast the current administration and leaders in Congress, it is fair to say that the deregulatory effort remains important.

Executive Branch

For the past few administrations, presidents have used their office to affect the organization and priorities of the regulatory agencies housed within the executive branch. During the 1970s, most presidential efforts were designed to develop agency accountability—that is, guarantees that they were conducting their affairs within specific performance guidelines. With the signing of Executive Order 12,291, President Reagan went a step beyond his predecessors.

The Reagan order began as an effort to consolidate oversight functions within the Office of Management and Budget, although the order has also rerouted the regulatory process. Designed to avoid potential problems associated with pending regulations, the order required an agency to demonstrate the benefits from proposed regulation changes in advance of their implementation. If the OMB has doubts about any benefits, it can delay publication of the proposed change until the regulatory agency satisfies its objections.

Observers differ on the impact of Reagan's order. A study conducted by the administration itself concludes that of 142 final and proposed rules subjected to OMB review during a two-year period, 86 percent were accepted without change, while another 8 percent were accepted after minor adjustments.[19]

But another school of thought contends that the administration's numbers are inaccurate, if not misleading. With respect to the advance relationship between agency goals and the OMB, the former chairman of President Carter's Regulatory Analysis Review Group cautions that the OMB now serves as a roadblock to many regulatory proposals. According to George Eads, the true importance of the new OMB role is that its interaction with agencies occurs "*before* a regulation has been formally proposed."[20] If such a relationship actually prevents a number of proposals from ever appearing, then the figures offered by the Reagan administration may be inaccurate.

Assessments aside, the OMB has emerged with increased power in the regulatory arena. Scholars and political leaders may dispute the wisdom of this change, but it is clear that enhanced executive authority is one result. For the moment, at least, that authority has placed significant new burdens on those who propose regulatory activity.

Agency Restructuring from Within

The twenty-two independent regulatory agencies and boards exemplify the definition of specialization. Often mired in technical questions of concern to a small constituency, the agencies and their personnel go about their business in an almost ghostlike manner. Yet, as has been demonstrated throughout this volume, their decisions have tremendous inputs not only on client industries but also on the public at large.

In recent years, the actions of the independent agencies have signalled a more aggressive "laissez-faire" attitude toward business activity. Although some regulatory units have been more aggressive than others, their collective posture seems to suggest a "live and let live" approach to politics and government. The tendency has thus been to decrease restrictions and increase industry self-government.

Much of this new approach has been connected to the view that consumers, rather than government, should have final say over industry performance. With the public determining the success of competitors in the marketplace, those offering goods or services would be accountable to consumer, instead of governmental, oversight. This idea was recently expressed by outgoing FCC chair Mark Fowler at a meeting of the National Association of Broadcasters. In defense of his agency's widespread deregulation of the radio and broadcast industries, he observed that regulation "didn't make sense five years ago, and it doesn't make sense today, for the government to be telling broadcasters how to run their businesses. Your work should take you to Main Street or Wall Street, not to M Street [address of the FCC]."[21] Fowler thus believed that self-regulation would make the industry more efficient and responsive to the public will.

A similar reassessment has been observed with the new deregulatory majority on the ICC. Congress became so concerned with lax ICC policies that it passed a new trucking-safety law in 1984 affecting agency standards. But a 1985 study found that the ICC continued its own safety policy, which accepted the testimony of cited carriers as the basis for clearing them of all charges. Within six months of the new law, 160 truck companies had applied for increased route authority even though they had unacceptable safety records by commission standards. Not one was refused, even though the commission relied exclusively on applicant statements as the means for reaching its decisions. Expressing his satisfaction with the procedure, one commissioner concluded that self-policing was an adequate mechanism for monitoring industry behavior, both in the past as well as the future. Thus, he asked rhetorically, "having corrected the problem, ought not the company have a chance to rehabilitate itself?"[22] Not all interested parties, however, have been content with an approach that gives the regulated elements so much power over themselves. Concluded one attorney who has testified before the ICC for twenty years, "the Commission hasn't denied a single request on the basis of safety. A rating of unsatisfactory doesn't mean a thing."[23]

The Future of Deregulation

The issue of regulation as an appropriate governmental activity has been considerably more controversial in the 1980s than at any time in the last fifty years. At the same time, the direction of regulatory activity seems to have shifted: Less regulation makes for a placated industry clientele, a less expensive—perhaps more competitive—product or service, and a pleased body of consumers. So many benefits, however, come with a price. The movement toward reduced governmental activity has also generated concerns over safety, quality control, and monopolistic industry behavior.

Whether the benefits outweigh the costs, whether the freedoms are worth the risks, whether the reduction in governmental oversight outweighs the ignorance of consumers—these are the questions that remain unanswered in the deregulated society. As with the long buildup during the period of increased governmental involvement, the answers may come not so much from the policies themselves as much as from the responses to those policies. In the meantime, it is safe to say that the deregulation movement is alive and well, although the final outcome of the movement remains to be seen.

Notes

1. *Free to Choose* (New York: Avon Books, 1980), p. 9.
2. The most prominent agency exception here is the Civil Aeronautics Board, which was deregulated out of existence by congressional action in 1978 (see chapter 5).
3. *Wall Street Journal*, December 14, 1983, p. 22.

4. *Ibid.*
5. Regulatory Information Center, Office of the Federal Register, August 11, 1983.
6. Richard M. Cooper, "Stretching Delaney Till It Breaks," *Regulation*, 9, no. 6 (November/December 1985): 11.
7. See Kenneth J. Meier, *Regulation* (New York: St. Martin's Press, 1985), p. 108, for a discussion about the FTC's early history.
8. *Ibid.*, p. 109.
9. Susan J. Tolchin and Martin Tolchin, *Dismantling America* (New York: Oxford University Press, 1983), p. 25.
10. George C. Eads and Michael Fix, *Relief or Reform?* (Washington, D.C.: Urban Institute Press, 1984), p. 195.
11. Tolchin and Tolchin, *Dismantling*, p. 92.
12. *The Politics of Deregulation* (Washington, D.C.: The Brookings Institution, 1985), p. 13.
13. *Ibid.*, chapter 6, "The Limits of Deregulation."
14. "Making Regulation Reasonable," *The Center Magazine*, 19, no. 2 (March/April 1986): 46.
15. Over the years, variations on this theme have been put forth by C. Wright Mills, *The Power Elite* (New York: Oxford, 1956), Theodore J. Lowi, *The End of Liberalism* (New York: Norton, 1969) and Derthick and Quirk, *The Politics of Deregulation*.
16. Such inconsistencies are pointed out in Tolchin, *Dismantling*, pp. 263–265, and A. Lee Fritschler and Bernard H. Ross, *Business Regulation and Government Decision-Making* (Cambridge: Winthrop Publishers, 1980), pp. 36–37.
17. "Reshaping the Financial System," *The New York Times*, July 14, 1985.
18. "Aviation's Worst Year Fuels Safety Fears," *San Jose Mercury News*, December 22, 1985.
19. Presidential Task Force on Regulatory Relief, Reagan Administration Regulatory Achievements, Washington D.C., August 11, 1983.
20. George Eads, "Harnessing Regulation," *Regulation*, 5, no. 3 (May/June 1981).
21. *The Dallas Morning News*, April 17, 1986.
22. *San Jose Mercury News*, May 12, 1986.
23. *Ibid.*

INDEX